HIKING CIRCUITS IN ROCKY MOUNTAIN NATIONAL PARK

Loop Trails, With Special Sections for Combining Circuits
and Using the Shuttle Bus to Complete a Circuit

Jack P. Hailman and Elizabeth D. Hailman

University Press of Colorado

© 2003 by Jack P. Hailman and Elizabeth D. Hailman

Published by the University Press of Colorado
5589 Arapahoe Avenue, Suite 206C
Boulder, Colorado 80303

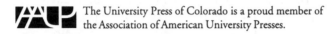 The University Press of Colorado is a proud member of
the Association of American University Presses.

The University Press of Colorado is a cooperative publishing enterprise supported, in part, by Adams State College, Colorado State University, Fort Lewis College, Mesa State College, Metropolitan State College of Denver, University of Colorado, University of Northern Colorado, and Western State College of Colorado.

The paper used in this publication meets the minimum requirements of the American National Standard for Information Sciences—Permanence of Paper for Printed Library Materials. ANSI Z39.48-1992

Library of Congress Cataloging-in-Publication Data

Hailman, Jack Parker, 1936–
   Hiking circuits in Rocky Mountain National Park : loop trails, with special sections for combining circuits and using the shuttle bus to complete a circuit / Jack P. Hailman and Elizabeth D. Hailman.
       p. cm.
Includes bibliographical references and index.
   ISBN 0-87081-721-3 (Paperback : alk. paper)
   1. Hiking—Colorado—Rocky Mountain National Park—Guidebooks. 2. Trails—Colorado—Rocky Mountain National Park—Guidebooks. 3. Rocky Mountain National Park (Colo.)—Guidebooks. I. Hailman, Elizabeth D. II. Title.
   GV199.42.C62R6253 2003
   796.51'09788'69—dc21
                                                                                2003007720

Design by Daniel Pratt

12 11 10 09 08 07 06 05 04 03   10 9 8 7 6 5 4 3 2 1

COVER PHOTOGRAPHS. *Front, top, from left:* Longs Peak from Mills Lake, bull Elk, Upper Copeland Cascades; *front, bottom:* Golden-mantled Ground Squirrel, Longs Peak from Estes Cone, Alpine Sunflower; *back, top:* Alpine Sandwort, Lily Lake, fall color near Bear Lake; *back, bottom:* Glacier Basin, Clark's Nutcracker, mountains with Andrews Glacier in background center; *spine, top:* North Inlet Trail; *spine, bottom:* Alberta Falls.

HIKING CIRCUITS IN
ROCKY MOUNTAIN NATIONAL PARK

For our siblings—
Jack's sister, Frances Hailman;
Liz's brother, Tom Davis;
and Tom's wife, Jane Loveless Davis

Contents

Preface   ix

Acknowledgments   xi

Map of Access Points for Circuit Hikes in RMNP   xii

Table of Circuits in Order of Hiking Times   xiii

Introduction   1
    Types of Hikes Included   2
    Types of Trail Ratings   4
    More About Trails   6
    Health, Safety, and Comfort   7
    Equipment and Its Use   11
    Fees and Permits   14
    A Few Relevant Park Regulations   15
    Final Words   15

About the Circuit Accounts   17
    Account Contents   17
    Account Maps   20

Circuit Hikes From Access Points on the East Side   23
    Introduction to East Side Circuits   23
    Lumpy Ridge Circuit (Twin Owls Trailhead)   25
    Deer Mountain Loops (Deer Ridge Junction Trailhead)   31
    Beaver Brook Circuit (Upper Beaver Meadows Trailhead) 39
    Wind River Circuit (East Portal)   45
    Lily Lake Loops (Lily Lake Trailhead)   51
    Longs Flank Circuit (Longs Peak Trailhead)   57
    Wild Basin Loops (Wild Basin Trailhead or Finch Lake
      Trailhead)   65
    Combining East Side Circuits   69

Contents

Circuit Hikes From Access Points Along Bear Lake Road   71
   Introduction to Bear Lake Road Circuits   71
   Moraine Park Circuit (Cub Lake Trailhead)   73
   Cub Lake Circuit (Fern Lake Trailhead or Cub Lake
     Trailhead)   79
   Steep Mountain Circuit (Mill Creek Basin Trailhead)   85
   Sprague Lake Circuit (Sprague Lake Picnic Area)   91
   Glacier Basin Loops (Sprague Lake Picnic Area)   95
   Bierstadt Moraine Loops (Bierstadt Lake Trailhead)   99
   Boulder Brook Circuit (Glacier Gorge Junction Trailhead)   105
   Alpine Lakes Circuit (Glacier Gorge Junction Trailhead or
     Bear Lake Trailhead)   111
   Bear Lake Circuit (Bear Lake Trailhead)   117
   Mount Wuh Circuit (Bear Lake Trailhead)   121
   Tundra & Glaciers Circuit (Glacier Gorge Junction
     Trailhead or Bear Lake Trailhead)   127
   Combining Bear Lake Road Circuits and Using the Shuttle
     Bus to Complete a Circuit   133
Circuit Hikes From Access Points on the West Side   135
   Introduction to West Side Circuits   135
   Grand Ditch Circuit (Colorado River Trailhead)   137
   Red Mountain Circuit (Colorado River Trailhead)   141
   Big Meadows Circuit (Green Mountain Trailhead or Onahu
     Creek Trailhead)   147
   Kawuneeche Valley Loops (Harbison Picnic Area)   153
   Green Mountain Circuit (Kawuneeche Visitor Center or
     Green Mountain Trailhead)   157
   Continental Divide Circuit (North Inlet Trailhead)   161
   Shadow Shore Circuit (East Shore Trailhead)   167
   Combining West Side Circuits   173

Natural History Appendix   175

Fee Schedules   195

Local Hiking Equipment Stores   197

Organizations You Can Join   199

Suggested Reading and Reference   201

Index   209

Preface

Oh, no! Not another hiking guide! More than a dozen guides devoted to trails in Rocky Mountain National Park (RMNP) already exist, and more than a dozen others covering a larger geographic area feature prominent RMNP trails. So why another guide? Because this one is different (otherwise, we would not have bothered to write it). It is the first and only guide to circuit hiking in RMNP.

Circuit (or loop) hikes are identified only occasionally in existing trail guides, perhaps because authors have not thought consciously in such terms. Existing guides do describe a few of the loops—mainly the shorter ones—or mention others in passing; our guide covers all of these in detail and includes many other circuits not described elsewhere.

We framed this guide with many different users in mind, from families desiring a pleasant walk within the reach of even small children to vigorous, seasoned backpackers planning a multiday trip across the tundra. We offer hikes for those who can enjoy RMNP only during summer vacations, those who are able to take advantage of fall's crisp air and brilliant color, and those who love hiking, snowshoeing, and cross-country skiing over wintery, snow-laden trails. Whether users are staying in tourist cabins, camps such as Cheley Camp, the YMCA complex, the historic Stanley Hotel, RMNP campgrounds, or private area residences, they will find this book valuable in planning outings. After all, from the complete novice to the old hand, we all share the desire to hike some of the best trails available anywhere.

Acknowledgments

First, we thank the many rangers of Rocky Mountain National Park whom we talked with in the field, in visitor centers, and at campfire programs; RMNP staff members such as those in the backcountry office; and employees of the Rocky Mountain Nature Association (RMNA) who run the visitor center bookstores. Special thanks go to RMNP staff member Judy Visty, who gave us access to key specimens in the park's collections, and to Barb Christian of RMNA, who so cheerfully helped us with myriad small issues.

We were exceedingly fortunate to have two wonderful manuscript reviewers. Alexander Drummond, who is exceptionally qualified both as an outdoorsman and author, provided many useful comments, gently goaded us to include more ancillary information about the places visited on the hikes, and even surprised us with a circuit we had overlooked. RMNP staff member Dick Putney helped us avoid several potential pitfalls in the manuscript, provided valuable information about the park, and took the trouble to write down from his own experience the fall and winter uses of every circuit in the book, which material we have shamelessly appropriated, almost verbatim in many cases.

For expediting production of this book we thank the University Press of Colorado's Director Darrin Pratt and his staff, especially Laura Furney and Daniel Pratt (no relation to Darrin), who processed the text and illustrations, respectively.

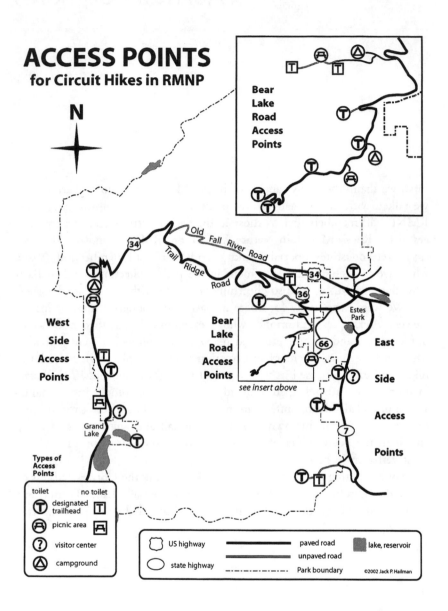

ACCESS POINTS
for Circuit Hikes in RMNP

N

Bear
Lake
Road
Access
Points

Old Fall River Road

Trail Ridge Road

34

West
Side
Access
Points

Bear
Lake
Road
Access
Points

see insert above

Estes
Park

East

Side

Access

Points

Grand
Lake

**Types of
Access
Points**

toilet   no toilet

Ⓣ designated   Ⓣ
trailhead

Ⓑ picnic area

Ⓠ visitor center

Ⓐ campground

US highway   paved road   lake, reservoir

state highway   unpaved road

     Park boundary   ©2002 Jack P. Hailman

TABLE OF CIRCUITS IN ORDER OF HIKING TIMES

Time[1]		Exertion[2]			
Circuit[3]	Max[4]	Circuit[3]	Max[4]	Circuit Name	Access[5]
0:15	—	0.7 stroll	—	Sprague Lake Circuit	BLR
0:18	—	0.9 stroll	—	Bear Lake Circuit	BLR
0:21	—	1.0 stroll	—	Inner Lily Lake Loop	ES
1:04	—	3.1 VE	—	North Glacier Basin Loop	BLR
1:09	—	3.3 VE	—	South Kawuneeche Valley Loop	WS
1:32	—	4.4 VE	—	South Glacier Basin Loop	BLR
1:44	5:56	4.9 VE	21.1 MS	Shadow Shore Circuit	WS
1:47	—	5.1 VE	—	Glacier Basin Loops (entire circuit)	BLR
2:22	—	6.8 E	—	Outer Lily Lake Loop	ES
2:25	—	7.0 E	—	Kawuneeche Valley Loops (entire circuit)	WS
2:41	—	7.5 E	—	Moraine Park Circuit	BLR
3:00	—	8.7 E	—	East Bierstadt Moraine Loop	BLR
3:18	4:45	9.2 E	13.4 ME	Cub Lake Circuit	BLR
3:49	6:58	11.4 ME	21.0 MS	Alpine Lakes Circuit	BLR
4:03	—	11.6 ME	—	Wind River Circuit	ES
4:03	—	12.0 ME	—	West Bierstadt Moraine Loop	BLR
4:07	—	12.0 ME	—	East Wild Basin Loop	ES
4:13	—	12.3 ME	—	Beaver Brook Circuit	ES
4:50	7:45	14.3 ME	22.7 S	Big Meadows Circuit	WS
4:55	—	14.4 ME	—	Bierstadt Moraine Loops (entire circuit)	BLR
5:11	—	13.7 ME	—	Deer Mountain Loops (outer circuit)	ES
5:31	—	16.1 M	—	Green Mountain Circuit	WS
5:46	—	17.2 M	—	Boulder Brook Circuit	BLR
5:56	6:21	17.3 M	18.6 M	South Deer Mountain Loop	ES
6:08	—	18.0 M	—	Wild Basin Loops (entire circuit)	ES
6:18	—	18.1 M	—	Steep Mountain Circuit	BLR
6:44	7:09	19.6 MS	20.9 MS	North Deer Mountain Loop	ES
6:57	11:09	19.8 MS	31.9 VS	Lumpy Ridge Circuit	ES
7:57	10:01	23.8 S	30.3 VS	Grand Ditch Circuit	WS
8:06	—	24.1 S	—	Red Mountain Circuit	WS
9:12	—	27.4 VS	—	Mount Wuh Circuit	BLR
9:26	—	28.7 VS	—	Tundra & Glaciers Circuit	BLR
11:46	17:07	36.7[6]	53.9[6]	Longs Flank Circuit	ES
16:19	22:42	51.1[6]	70.7[6]	Continental Divide Circuit	WS

[1] Walking times based on a standard formula explained in the Introduction.

[2] Exertion points based on a formula devised for this book and explained in the Introduction. Groupings in order of increasing exertion: VE = very easy, E = easy, ME = moderately easy, M = moderate, MS = moderately strenuous, S = strenuous, VS = very strenuous.

[3] Circuit (plus access trail, if any) without any side trips.

[4] Circuit plus all optional out-and-back side trip(s).

[5] BLR = Bear Lake Road, ES = East Side, WS = West Side.

[6] Exertion values are intended to characterize a continuous day hike; these "off scale" values for multi-day backpacking trips have limited usefulness for planning.

Introduction

Circuit, or loop, hikes have an almost magical feel: you begin at one place, walk without ever retracing your steps, and then emerge where you started from. True, a trail usually looks a little different when you walk it in the opposite direction, but once you have reached the goal of an out-and-back hike—that peak or pass, lake or waterfall—the return journey is often an anticlimactic trudge. By contrast, a loop hike has no humdrum second half; every step of the journey is infused with a sense of exploration.

Rocky Mountain National Park is one of the premier hiking parks in the nation. In certain respects, it is not unique. Other national parks, such as Glacier, also boast spectacular mountain scenery. Other national parks, such as Yellowstone, also afford superb wildlife viewing. Other national parks, such as Mount Rainier, also sport blankets of stunning wildflowers. And virtually all national parks contain well-maintained trails. What makes Rocky distinctive is the diversity of its hiking trails, from short and easy to long and strenuous. Several trails are accessible to wheelchairs, and there is even a wheelchair-accessible backcountry campsite. At the other end of the spectrum are trails well above tree line, where the thin air and rocky terrain challenge the body. Between these extremes are trails of diverse length, altitude, and steepness. You can walk to alpine tundra, lush meadows, shady forests, rushing creeks, scenic canyons, historic sites, noisy waterfalls, quiet lakes, and even a glacier or two. And you never have to look over your shoulder, because there are no Grizzlies in the park. That's a shame, in a sense, because the big bears once occurred here and belong to the ecosystem.

Three hiking seasons predominate in Rocky. The tourist season begins with Memorial Day at the end of May and ends on Labor Day at the beginning of September. Due to the sheer number of visitors then, we perforce emphasize summer hiking. In autumn, when the aspens turn gold against the conifer-covered hills, fall hunting season chases most Colorado hikers and backpackers out of the national forests, but they can tread safely here in Rocky. Finally, winter and early spring bring heavy snow to the high country, although many trails below 10,000 feet still beckon the outdoor enthusiast. Hiking in snow, snowshoeing, and cross-country skiing require special skills and equipment beyond the purview of this book, but, having enjoyed the winter outdoors for decades in Wisconsin, we highly recommend exploring snow-covered trails once you are properly prepared.

TYPES OF HIKES INCLUDED

Circuits, loops, and side trips. According to the dictionary, the definitions of *loop* and *circuit* are similar, but only *circuit* specifically means "a path or route the complete traversal of which without local change of direction requires returning to the starting point." By contrast, *loop* is a more general term, various meanings of which do not involve returning to the exact starting point (*e.g.*, loop stitches in sewing, loops on roller coasters). So we call our hiking routes circuits, but do use the term *loop* for component circle routes. A circuit may be composed of an inner and outer loop with at least one cross-connection, though it more commonly consists of two loops arranged somewhat like a figure 8, where it is possible to hike either the entire circumference or one (or both) of the individual loops. A side trip is an optional out-and-back route from a circuit.

Criteria for inclusion. We have tried to incorporate every possible circuit meeting the following four criteria. First, the circuit must be wholly within Rocky Mountain National Park. We don't want to incur the ire of any private landowners. Second, the trail must describe a true circuit, leaving from a parking area and returning to that same place without retracing steps (excepting short access trails for a few circuits). Recommended side trips from the circuit require out-and-back walking, but these are optional diversions for those hikers desiring a longer outing. Third, the circuits included must not involve walking on heavily traveled, paved roads amid the carbon monoxide and hazards of traffic. A couple of circuits do incorporate a short section along an unpaved road, but the vast majority do not even cross a paved road. Fourth, the route must be a true hike not requiring the use of special equipment such as crampons for negotiating an ice field or pitons and ropes for climbing a rock face. This is not to say that every inch of the way is necessarily on manicured trail. You may have to traverse a snowbank, cross open tundra, or scramble (gently) through a rock field. The route, however, is always well defined.

Most of the circuits are intended as day hikes. Even the longest hikes (save two) could be completed during a long summer's day by a strong walker in good shape. Nevertheless, length was not a criterion for inclusion. A few of the longer circuits that could be walked in a day are perhaps better done as overnight backpacking trips. Backcountry campsites are shown on our trail maps; permits are required for all backcountry camping, and advanced reservations are strongly recommended.

Side trips. Some accounts suggest optional side trips. Like the circuit itself, each side trip usually includes at least one interesting natural or historical feature such as a lake, waterfall, cabin site, or scenic vista; most side trips go specifically to such a feature. In some cases a side trip can be extended beyond the stated goal (*e.g.,* the side trip to Mills Lake from the Alpine Lakes Circuit can be extended to Jewel Lake—another 0.4 mile—or even Black Lake—2.2 miles from Mills Lake). Such extensions are not included in the accounts. Finally, side trips leave from the circuit itself, not from a trailhead (Nymph Lake, for instance, is a mere half mile from Bear Lake but is not listed as a side trip from the Bear Lake Circuit because the trail to Nymph Lake leaves directly from the Bear Lake Trailhead).

Turn to the account of a circuit for specific information on formula times for each side trip (more on formula times follows). For example, the basic Lumpy Ridge Circuit is listed as 6 hours, 57 minutes, with two possible side trips for a maximum hike of 11 hours, 9 minutes. When we hiked it, we chose only one of the side trips (Bridal Veil Falls at 1 hour, 37 minutes) and so planned a hike that we estimated would take 8 hours, 34 minutes (6:57 + 1:37 = 8:34); our actual time proved to be 7 hours, 58 minutes, including a short lunch stop.

Other circuits. There are at least three other ways to make circuit hikes wholly within Rocky Mountain National Park. One is to combine two or more contiguous circuits. We provide specific suggestions at the end of each major section of the book, which is divided by access points (East Side, Bear Lake Road, and West Side). At the end of the Bear Lake Road section, we also discuss using the park's free shuttle bus as a part of a circuit. Finally, hiking parties with two vehicles can devise still other hikes requiring no retracing of steps, but possibilities are too numerous to include in this guide.

TYPES OF TRAIL RATINGS

In planning a hike, people usually want to know how far they will be walking and, even more importantly, how long it will take, the duration depending upon both distance and elevation gain. Most people also want to know how strenuous the hike will be, an equation involving what (if any) physical exertion besides walking is involved and how distance, elevation gain, and altitude combine to tax a hiker's stamina. We provide basic data about such factors for each trail.

Formula hiking times. Hiking times set forth in this book are standard durations based on a widely used formula: an hour for every 2.0 miles walked and an hour for every 1000 feet of total elevation gained. Elevation loss does not speed hiking time because negotiating your way downhill can be even slower than walking level ground, but on the whole is about the same. Formula hiking times also provide a first indication of hiking exertion, in that usually the longer the formula time, the more strenuous the hike will be. We order circuit hikes first by access area and then by location from north to south within that area; a listing by formula hiking times is provided in the Table of Circuits on page xiii.

Formula times have proven reasonably accurate predictors of our actual times on day hikes, during which we carry ample day packs with plenty of water, raincoat, lunch, maps, binoculars, and camera. Admittedly, we often pause to identify a bird, photograph a flower, or admire a view, so even we can hike faster than we usually do. Therefore, formula times may err on the conservative side. Your actual hiking times may be shorter or longer, and after a little experience you can calibrate your actual times against the formula times. Here are some other factors that influence hiking times:

Slower	*Faster*
Newly arrived from low altitudes	Acclimated to high altitudes
Walking in heavy leather boots	Walking in light but strong boots
Carrying overnight backpack	Carrying day pack
Carrying full day pack	Carrying essentials only
Stopping to take pictures, watch animals	"Always keep amovin' and don't stand still"
Smoker	Nonsmoker
Overweight for height	Correct weight for height
Poor physical condition; couch potato	Good physical condition; regular exercise
Old and wise	Young and vigorous

If you are newly arrived from the flatlands—Madison, Wisconsin, where we lived for years, is only 300 feet above sea level—you would be wise to begin hiking circuits with shorter formula times at lower altitudes and work your way up to longer hikes at higher elevations. You may want to travel light on these initial short hikes, carrying only essentials such as those listed on page 13, until your shoulders can bear a day pack weighted down with optional items such as camera, binoculars, or field guides.

Route classification. Those who frequent high places, especially climbers, have devised a classification of routes based on the physical activity and skills demanded. With one exception, all the basic circuits in this book are Class 1, "hands-in-pockets" walking hikes. (Several optional side trails require some rock scrambling, making them Class 2 excursions.) That exception is a circuit that involves descending over or alongside a glacier, which is usually possible without equipment; if ice axe and crampons are necessary, however, the rating jumps to Class 3. As all our circuits can be considered Class 1, we do not provide this type of rating.

An exertion rating system. Difficulty ratings in most other guides are assigned subjectively, typically as easy, moderate, or difficult. In fact, there is often ambiguity about what an author means by "difficulty," as the term can refer either to the skills or the exertion required. As we have noted, the skills required for the circuits in this book are minimal: walking, some gentle scrambling over rocks, and in one case negotiating your way down a glacier. We are more concerned with difficulty in the sense of exertion. A system used in at least one guide to certain trails in RMNP does attempt to quantify exertion levels objectively, but that system is merely a rescaling of the distance walked and altitude gained and there-fore differs little from formula hiking time. The missing factor is altitude.

A new formula. For this book we devised a formula that yields an objective exertion (difficulty) rating in points. This formula recognizes the fact that a given hike at an altitude of 11,000 feet is more strenuous than a hike of the same distance and total elevation gain at 7000 feet. Our formula assigns one point for each mile walked and one point for each 500 feet of total elevation gained, the sum divided by a percentage ex-pressed as a decimal fraction determined by the average altitude of the hike (details follow). The average altitude is calculated by adding the low-est and highest elevations and dividing by 2.

Technical stuff. The hiker need not understand how the altitude divi-sor is calculated, but for those interested in the technicalities, here is an

5

explanation. The body harnesses energy by oxidizing, or burning, stored food derivatives such as carbohydrates and fats. The relative amount of oxygen in the air is a constant 21 percent (air is mostly nitrogen), but air pressure decreases with altitude, meaning that the partial pressure of oxygen in the lungs (called the alveolar pressure) decreases accordingly. We assume that exertion is directly related to this scarcity of oxygen at high elevations. It turns out that the logarithm of the alveolar pressure, relative to that at sea level, is proportional to the altitude above sea level. Therefore, the relative alveolar pressure *(P)* is calculated by the formula log P = $sA + i$, where A is the altitude (in thousands of feet), s is the slope (which we determined to be -0.02), and i the intercept (determined to be 2.02). If this formula were perfectly accurate, the intercept would be exactly 2.00, so that the relative pressure at sea level would be exactly 100 percent instead of a slightly higher calculated value. Nevertheless, the equation is 99.6 percent accurate in a statistical sense, so it is far and away accurate enough for our purposes. Using this formula, we can calculate the relative alveolar pressure at 7000 feet as 75 percent and at 11,000 feet as 63 percent of the pressure at sea level. Thus, a hike of 15 points for distance and elevation gain would have an exertion rating of 15/0.75 = 20.0 points at an average altitude of 7000 feet and 15/0.63 = 23.8 points at 11,000 feet.

Categories. We classified exertion points by inspecting how circuit point totals grouped themselves, and we identified eight categories: stroll, very easy, easy, moderately easy, moderate, moderately strenuous, strenuous, and very strenuous. Consider this new exertion rating experimental and let us know how useful you find it.

Effect on hiking times? If altitude usefully figures into an exertion rating, why, you may wonder, doesn't it also contribute to hiking time, at least as we calculate it? The answer is that it probably does to some extent: at or above 10,000 feet, most hikers do slow their pace, so the formula time may underestimate the true duration of a hike. Nevertheless, our observation is that most people try to maintain a given hiking pace, which means that the exertion increases while the hiking time stays the same. In any case, an hour for every 2.0 mile and for every 1000 feet of total elevation gain is such a widely used formula that we decided not to tamper with it.

MORE ABOUT TRAILS

Trailheads vs. access points. The starting point of a trail is commonly called a trailhead, but we prefer the term *access point* to avoid confusion:

in Rocky Mountain National Park there are many trail access points, but only some of them are officially designated trailheads (with a capital T). Therefore we use *access point* as the general term in all our circuit accounts. Where an access point is also an official trailhead, we also give its name.

Heraclitean Warning! Things change. Trails are rerouted, footbridges are carried away by storms, cairns are toppled, trail segments wash out, backcountry campsites are relocated, and so on. Above all, trail signs and markers change (or are obliterated by vandals or other beasts), and for that reason, this guide makes little mention of them.

We recommend carrying a topographic map on every hike. True, mountains move (slowly), creeks reroute themselves (sometimes), and avalanches alter contour lines (a little). Nevertheless, geographic features remain remarkably constant on a human time scale, so even an old topographic map will be helpful if you become lost. Newer, more useful maps are printed on plastic, which not only resists wear and tear but is completely waterproof: you can read them in a rainstorm with impunity. These tend to be large-scale maps (1:59,000, for example) although they are adequate for most purposes. These and more detailed U.S. Geological Survey (USGS) quadrangle maps are available for purchase in RMNP visitor centers and outdoor shops in Estes Park and Grand Lake.

HEALTH, SAFETY, AND COMFORT

Water. Nearly every hiker knows not to drink untreated water from lakes and streams. Boiling water is time-consuming, and not terribly practical for day hikes, so many hikers rely on chemical treatments or filters to purify drinking water they collect on the way. Certain older water-treatment tablets are insufficient because they kill bacteria but not *Giardia,* a protozoan that causes major intestinal distress. Newer chemical treatments do kill *Giardia,* but check the label to be sure. *Giardia* can also be removed from water by using a ceramic micropore filter. There are many small filter systems now on the market for hikers and campers; they are not cheap (starting at around $50), but they work well, allowing you to fill a water bottle from a stream with a few minutes of pumping. Come to think of it, the filters *are* cheap compared with the cost of extensive medical treatment, not to mention the agony of *Giardia* infection.

Always carry water. You can go days without food and suffer few ill effects save hunger and decreased energy, but dehydration is a serious problem. Very few of the trail access points provide sources of drinking water. Therefore, you must remember to fill your water bottles before setting out for the day.

Glass bottles are a no-no because of the possibility of breakage; they are also heavy. In a pinch you could use half-gallon plastic soft-drink bottles; they have thin, weak sides but usually do not flavor the water. We recommend a good, modern plastic water bottle. If you don't already own one, go to an outdoor supply store in Estes Park or Grand Lake and buy one that meets your particular needs.

During the hike, drink even though you may not feel thirsty. The dry mountain air dehydrates the body faster than thirst signals can keep pace. A good rule of thumb is to drink at least a pint of water for every two hours on the trail.

The elements. Winter hiking poses certain dangers—hypothermia, frostbite, and a bevy of other special problems beyond the scope of this book— but summer and fall hiking, too, present their share of risks. The most serious is being struck by **lightning**. The trails in this book are mostly well below tree line, but even if you are not on the alpine tundra, lightning is still extremely dangerous. If you are one of the tallest objects around, or are next to such an object—for example, a Ponderosa Pine in open parkland—you are in danger in an electrical storm. If possible, move into forest immediately; in any case, crouch as low as you can, keeping minimal contact with the ground. Squat or kneel but do not lie or sit. Pick as dry a spot as you can find quickly. Do not get directly under a tree or rock overhang, or duck into a cave, where lightning can sometimes enter. It's better to get soaked by rain than struck by lightning.

Hypothermia can be of concern even in summer, especially if you get drenched in a rainstorm. A body that was soaking up the rays just minutes before can quickly begin soaking up the rain and shivering. The most important area to keep dry is the torso: its large surface area promotes massive evaporative heat loss when wet. We always carry simple, hooded rain jackets, which double as windbreakers when needed. We usually hike in shorts in summer and let our legs get wet; they stay warm while walking because muscle contraction generates heat.

Add hail to the wraths of **afternoon storms** and you know why we always get an early start on hikes that take us high into the mountains. Moist air rises as the morning warms, and then cools at high altitudes, forcing moisture out of the air. In Rocky, clouds begin forming by late morning; by early afternoon you can find yourself in a fierce electrical storm. If your hike takes you above tree line, plan to reach the high point before noon and get below tree line as soon after midday as possible.

The flip side of the weather coin involves **sunburn**, heat exhaustion, and sunstroke. Sunburn is caused by ultraviolet (UV) radiation, which increases with elevation. UV rays penetrate clouds, so you can burn even on cool, overcast days. We always wear hats when hiking, put sunscreen on all exposed skin, and carry the sunscreen in our day packs. Dermatologists agree on the importance of using sunscreen but may differ in specific recommendations. One dermatologist we talked with said that an SPF of more than 30 was not necessary, but frequent renewal was essential because perspiration and other factors diminish the protection. Another dermatologist recommended sunscreen of at least SPF 30 or one containing Parsal 1789, with renewal at least every 4 hours. Heat exhaustion and sunstroke are less common but more serious. **Heat exhaustion** is characterized by weakness, nausea, and profuse sweating. The afflicted person pales and becomes dizzy. If this happens to you, sit down immediately so that you don't fall and injure yourself. If possible, lie with your feet slightly higher than your head. Rest until you feel normal again, then take things slow and easy. **Sunstroke** is more dangerous: characterized by flushed skin and increased body temperature, it leads to convulsions and possibly coma. At the first sign of possible sunstroke, get into shade or put a jacket over your head. Sit upright and dampen your face and head in particular. If you go into convulsions, you will need a rescue team with competent medical help, so your hiking companion will have to act quickly.

Elevation. Altitude sickness afflicts many people at elevations of 8000 feet and higher. Headaches and listlessness are the two most common complaints, but a more severe manifestation is nausea. These symptoms constitute acute mountain sickness, or AMS, and the best cure is to descend to a lower altitude. You are more likely to suffer the effects of elevation while driving along Trail Ridge Road than while taking any of the hikes in this guide because the climb is faster and the road goes higher than most of the trails. It is common to find yourself short of breath in the thinner air above 10,000 feet; pace yourself to keep your breathing and heart rates within reasonable limits. The nausea that sometimes occurs is due partly to chemical responses that render the gut more acidic than usual; an antacid tablet (we carry a roll when hiking at high elevations) should offer some relief.

Effects that are more serious are rare. If you have a cold that has blocked your eustachian tubes, preventing pressure adjustments in the middle ear, do not venture into the high country and risk permanent hearing damage. Some people can develop a life-threatening condition called high-altitude pulmonary edema (HAPE), which is basically an accumulation of fluid in the lungs. If you suspect you are suffering from HAPE, descend immediately, and if the symptoms do not completely abate, see a doctor.

Animal dangers. Grizzlies no longer range as far south as RMNP, and Black Bears (which are often more frightening than truly dangerous) are uncommon. In all our decades of picnicking, hiking, camping, and backpacking in RMNP, we have never come across a bear or venomous snake. Nevertheless, increased use of the backcountry has raised the number of bear encounters. Television may promote the image of bears as furry, cuddly animals, but in reality they are smart, efficient killing machines. In an unlikely encounter with a bear, give it a wide berth, move slowly, and never turn your back to it. If attacked by a bear, or even a Mountain Lion, fight back. Rocky Mountain Black Bears average only about 150 pounds and therefore pose much less of a threat than the 400-pound bears of the eastern United States.

The greatest potential danger from animals may come from Elk, simply because they are so common. The Elk population, like the visitor population, has increased greatly over the years, raising the number of Elk-visitor encounters. Usually, Elk pay little attention to people, but if a crowd of photographers and wildlife admirers surrounds one, the animal is likely to bolt, probably toward someone in the circle. You also don't want to blunder into a harem, especially during rutting season, and be treated like a trespassing bull. Nor do you want to approach a mother and her calf. Common sense will usually keep you out of trouble.

Moose also deserve mention because they have begun infiltrating the west side of the park from other areas. Alaskans, who have extensive experience with wildlife, consider the Moose second only to the Grizzly Bear in terms of danger to humans. Both bulls and cows can be aggressive; never, ever approach a Moose.

People most often get into trouble with large animals when they try to photograph or feed them. Simple point-and-shoot cameras tempt would-be photographers to approach animals too closely. Use a telephoto lens—at least a 200mm is recommended. (Jack uses a 640mm lens for wildlife.) Or buy your animal photos in a gift shop.

Feeding the animals is prohibited in RMNP. Like all park rules, this one has been established with good reason. In addition to triggering complex ecological disturbances, offering handouts to the animals creates junk-food junkies who forget how to forage. Summer is when young animals must learn how to obtain food in nature, else they may die in winter when food becomes scarce. And let's not forget that people who feed the animals run the risk of being bitten. That cute chipmunk or ground squirrel may be willing to take food from your hand, but if something frightens the animal at just the wrong moment, you may feel rodent teeth sink into your finger. The tetanus bacterium loves puncture wounds such as animal bites. Rabies is always a possibility with any mammal bite. And rodent populations in the western United States carry bubonic plague—yes, the scourge of the Middle Ages. It's not likely you'll contract plague, but any unnecessary risk is unacceptable.

EQUIPMENT AND ITS USE

Footwear and blisters. Traditionalists advocate wearing strong, well-broken-in, ankle-height boots, and we agree. Nevertheless, two other opinions exist among experienced hikers. The first is that once your ankles are sufficiently strong, lower, shoe-height boots are preferable because their lighter weight translates into less energy expended while hiking. The other opinion is that ankle-high athletic shoes provide (almost?) as much support as boots yet weigh noticeably less. Your feet belong to you, so you decide; we're sticking to boots with ankle support in rough terrain or when carrying lots of weight for backpacking. At lower elevations on easy trails, lightweight athletic shoes are usually adequate. Whatever your footwear, be 100 percent certain it is well broken in before setting off on a long hike.

One pair of socks or two is another decision. We recommend wearing a thin inner sock and thick, cushioning outer sock so that slippage occurs mainly between the socks rather than between foot and sock. Liz wears ordinary light inner socks and Jack prefers wicking nylon inner socks sold especially for hikers. A few experienced hikers we know wear only one pair of socks but treat their feet to promote slippage without abrasion and blisters. Two methods of treatment are taping the heel area with duct tape and greasing the foot with Vaseline or a similar agent. In any case, we caution against cotton socks because once they get wet, they loose all insulating value and won't dry even if you take them off and hang them on your pack.

If you feel a hot spot that could be a blister forming, stop immediately and inspect the area. If there is no blister yet, put something over the area so that slippage occurs between the buffer material and your sock. You can use special products for hiking, such as moleskin, but we find that duct tape works just as well. Some people say never to drain a formed blister, but we always do. Take the needle from that little first-aid kit that you always carry hiking, sterilize it with one of the matches you also carry, and then pierce the blister at the edge, with the needle parallel to the skin. Then apply moleskin or build up tape *around* the drained blister so that nothing sticks to the blister itself and the blister is protected from further rubbing.

Clothing. We like nylon pants with zip-off lower legs for conversion to shorts. Jeans are tough, but like other cotton garments they lose insulating power when wet and simply will not dry out while you're wearing them. If you wear shorts, put a pair of long pants or rain pants in your day pack.

In warm weather we often hike in tee shirts, but again, not those made of pure cotton. Stuffed in our day packs, though, is a long-sleeve shirt. Once again, we eschew cotton, and use instead one of those expensive, vented nylon shirts made popular by Columbia Sportswear but now manufactured by several companies. We also carry a fleece vest or jacket for warmth; a wool sweater would serve the same purpose.

Hat. We always wear hats, especially to shade our faces in open areas where the UV radiation is high. A hat is also useful beneath the hood of a raincoat or poncho: when you turn your head, the hood turns with it. There are many different kinds of sun-shading hats; selecting one is a matter of personal preference.

Walking stick? In general, we rarely take our walking sticks on easy day hikes, although we always take them when backpacking. On relatively flat land, a stick staves off leg fatigue, and on steep trails, it is useful on the uphill struggle and will save your knees on the downhill trek. When crossing a stream on a slippery log, a walking stick can prevent disaster. Nevertheless, if you don't really need them, walking sticks can get in the way, and we have found that even on flat land they tend to slow us down. Furthermore, Jack likes to have his hands free to use binoculars, camera, and microtape recorder. One compromise is to carry your stick horizontally whenever you don't need it. Jack has devised another solution: he hangs his stick from a clip sewn onto the upper part of his day pack, securing the stick to the bottom of the pack with a small strap.

Day pack contents. Authorities more or less agree on the essentials for day hiking. Here is a suggested list (in addition to the extra clothing we have already mentioned) distilled from three different sources:

- Water bottle
- Topographic map
- Compass (know how to use it with your map)
- Pocket knife (a Swiss Army type with useful gadgets such as scissors)
- First-aid kit (appropriate for blisters, cuts, burns, headaches, etc.)
- Rain gear (raincoat or poncho)
- Food (trail mix, high-energy bars; lunch, if applicable)
- Fire-starting kit (*e.g.,* waterproof matches and candle stub)
- Small flashlight with extra batteries
- Sunglasses and sunscreen
- Signaling devices (*e.g.,* whistle and metal mirror)

Other useful items that some might also place on the essential list include space blanket, nylon line, extra socks, bandanna, and toilet paper. If you wear glasses, be sure to take a pair (especially if you need them for map reading) and remember to pack any medications that you take regularly. Finally, we strongly urge you to bring along a plastic trash bag.

Popular optional items include camera, binoculars, field guides for natural history, and trail guides (for instance, this book!). Small point-and-shoot cameras are both popular and lightweight. Until recently, serious photographers had to lug along heavy equipment, but those who have switched to digital photography can now carry sophisticated, lighter-weight instruments. Small, center-focus binoculars of sufficient quality can be bought for about $100. Jack carries such binoculars (a 10x model) while hiking, leaving locked up at home his optically superb Zeiss pair that cost ten times as much and are probably nearly ten times as heavy. Books, of course, still weigh what they always have, so choose your reading material carefully.

Backpacking gear. If you want to turn some of the circuits into backpacking trips, consult quality reference materials for advice on gear and techniques. The Suggested Reading and Reference list at the end of this book will get you started. Of course, we recommend *Backpacking Wisconsin,* not because it is the most appropriate reference in this case, but because we like the authors (us!).

About cell phones and other electronic toys. In writing *Backpacking Wisconsin,* we were taken to task by one reviewer for suggesting that cell phones be left at home. Our recommendation, however, reflected the strong consensus of the hiking community. The following story illustrates but one reason why carrying cell phones while hiking is frowned upon. We choose this story because it comes firsthand from the people who actually made the call from their tent in a Wisconsin state park. After hearing scary noises in the middle of the night, they dialed 911. Their call was picked up by an emergency station on the far side of Lake Michigan. The Michigan authorities contacted a sheriff's office in Wisconsin, which dispatched a patrol car to the scene. The officers involved spotted nothing more threatening than a raccoon roaming the campground. Your tax dollars at work!

We have yet to talk to a seasoned camper, backpacker, or hiker who condones using cell phones in the woods. If you are lost, a cell phone is no help because its signal cannot be traced (if you require medical assistance and know where you are, however, then, of course, a cell phone would be useful). If carrying a cell phone in your pack makes you feel more secure, by all means go ahead—but please, keep it turned off completely except for true emergency situations.

A new craze has hit the market: GPS (global-positioning system) receivers. Jack has an old one that he sometimes uses to check a trail distance, but we don't recommend depending on GPS receivers to find your way. The system works well for boaters on large expanses of open water; they can receive signals from many satellites and require accuracy only within a few hundred feet. In the mountains, however, reception is usually quite limited and the resulting geographic coordinates are not very reliable.

FEES AND PERMITS

In Rocky Mountain National Park, there is no charge for hiking a trail, or even for riding the shuttle buses on Bear Lake Road. There is, however, a park entrance fee, waived for holders of the National Parks Pass, the Golden Age Passport (for those 62 or older), or the Golden Access Passport (for those with disabilities). Anyone can purchase a Golden Eagle Passport, good for one year, which covers entrance to most federal fee areas, including RMNP.

Camping involves fees, too. The Golden Age and Golden Access Passports offer a 50 percent discount on campground fees (the Golden Eagle Passport does not). Backpacking requires a permit for a specific site on a given night, and there is now an administrative fee for this permit, which formerly was free. The funds may, of course, be needed to defray expenses in an era of decreasing support from Congress. Nevertheless, we think the charge is unfair because backpacking is a low-impact, low-cost activity. Picnicking is just the opposite—there are roads to maintain and trash to dispose of—yet it is free. Even more unfortunate is the fact that the Golden Age Passport does not apply to the backpacking fee. Ironically, it is cheaper for someone 62 or older to stay in a campground with all its amenities than it is to hike to a primitive site in the backcountry.

See the "Fee Schedules" appendix for more information on fees.

A FEW RELEVANT PARK REGULATIONS

Fortunately, unlike many state parks, national parks do not bombard you with rules upon entry. There is no huge sign awaiting you with illegibly tiny writing delineating all the things that are forbidden. Nevertheless, RMNP does have some regulations. Most are benign and little more than codified common sense.

Here are a few regulations of special relevance to hikers. Pets and bicycles are not allowed on any trail. No wild animal may be fed or touched, and no wildflower may be picked. (You may, however, pick berries for immediate consumption. Yum!) In fact, no natural, historical, or archaeological item or area may be damaged, destroyed, collected, or disturbed in any way. If you will be camping, backpacking, or fishing, inquire about further regulations applicable to those activities.

FINAL WORDS

You can help preserve our scenic trails in small but important ways while on your hike. First, remember to include a plastic trash bag in your pack and pick up those drink cans, film wrappers, cigarette butts and other detritus that thoughtless hikers have discarded on the trail. Second, ask anyone picking wildflowers to stop. We simply say, "Please leave the flowers for others to enjoy." Sometimes our request may be ignored, but most people desist if they know others are watching and do not approve. Finally, in a similar vein, try to prevent people from shortcutting switchbacks (kids are especially prone to this unfortunate behavior). Just say something like, "Please stay on the trail; shortcuts cause erosion."

About the Circuit Accounts

Within the major access sections (East Side, Bear Lake Road, West Side), accounts are ordered by access point from north to south. If the name of a circuit ends in "Loops," that circuit has component circles (either concentric, or, more commonly, adjacent to one another). For planning purposes, a complete table on page xiii shows formula hiking times for all circuits and any component loops. Many circuits also have one or more optional, out-and-back side trips, which extend the hiking time, so the table provides maximum formula times that include all possible side trips.

ACCOUNT CONTENTS

FORMULA TIME(S): This section provides formula walking times (in hours and minutes) for the circuit only (shortest hike) as well as the circuit plus all optional side trips (longest hike). As explained in the Introduction, formula time is calculated by allotting an hour for each 2.0 miles walked and each 1000 feet of total elevation gained. Formula time is the actual walking time and does not include lunch stops, lengthy rests, sightseeing, photography, or other diversions.

HIKING ELEVATIONS: This section provides the lowest and highest elevations of the circuit. Often, an optional side trip will take the hiker up from the circuit; these higher elevations are also given. Total elevation gain may be much greater than the difference between highest and lowest elevations.

EXERTION RATING(S): As explained in the Introduction, we have devised a rating system to reflect the strenuousness of a hike. The formula incorporates factors for distance walked, total elevation gained, and average altitude. Minimum rating is for the circuit itself; the maximum figure includes all optional side trips.

FEATURES: Here we describe the general character of a hike and its main attractions—obviously a matter of judgment.

ACCESS POINTS: The access points are the named trailheads, picnic areas, or other places where hikers can park a car. Details on how to find the access point(s) are given later in the account.

SEASONS: Notes on appropriate seasonal use are based on information kindly provided by RMNP staff member Dick Putney.

SUMMARY: Here we provide a table showing the distance, elevation gain, formula time, and exertion rating for the circuit itself and for each component loop and optional side trip. If you wish to plan an outing involving at least one but not all possible side trips, add the formula times for the desired side trip(s) to the formula time for the circuit itself to estimate walking time. The exertion ratings also add in the same way.

FINDING THE ACCESS POINT(S): Sometimes the most confusing thing about a hike is finding the starting place. This section provides directions to the access point (or points, if more than one choice is available), and to the trail from the parking place if the way is not obvious. We also state whether drinking water and toilets are available at the access point. *Warning:* Access points rarely provide sources of drinking water. Fill your bottles before setting out for the day.

TRAIL DESCRIPTION: This section includes notes for each leg of the hike (including the formula time for that leg) and indicates whether the hike should be done clockwise or counterclockwise. If we favor walking the circuit in a particular direction, we state why. We may also say a few words about the general ecology and terrain here, but if our notes are more extensive, we save them for the hiking notes. Note that summing individual formula times may differ from the overall time by 1 minute because of rounding.

The component leg times are useful for predicting when you should reach a specific point, such as a planned lunch stop. They are also helpful for orienting yourself. If you should have reached a particular place after 20 minutes of walking and have not reached it after 40, you've probably missed it. The notes also provide times for side trips, and often some notes about what you may see on a given leg of the hike. Ancillary information—on natural history, for example—is shown in *italics*.

Walking a circuit in the other direction from that described in detail will involve the same time overall, but individual segments will differ because the elevation gains are in different places. Therefore, following the main description, we offer a summary of the trail segments in the opposite direction. The optional out-and-back side trips are the same regardless of which way the circuit is walked.

OUR HIKING NOTES: For those circuits we've taken notes on (most of them), we share our experiences. If we timed our hike, we begin by comparing the actual duration with the formula time. We try to mention the habitats (including component trees) passed through, smaller plants noticed (principally wildflowers), birds seen or heard, and mammals spotted. These are not necessarily the things you will find or notice, but at least you are alerted to possibilities. Some guidebooks tend to highlight the larger animals, even if people are extremely unlikely to see one. For example, Mountain Lions do inhabit Rocky Mountain National Park, but they have huge home ranges and are both nocturnal and shy, so your chances of seeing one are very slim. You do have a good chance, however, of seeing the same things we did on a particular route.

About names of animals and plants: Following a convention universal in ornithology and widespread among wildflower enthusiasts, we use initial caps on proper names of plant and animal species ("a grove of Engelmann Spruce") but lowercase generic categories ("a grove of spruce trees"). This orthographic device is useful in distinguishing between, for instance, a Blue Jay (a particular species of jay) and a blue jay (a jay that is blue, which is true of both the Blue Jay and Steller's Jay).

To avoid burdening the book with Latinized scientific names we use standard common names for which the exact scientific name can be found in an appropriate reference. Common names of plants follow *Plants of Rocky Mountain National Park* by L. H. Beidleman, R. G. Beidleman, and B. E. Willard. We list wildflowers in the sequence they are found in this book, except that we follow the usual practice of listing monocots before dicots. Fungi are no longer considered plants, but rather compose a separate kingdom paralleling plants and animals. Mushroom common names are taken from *A Field Guide to Mushrooms of North America* by K. H. McKnight and V. B. McKnight. Bird names, and the sequence in which birds are listed, follows the authoritative *A. O. U. Check-list of North American Birds,* 7th ed., published by the American Ornithologists' Union. You needn't bother tracking down this academic monograph in a college library, however, because the species list is available on the World Wide Web at http://pica.wru.umt.edu/aou/birdlist.html. For mammals, we follow the names and sequence in J. O. Whitaker's *National Audubon Society Field Guide to North American Mammals*. Finally, some of the more common plants and animals can be found in the Natural History Appendix near the end of this book.

ACCOUNT MAPS

Each account begins with a trail map drawn specifically for this book. These maps coordinate with the trail descriptions: trail points (solid triangles) mark the divisions between legs described in text. The elevations (in feet) at the trail points, and the distances between trail points (in miles to the nearest tenth), are also provided (except for extremely short trails such as Lily Lake Inner Loop, Sprague Lake Circuit, and Bear Lake Circuit).

We have always taken elevations and trail distances from authoritative sources when possible (*e.g.*, USGS topographic maps and official RMNP publications). When comparing distances given in different trail guides for the same trail, we have found discrepancies—occasionally significant ones— so use such data cautiously. When there was any doubt or we could not locate a trail distance in a reliable source, we have measured trails with a map wheel on topographic maps as carefully as possible. We then compared a reputed distance with our walking time to see if the values were reasonable.

Accurate elevations are easier to come by than accurate distances (assuming the trail route is located correctly on the map). The elevations we provide are accurate within one contour line (plus or minus 80 feet maximum discrepancy). Some of our map distances will no doubt prove slightly off, but not enough, we trust, to noticeably affect the formula walking time or exertion rating of a circuit.

Jack has also measured distances on some circuits with a handheld GPS unit, but comparisons with other sources reveal that GPS always underestimates trail distances. The main reason appears to be that GPS calculates distances by comparing the latitude and longitude of successive points. As far as GPS is concerned, if you fall off a sheer cliff that is 1000 feet high, your body will have almost the identical geographic coordinates it did the instant before you fell. In this case, GPS cannot detect that you did indeed travel 1000 feet.

Account maps also provide information that may not be included in text. For example, backcountry campsites are shown even though they are not mentioned in text. Watercourses (brooks, streams, creeks, rivers) are usually identified by name on the maps but only rarely in text. Even though a trail map is probably sufficiently accurate and detailed to stand alone as a guide, we urge once again that you carry a topographic map. If you lose the trail (as in a violent rainstorm) or for some reason need to go cross-country, a topographic map is an absolute necessity.

Ouzel Falls in Wild Basin, one of the many places on the East Side of Rocky Mountain National Park offering circuit hikes.

Circuit Hikes From Access Points on the East Side

INTRODUCTION TO EAST SIDE CIRCUITS

East Side circuits are those located on the eastern side of RMNP, excluding those accessed from Bear Lake Road, which we have placed in a separate category. In order to access most of these East Side circuits, you will find you must leave the Park and drive to an access point on or just inside the park's eastern boundary.

Those staying in campgrounds may find it convenient to do a circuit hike that begins right by their campsite. Unfortunately, most of the East Side circuits cannot be hiked in this way. The exception is the Wind River Circuit, which could be hiked from the Glacier Basin Campground on Bear Lake Road. The Longs Flank Circuit is indeed accessed from Longs Peak Ranger Station and Campground, but it is not a circuit one could hike while camping in this tents-only, limited-stay small campground. Longs Flank is one of only two circuits in this book that cannot be done as a day hike, so special planning for a multiday trip is necessary.

The accounts in this section are ordered geographically by access point from north to south. All have different access points.

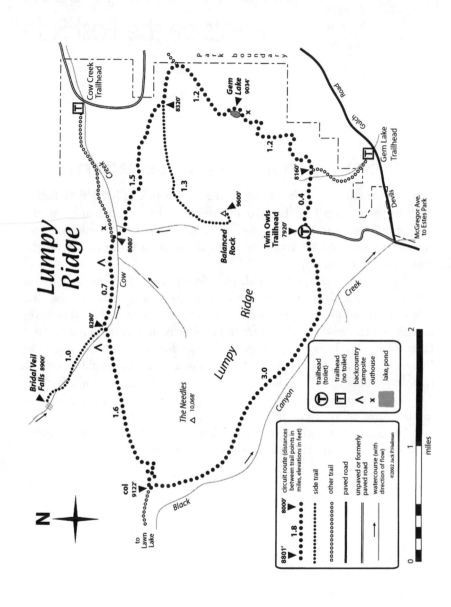

Lumpy Ridge

Cow Creek Trailhead

Gem Lake Trailhead

Twin Owls Trailhead 7920'

Gem Lake 9034'

8320'

8160'

8080'

8280'

Bridal Veil Falls 8900'

col 9122'

The Needles △ 10,068'

Balanced Rock 9600'

Lumpy Ridge

Cow Creek

Black Canyon Creek

Devils Gulch Road

McGregor Ave. to Estes Park

to Lawn Lake

park boundary

N

1.2
1.2
1.5
1.3
0.4
0.7
1.0
1.6
3.0

Legend

8801' 8000'
▲   ▲
1.8

●●●● circuit route (distances between trail points in miles, elevations in feet)

•••• side trail

•••• other trail

ooooo unpaved or formerly paved road

━━━ paved road

→ watercourse (with direction of flow)

Ⓣ trailhead (toilet)

🅃 trailhead (no toilet)

∧ backcountry campsite

✕ outhouse

▨ lake, pond

miles
0   1   2

©2002 Jack P.Hailman

LUMPY RIDGE CIRCUIT

FORMULA TIMES: 6 hours, 57 minutes for the circuit; 11 hours, 9 minutes including both side trips.

HIKING ELEVATIONS: 7920 to 9122 feet.

EXERTION RATINGS: 19.8 (moderately strenuous) for the circuit itself to a maximum of 31.9 (very strenuous) with both side trips.

FEATURES: Geologic formations (Lumpy Ridge), wildflowers and birds, views of Estes Park, and the unusual Gem Lake; side trips to Balanced Rock and Bridal Veil Falls. Unlike most circuits on the eastern side of RMNP, this one is fairly deserted, except for Gem Lake and Bridal Veil Falls, which are popular spots. You'll also see technical climbers on the south face of Lumpy Ridge. The area around Twin Owls Trailhead and along the trail to Gem Lake is one of the best places to see birds in Rocky Mountain National Park.

ACCESS POINTS: Twin Owls Trailhead (East Side, north of Estes Park). The circuit is also accessible from Gem Lake and Cow Creek Trailheads, neither of them directly on the trail (see accompanying map) and therefore not considered alternate access points.

SEASONS: Summer and fall hiking are great. The south side of Lumpy Ridge is good in winter; the north side, however, collects a lot of snow, rendering a loop hike difficult.

SUMMARY:

Route	Distance (mi.)	Total Elevation Gain (ft.)	Time (hr.:min.)	Exertion Rating
Basic circuit	9.6	2156	6:57	19.8
Roundtrip to Balanced Rock	2.6	1280	2:35	7.5
Roundtrip to Bridal Veil Falls	2.0	620	1:37	4.6
Totals	14.2	4056	11:09	31.9

FINDING THE ACCESS POINT: From the intersection of US 34 and US 36 in Estes Park, go westbound (actual direction is initially north, then curving west) uphill on the US 34 bypass for 0.4 mi. and turn right (north) on McGregor Avenue. McGregor Avenue is the first road west of the historic Stanley Hotel on the US 34 bypass. Drive 0.8 mi. to the end of McGregor Avenue (where the road makes a sharp right and continues as Devils Gulch Road) and enter the McGregor Ranch by continuing straight ahead for 0.9 mi. (Do not bear right on Devils Gulch Road.) Follow the ranch road left around and past the small museum and then other buildings to the RMNP parking lot at the end. (Absolutely no parking is allowed on ranch land; violators will be towed.)

Water is available from a spigot on the uphill side of the parking lot. *Warning:* this is a hot hike at relatively low elevation through much open parkland, with natural water available only at Gem Lake and Cow Creek. Carry more water than you would for most hikes of the same duration.

Outhouses are located beyond the eastern end of the parking lot, at the start of the trail. Lumpy Ridge is a favorite climbing spot, and the small parking lot fills early; arrive before 9 A.M.

TRAIL DESCRIPTION (counterclockwise): The circuit can be walked in either direction, but we recommend counterclockwise; this direction allows you to traverse the good bird-watching stretch between Twin Owls Trailhead and Gem Lake early in the morning, when birds are most active.

Lumpy Ridge is popular for technical climbing for several reasons. First, the outcrop is granite, a favorite rock of climbers because it is hard, does not crumble, and provides hand- and footholds. Second, the vertical surfaces are steep enough and high enough to be challenging. Third, the elevation is low, so the climate is not as harsh and the chances of afternoon thunderstorms in summer are lower. Fourth, the climbing routes are immediately accessible via a short walk from the parking lot, whereas high-country climbing often requires a lengthy hike in and out. And last, the skill required and the risk involved are lower at Lumpy Ridge than high-country sites.

The area between the trailhead and Gem Lake is popular among bird enthusiasts for its easy accessibility and diversity of good habitat. The cliffs provide nesting places for White-throated Swifts, this being the best place in the park to find them. The low elevation, open forest, burned forest, ranch fields, and other factors contribute to the ecological diversity that promotes good birding.

1) *Before leaving the parking lot, look south into the ranch meadow for sky-blue Mountain Bluebirds commuting between scattered bushes.* Begin walking the trail uphill (east), taking about 26 min. to reach the junction with the trail leaving right to the Gem Lake Trailhead. *This stretch is good for birds and wildflowers.*

2) At the junction, go straight, continuing 1 hr., 28 min. to **Gem Lake.** *As you move through an old burned area of Ponderosa Pine, watch especially for Abert's (tassel-eared) Squirrels and various birds.* The trail ascends to Gem Lake, passing through aspens and conifers, such as Douglas-

Abert's Squirrel foraging in pine needles in a patch of sunlight, one of several special wildlife species to look for on the Lumpy Ridge Circuit.

fir, with views to the south. Marring the scenery is an outhouse perched on the approach below Gem Lake. *Gem Lake is one of the few lakes in Rocky Mountain National Park that is not located in a high-mountain cirque. This small, shallow lake is a rain-filled depression in the rocky surface, having no inlet or outlet. Gem Lake is usually a good place to find birds.*

3) The unimproved but perfectly adequate trail descends from Gem Lake for about 36 min. through Ponderosa Pine and mixed forest to meet a trail leaving left for Balanced Rock. Along the way, it passes a trail on the right that leads out of RMNP.

3a) We have not made the side trip to **Balanced Rock,** which is 1.3 mi. distant (elevation gain about 1280 ft.); allow 2 hr., 35 min. roundtrip walking time.

4) From the junction with the trail to Balanced Rock, continue northwest for about 45 min., passing another trail on the right that leads to private land, then crossing Cow Creek on a bridge and ascending briefly to Cow Creek Trail. Cow Creek Trailhead is about 1.2 mi. to the east (right). Remember to filter or treat any water you take from Cow Creek.

5) Head west on Cow Creek Trail for about 33 min. to reach a fork in the trail. Along the way, the route follows above Cow Creek, where beaver dams create small impoundments.

5a) At the fork, bear right for a side trip to **Bridal Veil Falls**; allow 1 hr., 37 min. roundtrip. The trail follows Cow Creek up to the falls, crossing the creek twice on log bridges. At the triangular hitching post, we found the sign "NO HORSES BEYOND THIS POINT" and Liz remarked a few moments later, "And no trail, either." On the short stretch over bare rock, stay above the creek to regain the trail. Expect to find other hikers at the falls, usually lots of them.

---

6) At the fork, bear left (bear right if you are descending from the falls) and soon cross Cow Creek on a bridge. Again, be sure to filter or treat any water you take from Cow Creek; this is the last certain source of water on the hike. Follow the trail for about 1 hr., 39 min. up the valley, first through open Ponderosa Pine parkland and then through denser forest as the trail climbs to a col that traverses the western end of Lumpy Ridge. The route ends shortly thereafter at the trail connecting Twin Owls Trailhead (where you started) with Lawn Lake. The creek bed in this valley is ordinarily dry in summer. *Along this section of the trail, we found marvelous yellow mushrooms more than half a foot in diameter, decorated with profuse, tiny brown spots. As the trail approaches the col, it follows some gentle switchbacks, and here we saw a small herd of Mule Deer.*

7) After crossing the col, turn left (southeast) on the trail from Lawn Lake and begin the long walk back to Twin Owls Trailhead: about 1 hr., 30 min. Most of the way, the route passes through Ponderosa Pine parkland, which becomes increasingly open and eventually yields to meadow before the trail regains the parking lot. The trail stays well above Black Canyon Creek, which is always out of sight. The rounded formations of Lumpy Ridge, almost constantly visible through the trees, are the scenic attraction of this final leg of the circuit. *The rounded granite formations are created by water penetrating the rock, dissolving certain minerals, and expanding when freezing, causing bits of rock to flake off—a process called* exfoliation. *Famous exfoliated granite domes are found in Yosemite National Park, California; few visitors to Rocky come to Lumpy Ridge to see the rounded formations here, and fewer yet walk the trail west of Twin Owls Trailhead to admire the ridge. The last half mile or so of the circuit is an excellent stretch for spotting birds.*

Clockwise walking time is the same overall, but individual segments differ from the counterclockwise circuit because the elevation gains are in different places. From Twin Owls Trailhead clockwise: **(7)** walk 2 hr., 42 min. to the western col, where the trail continues to Lawn Lake but you turn right at the junction; **(6)** descend 48 min. to Cow Creek; **(5)** continue 21 min. to the trail leaving for Gem Lake, where you bear right; **(4)** walk 59 min. to the junction where the trail leaves right for Balanced Rock; **(3)** continue straight and ascend 1 hr., 19 min. to Gem Lake; **(2)** descend 36 min. to the junction where the trail leaves left for Gem Lake Trailhead; and **(1)** go straight at the junction, continuing 12 min. to the Twin Owls Trailhead. **Side-trip times,** based on out-and-back roundtrips, are same as in main description.

OUR HIKING NOTES: The formula time for the hike including the side trip to Bridal Veil Falls is 8 hr., 34 min.; our actual walking time was 7 hr., 55 min. in late August.

Hummingbird display. Between the Twin Owls Trailhead and Gem Lake, we were treated to the courtship display flights of a Broad-tailed Hummingbird. From a height of about 10 ft. above the perched female, the male flew a steep U-shaped path, pulling out of the power dive right in front of the female. He made one or two passes and then moved out of sight above us, only to reappear and make another one or two display flights. We watched this spectacle for about a half dozen cycles before continuing with our hike.

Habitats traversed: Largely Ponderosa Pine parkland, some of it quite open, with aspen groves and some pockets of mixed conifers. **Wildflowers noted:** Black-eyed Susan, Canada Thistle, Diffuse Knapweed, Salsify, yellow composites, Monument-plant, Horsemint, Common Evening-primrose, and Butter-and-eggs.

Birds seen or heard: Red-tailed Hawk, Broad-tailed Hummingbird, Hairy Woodpecker, Northern Flicker, *Empidonax* flycatcher, Olive-sided Flycatcher, Steller's Jay, Clark's Nutcracker, Common Raven, Mountain Chickadee, Red-breasted Nuthatch, White-breasted Nuthatch, Pygmy Nuthatch, Brown Creeper, Ruby-crowned Kinglet, Mountain Bluebird, Townsend's Solitaire, American Robin, Yellow-rumped Warbler, Wilson's Warbler, Green-tailed Towhee, Dark-eyed Junco, and Red Crossbill. **Mammals encountered:** Chipmunk (perhaps both Least and Uinta), Golden-mantled Ground Squirrel, Abert's (tassel-eared) Squirrel, and Mule Deer; beaver ponds (on Cow Creek).

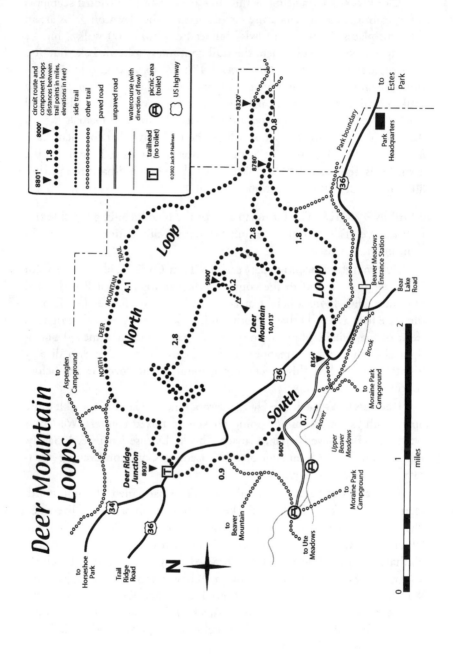

Deer Mountain Loops

North Loop

South Loop

Deer Mountain
10,013'

Deer Ridge Junction
8930'

Legend:
- circuit route and component loops (distances between trail points in miles, elevations in feet)
- 8801' ▲   1.8   8000' ▲
- side trail
- other trail
- paved road
- unpaved road
- watercourse (with direction of flow)
- Ⓐ picnic area (toilet)
- trailhead (no toilet)
- US highway

©2002 Jack P Hailman

to Horseshoe Park

Trail Ridge Road

to Aspenglen Campground

to Beaver Mountain

to Ute Meadows

to Moraine Park Campground

to Moraine Park Campground

Upper Beaver Meadows

Beaver Meadows Entrance Station

Bear Lake Road

Park Headquarters

to Estes Park

Park boundary

DEER MOUNTAIN NORTH TRAIL

8320'
8780'
9800'
8364'
8400'

2.8
2.8
4.1
1.8
2.8
0.8
0.7
0.9
0.2

US 34
US 36
US 36

Beaver Brook

N

miles
0   1   2

DEER MOUNTAIN LOOPS

FORMULA TIMES: 5 hours, 11 minutes for the outer circuit. A peculiarity of the Deer Mountain circuit is that the component loops are both longer than the outer circuit because the loops wind over the mountaintop, whereas the circuit goes around the mountain. Formula times are 6 hours, 44 minutes for the North Loop (7 hours, 9 minutes with the virtually mandatory side trip to the summit), and 5 hours, 56 minutes for the South Loop (6 hours, 21 minutes with the side trip to the summit).

HIKING ELEVATIONS: 8320 to 8930 feet on the outer circuit, to 9800 feet on the component loops, to 10,013 feet on the side trip to the summit.

EXERTION RATINGS: 13.7 (moderately easy) for the outer circuit; 19.6 (moderately strenuous) for the North Loop, to 20.9 (moderately strenuous) with the side trip to the summit; 17.3 (moderate) for the South Loop, to 18.6 (moderate) with the side trip to the summit.

FEATURES: Great vista featuring Longs Peak. There is a good possibility of sighting the Mule Deer for which Deer Mountain is named. The climb to the summit is one of the most popular out-and-back hikes in the park.

ACCESS POINT: Deer Ridge Junction (East Side of the park).

SEASONS: Summer and fall are fine for the entire circuit and both loops. The South Loop is also fine in winter, but the north side of Deer Mountain collects so much snow that neither the North Loop nor the entire circuit is recommended during that season.

SUMMARY:

Route	Distance (mi.)	Total Elevation Gain (ft.)	Time (hr.:min.)	Exertion Rating
Outer circuit	8.3	1026	5:11	13.7
North Loop	10.5	1480	6:44	19.6
Roundtrip to summit	0.4	213	0:25	1.3
North Loop with side trip	10.9	1693	7:09	20.9
South Loop	9.0	1436	5:56	17.3
Roundtrip to summit	0.4	213	0:25	1.3
South Loop with side trip	9.4	1649	6:21	18.6

FINDING THE ACCESS POINT: From the Beaver Meadows Entrance Station, drive 3.1 mi. west on US 36 to Deer Ridge Junction (4.3 mi. from the Beaver Meadows Visitor Center). The trailhead is on the right (north) just before the junction with US 34. Park along the road. There are **no outhouses** and **no water** at the trailhead, and **no reliable natural water** along the trail (although there are a few seepage trickles along the North Deer Mountain Trail). Carry plenty of water as this can be a hot, dry hike.

TRAIL DESCRIPTIONS:

Outer circuit (clockwise): The outer circuit can be hiked in either direction. We choose to describe it clockwise, the direction that saves the most varied terrain for the second half of the hike.

1) Take the path less trodden from Deer Ridge Junction and walk for 2 hr., 3 min. around the north side of Deer Mountain to the easternmost point of the hike. You will at first lose some altitude. Along the way, pass a trail leading left that later splits to go to Horseshoe Park or Aspenglen Campground. The trail on the back side of the mountain is fairly level, crossing few contour lines. On this stretch, the only people we encountered were a couple jogging and a chap with a fancy GPS receiver on a tripod. He told us that the North Deer Mountain Trail was located incorrectly on all the maps, which may be true; nevertheless, the maps are sufficiently accurate for the hiker.

2) Eventually, the trail approaches a sparsely wooded col where a trail heads left to Estes Park. Here bear right, keep right to pass another trail leading out of the park, and begin climbing, moving west for 52 min. until you reach a junction with the trail coming up on the left from Upper Beaver Meadows.

3) At the junction, go left and walk west downhill for about 54 min. to US 36 at a bend in the road, losing almost all the elevation you gained on the previous leg. Along the way, pass two trail junctions, keeping right in both cases.

4) At the bend in the highway, an unpaved road leaves west for the picnic areas in Upper Beaver Meadows. You must cross the highway and walk this unpaved road for about 23 min. Keep to the left on the road, facing any vehicles you might encounter. Pass the RMNP helicopter pad on this segment.

5) At a noticeable bend in the unpaved road, you will see a trail on the right. Leave the road and follow this trail, walking mostly uphill for about 59 min. to complete the circuit at Deer Ridge Junction. On the way, pass a trail coming in from the left.

Counterclockwise walking time for the outer circuit is the same overall, but differs from the clockwise circuit for individual segments

Park headquarters area seen from Deer Mountain.

because the elevation gains are in different places. From Deer Ridge Junction cross the road and **(5)** walk downhill for 27 min. to the unpaved road in Upper Beaver Meadows. **(4)** Head east on the unpaved road for 21 min. to US 36. **(3)** Cross the highway and take the trail east for 1 hr., 19 min., passing two trails on the right before reaching the junction where the trail up Deep Mountain leaves left. **(2)** At the junction, continue east for another 24 min. Along the way, the trail dips into a col, passing a side trail (right), before arriving at the junction where the circuit trail turns sharply left. **(1)** Walk the "back side" of Deer Mountain staying virtually on the same contour line for nearly 2 hr. Pass a trail to Aspenglen Campground (right), and gain some elevation before arriving back at Deer Ridge Junction 2 hr., 40 min. after starting off from the col on the east side of the outer circuit.

North Loop (counterclockwise): This circuit can be walked in either direction, but we have chosen counterclockwise to get the summit climb over with early on. **Special warning:** For the first 2.0 mi. from Deer Ridge Junction to the summit trail (about two-thirds of the way), the route is rife with ticks from early April into June.

1) From the trailhead at Deer Ridge Junction, walk mainly uphill for about 2 hr., 16 min. to the junction where a side trail leaves right for the summit. Soon after leaving Deer Ridge Junction, pass two local branches of the North Deer Mountain Trail returning to the trailhead area, bearing right at both. After climbing the switchbacks on the western side of Deer Mountain, the trail wanders up and down along the broad top, but keep the faith: eventually you will arrive at the junction with the trail to the true summit.

1a) The side trip to the **summit of Deer Mountain** takes about 25 min. out and back (really up and down, with more than 200 ft. gained). It's a worthy side trip with one of the finest views of Longs Peak anywhere in the Park.

---

2) Upon descending the summit trail, turn right on to the main trail and descend the east side of Deer Mountain, encountering a series of switchbacks, for about 1 hr., 24 min. to a trail junction just inside the park boundary.

3) Continue straight (east) at the junction, walking for another 24 min. until the trail dips into a col, with several side trails leading downhill to the Estes Park area. At one junction, the circuit trail turns sharply left; there may or may not still be a sign there to North Deer Mountain Trail. This sparsely wooded col is potentially confusing, but we had no trouble "following our noses."

4) After the left turn, walk the back side (north side) of Deer Mountain on a trail that stays virtually on the same contour line for nearly 2 hr. Pass a trail to Aspenglen Campground on the right and gain some elevation before arriving back at Deer Ridge Junction 2 hr., 40 min. after starting off from the col at the easternmost end of the hike.

Clockwise walking time for the North Loop is the same overall, but individual segments differ from the counterclockwise circuit because the elevation gains are in different places. From Deer Ridge Junction clockwise: **(4)** walk 2 hr., 3 min. on the long back side of the mountain to the easternmost point; **(3)** turn right (west) and walk 52 min. uphill until you pass the intersection with the trail coming uphill on the left from US 36; **(2)** continue for 2 hr., 25 min. uphill on the east slope of Deer Mountain to the summit trail; and **(1)** head down 1 hr., 24 min. on the west side to arrive back at Deer Ridge Junction. The side-trip time to the summit, based on the out-and-back roundtrip, is the same as in the counterclockwise description.

South Loop (clockwise): This circuit can be walked in either direction. We've chosen clockwise because almost everyone starts out by heading for the summit. Dare to be different: do the circuit counterclockwise instead. The formula time to the summit from Deer Ridge Junction is 2 hr., 29 min.; we did it with young and vigorous boys in 1 hr., 35 min., but if you are going to do the entire loop, you probably will not want to prance up the mountain like a Bighorn Sheep. *The habitat is mainly Ponderosa Pine woods.* **Special warning:** For the first 2.0 mi. from Deer Ridge Junction to the summit trail (about two-thirds of the way), the route is rife with ticks from early April into June.

1) From the trailhead at Deer Ridge Junction, walk mainly uphill for about 2 hr., 16 min. until you reach the junction where a side trail heads right, up to the summit. Soon after leaving Deer Ridge Junction, pass two more junctions, bearing right at both. After climbing the switchbacks on the western side of Deer Mountain, the trail wanders up and down along the broad top, but keep the faith: eventually you will arrive at the junction with the trail to the true summit.

1a) The side trip to the **summit of Deer Mountain** takes about 25 min. out and back (or, more accurately, up and down—you will climb [and descend] approximately 200 ft. in 0.2 mi.). But the vista from the summit is worth it; trust us.

---

2) Upon descending the summit trail, turn right and descend the east side of Deer Mountain, encountering a series of switchbacks, for about 1 hr., 24 min. to a trail junction just at the park boundary.

3) At the junction, make a sharp right and walk west for about 54 min. to US 36 at a bend in the road. Along the way, pass two trail junctions, keeping right at both.

4) At the bend in the road, an unpaved road leaves west for the picnic areas in Upper Beaver Meadows. You must walk this road for about 23 min. Keep to the left on the road, facing any vehicles you might encounter. Pass the RMNP helicopter pad on this segment.

5) At a noticeable bend in the unpaved road, you will see a trail on the right. Leave the road and follow this trail for about 59 min. to complete

Deer Mountain seen from near the Beaver Meadows Entrance Station.

the circuit at Deer Ridge Junction. On this leg, you will pass one trail junction on your left. Sorry about the uphill climb on the home stretch; if you do the circuit counterclockwise, you can come home downhill.

Counterclockwise walking time for the South Loop is the same overall but differs from the clockwise circuit because elevation gains are in different places. From Deer Ridge Junction, cross the road and **(5)** walk downhill for 27 min. to the unpaved road in Upper Beaver Meadows; **(4)** turn left and head east on the unpaved road for 21 min. to US 36; **(3)** cross the highway and continue east on the trail for 1 hr., 19 min., passing two trail junctions on the right and coming to a third just inside the park boundary; **(2)** at this third trail junction, turn sharply left and ascend Deer Mountain for 2 hr., 25 min.—the only significant elevation gain on the counterclockwise circuit, but admittedly a whopping one—to the junction with the side trail to the summit; **(1)** descend Deer Mountain to the west, taking an additional 1 hr., 24 min. to complete the circuit. The side-trip time to the summit, based on an out-and-back roundtrip, is the same as in the North Loop (counterclockwise) description.

OUR HIKING NOTES: We hiked the North and South Loops separately, the former in late September, the latter in early August. The formula time for the North Loop, including the side trip to the summit, is 7 hr., 9 min.; we hiked it in 7 hr., 6 min. (yes, really), with an additional 19 min. for lunch and 8 min. for a "long" rest stop. Our walking time does include brief rests of 5 min. or less each. We did not time the South Loop hike, though on another occasion we did hike only to the summit with small children in 1 hr., 35 min. (formula time, 2 hr., 16 min.). The formula time for the entire South Loop is 5 hr., 56 min.—not quite as long as the North Loop.

Habitats traversed: Varied forests of mainly coniferous trees including Ponderosa Pine, Douglas-fir, Quaking Aspen, and Mountain Maple. **Wildflowers noted:** A coralroot (probably Spotted), a goldenrod, a purple aster with yellow center, a rabbitbrush, a white fleabane or aster, an aster, Yarrow, Plains Pricklypear, a harebell, Monument-plant, a buckwheat, and Scarlet Paintbrush. **Other plants found:** Common Juniper and Threeleaf Sumac (shrubs), and Salsify in seed.

Birds seen or heard: Golden Eagle, a sapsucker, Three-toed Woodpecker, Steller's Jay, Clark's Nutcracker, Common Raven, Mountain Chickadee, Pygmy Nuthatch, Rock Wren, Townsend's Solitaire, American Robin, and Dark-eyed Junco. **Mammals encountered:** Golden-mantled Ground Squirrel, Red Squirrel, and a bull Elk with his harem (seen in Beaver Meadows from the summit in September).

Beaver Brook

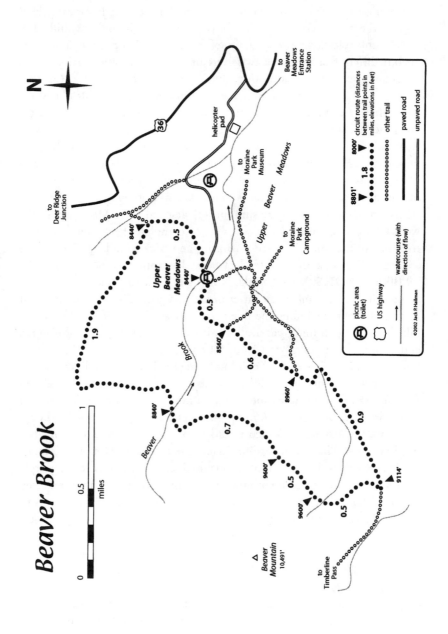

N

to Deer Ridge Junction

36

helicopter pad

to Beaver Meadows Entrance Station

to Moraine Park Museum

Upper Beaver Meadows

Upper Beaver Meadows

to Moraine Park Campground

8440'

0.5

8440'

0.5

1.9

8560'

0.6

8960'

0.9

8840'

Beaver Brook

Brook

0.7

9600'

0.5

9600'

9114'

0.5

Beaver Mountain
10,491'

to Timberline Pass

miles
0   0.5   1

Legend:

- 🚻 picnic area (toilet)
- ⬡ US highway
- ↑ watercourse (with direction of flow)
- 8801' ▼ ••••••• 1.8 ▼ 8000' circuit route (distances between trail points in miles, elevations in feet)
- ooooooo other trail
- ▬▬▬ paved road
- ────── unpaved road

©2002 Jack P. Hallman

BEAVER BROOK CIRCUIT

FORMULA TIME: 4 hours, 13 minutes

HIKING ELEVATIONS: 8440 to 9600 feet.

EXERTION RATING: 12.3 (moderately easy).

FEATURES: Views of Upper Beaver Meadows and Moraine Park. This is also a great birding hike on a lightly used trail.

ACCESS POINT: Western picnic area near Upper Beaver Meadows Trailhead (East Side of the park).

SEASONS: Year-round; especially in the fall, Elk herds are commonly in evidence.

SUMMARY:

Route	Distance (mi.)	Total Elevation Gain (ft.)	Time (hr.:min.)	Exertion Rating
Circuit	6.1	1160	4:13	12.3

FINDING THE ACCESS POINT: From the Beaver Meadows Entrance Station, drive 0.8 mi. west on US 36 to the unpaved road leading west into Upper Beaver Meadows. Turn left onto the road and drive 1.5 mi. to a picnic area at the very end (passing another picnic area on the way). The trail begins at the bridge over Beaver Brook, by the edge of the parking lot. There is an **outhouse** but **no drinking water** near the Upper Beaver Meadows Trailhead. Remember to treat or filter any water you take from Beaver Brook, which you will also cross about halfway along the circuit, and any other natural sources.

TRAIL DESCRIPTION (clockwise): This circuit could be walked in either direction; we chose clockwise.

1) Cross the footbridge over Beaver Brook and immediately turn right, continuing along nearly level ground for 22 min. to a trail junction.

2) At the junction, continue straight (do not head out across the meadow on the trail that leads southeast to Moraine Park). The trail heads uphill (west) into woods of Ponderosa Pine and Quaking Aspen, passing a spur leading right to a horse hitching post. After about 42 min., a trail from the meadows comes in on the left.

3) Keep right at the trail junction (left would take you east along the moraine) and walk for 36 min. over gently rising land to reach a third junction, with a trail to Timberline Pass. On the way, the Beaver Brook

Upper Beaver Meadows is one of many good places to see Elk; two cows running (above), bull quietly foraging (below).

Circuit angles along a hillside of fairly open Ponderosa Pine parkland that burned long ago, then breaks out into more open terrain with views of a large rock dome ahead on the right. The trail follows the creek valley between Beaver Mountain to the northwest and the moraine to the south, rising above and then passing below the rock dome before climbing nearly to the top of the moraine. *Below the dome look for immense (end-table-sized) chunks of white quartz with small amounts of pink.*

4) Turn right at the trail junction (straight leads to Ute Meadows and eventually to Trail Ridge Road) and climb for 44 min. to the circuit's highest elevations.

5) Continue northeast along essentially flat land for 15 min. Somewhere on this half-mile stretch, you will reach the precise high point of the circuit.

6) The trail descends for 21 min., offering vistas of Longs Peak to the south, Moraine Park to the southeast, and Upper Beaver Meadows to the east. Pass a triangular hitching rail and angle along the slope of Beaver Mountain, then enter a Lodgepole Pine forest before eventually crossing Beaver Brook on a half-log bridge.

7) From the bridge, walk 57 min. to a trail junction in open meadow 1.9 mi. away. Past the bridge, the route opens out, then passes through denser woods before opening out again in meadowland with scattered aspens. As you near the junction, the trail descends gently down a fairly open hillside with scattered Ponderosa Pines and sagebrush. **Note:** One recent book shows a trail crossing this segment. This trail, which runs from the Upper Beaver Meadows Trailhead to Many Parks Curve on Trail Ridge Road, does not appear on topographic maps of RMNP, nor does it show up in our hiking notes.

8) Turn right at the trail junction and walk about 15 min. back to the Upper Beaver Meadows Trailhead.

Counterclockwise walking time is the same overall, but individual segments differ from the clockwise circuit because the elevation gains are in different places. **(8)** From the Upper Beaver Meadows Trailhead, walk back along the road a short distance to the trail that leaves left, gently ascending as you cross the dry hillside, and walk for 15 min. to a trail junction; **(7)** turn left and walk for 1 hr., 21 min. to Beaver Brook; **(6)** continue mainly uphill for 1 hr., 7 min. to the higher ground of the circuit (this will not be obvious); **(5)** walk for 15 min. over the highest elevations; **(4)** continue 15 min. downhill to a trail junction; **(3)** turn left and descend gently, reaching another junction in 27 min.; **(2)** keep left (do not go right, out toward the meadows) and continue 18 min. downhill to yet another junction; and **(1)** bear left again, taking another 15 min. to arrive back at the Upper Beaver Meadows Trailhead.

Upper Beaver Meadows, where the Beaver Brook Circuit begins, with Longs Peak in the background.

OUR HIKING NOTES: This circuit could be walked in either direction; we did it clockwise. The formula time is 4 hr., 13 min.; our time was 3 hr., 31 min. on a hike in mid-July.

Nesting birds. Bird nests are often very difficult to find, but species that nest in cavities are less secretive because they are less vulnerable to nest predators. It was a delight on this hike to discover both nesting cavities and parents feeding fledged young. On the stretch past the trail to Timberline Pass, we discovered the nesting cavity of a pair of Pygmy Nuthatches at the top of an aspen tree broken off about 18 ft. above the ground and watched an adult Three-toed Woodpecker feeding its fledged young. Along the highest leg of the circuit, we found the nesting cavity of a Williamson's Sapsucker about seven feet up in a live aspen. On the long stretch after crossing Beaver Brook, in the upper meadow, we watched a family of Red Crossbills, the parents apparently foraging for their fledged young. We also found the nesting cavity of Violet-green Swallows about 10 ft. high in an old, partially dead pine. For us, that was a record number of species nesting spotted on a single hike.

Habitats traversed: Meadow, Ponderosa parkland, mixed coniferous woods. In addition to Ponderosa Pine, we commonly found Lodgepole Pine (especially between the east shoulder of Beaver Mountain and Beaver Brook), Engelmann Spruce, and Douglas-fir and saw a pretty grove of Quaking Aspen near the start of the clockwise circuit. **Wildflowers noted:** A chickweed, Blanketflower, Mountain Sagebrush (in open areas northeast of the picnic grounds), Salsify, Miners-candle, a wallflower, a harebell, Yellow Stonecrop, Golden Banner, Fremont Geranium, a nonwoody cinquefoil, a rose, Scarlet Paintbrush, and a penstemon. **Shrubs found:** Common Juniper and Shrubby Cinquefoil.

Birds seen or heard: Broad-tailed Hummingbird, Williamson's Sapsucker, Red-breasted Sapsucker, Hairy Woodpecker, Three-toed Woodpecker, Olive-sided Flycatcher, Warbling Vireo, Steller's Jay, Black-billed Magpie, Violet-green Swallow, Mountain Chickadee, White-breasted Nuthatch, Pygmy Nuthatch, Brown Creeper, House Wren, Ruby-crowned Kinglet, Mountain Bluebird, Townsend's Solitaire, American Robin, European Starling (ugh!), Yellow-rumped Warbler, Western Tanager, Rufous-sided Towhee, Chipping Sparrow, Dark-eyed Junco, Red Crossbill, and Pine Siskin. **Mammals encountered:** Mountain Cottontail, Least Chipmunk, Wyoming Ground Squirrel, Golden-mantled Ground Squirrel, Red Squirrel, and Mule Deer.

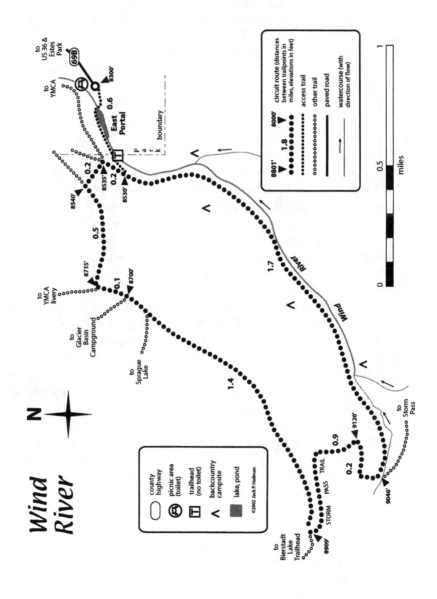

Wind River

N

Legend (top)

- ⬭ county highway
- 🅷 picnic area (toilet)
- 🛈 trailhead (no toilet)
- ∧ backcountry campsite
- ▓ lake, pond

©2002 Jack P. Hailman

Legend (bottom)

▶ 8801' ▶ 8000'
  1.8

- ●●● circuit route (distances between trailpoints in miles, elevations in feet)
- ••• access trail
- ooo other trail
- ▬▬ paved road
- → watercourse (with direction of flow)

miles
0   0.5   1

Map labels

to US 36 & Estes Park
69B
to YMCA
8300'
East Portal
0.6
park boundary
8535'
0.2
8530'
0.2
8540'
0.5
to YMCA livery
8715'
to Glacier Basin Campground
8700'
0.1
to Sprague Lake
1.7
Wind River
1.4
9120'
0.9
STORM PASS TRAIL
0.2
9046'
to Storm Pass
8909'
to Bierstadt Lake Trailhead

WIND RIVER CIRCUIT

FORMULA TIME: 4 hours, 3 minutes, including out and back on the access trail from East Portal.

HIKING ELEVATIONS: 8300 to 9120 feet, including the access trail from East Portal.

EXERTION RATING: 11.6 (moderately easy), including the access trail from East Portal.

FEATURES: Fairly level trail through quiet backcountry, with a lengthy stretch along the Wind River (actually a brook) that sports wildflowers and an interesting rock formation; some good birding.

ACCESS POINT: East Portal.

SEASONS: Year-round. In summer, expect to encounter equestrian traffic (although we found this to be minimal on our hike in early August). Fall, when the aspens have turned, is especially nice, and winter snows afford very good cross-country skiing and snowshoeing.

SUMMARY:

Route	Distance (mi.)	Total Elevation Gain (ft.)	Time (hr.:min.)	Exertion Rating
Circuit, including access trail	6.4	835	4:03	11.6

FINDING THE ACCESS POINT: From US 36 on the west side of Estes Park, follow Colorado 66, which turns into county highway 69B, for 3.4 mi., past the giant YMCA complex, to the end of the road at a turnaround circle near the dam at East Portal. On the northwest side of the road is a tiny county park with **outhouses** but **no water.** Leave your vehicle either alongside the circle or in the county park.

After the 9/11 terrorist attacks, the road to the dam was blocked off to prevent vehicle access. You can still reach the East Portal Trailhead by walking up this road past the government No Trespassing sign, crossing the dam, and turning left, following the path along the small lake beyond the East Portal of the water tunnel to the trailhead sign at the park boundary. An alternative route is to follow the horse trail from the county park, cross an open area (keeping right of the dam), and then climb to meet the trail (see map). Using this route, you will not pass the trailhead signboard.

TRAIL DESCRIPTION (counterclockwise): The circuit can be walked in either direction; we chose counterclockwise because this direction ends with a long, pleasant downhill stroll along the Wind River.

1) From the end of the county highway, walk for about 32 min. up the old road, across the dam, along the small reservoir, past the East Portal itself, and uphill past the trailhead sign to reach the junction with the Wind River Trail and the start of the circuit per se. You might spot interesting birds over the reservoir and around its edges, especially near the portal end. After the trailhead sign, pass a small pond created by a small cement dam on the Wind River.

2) Make a sharp right at the junction and continue climbing for 6 min. to an intersection where a horse trail comes in from the lower right and the circuit route turns left. (Straight ahead is unmarked.) This stretch overlooks the East Portal area and is good for spotting both birds and wildflowers that favor open habitat, such as Scarlet Paintbrush. If you came up via the alternative access, you meet the circuit here and go straight across the trail intersection.

3) Continue climbing for about 6 min. through scattered Douglas-firs and pines until you reach a T-junction, where you go left.

4) Walk for 26 min., still in the open for a while. Look for micaceous rocks sparkling in the sunshine. On your left, enjoy fine views of Estes Cone and, farther away, the top of Longs Peak. Still climbing the side of the moraine, the trail enters a grove of Elk-chewed aspens before passing through pinewoods. The way climbs more gently to cross a less heavily wooded pass between higher ground on both sides, then ends at another T-junction. The right arm leads to the YMCA livery; the circuit route goes left.

5) After turning left, soon pass a big water tank for the Glacier Basin Campground and, in a short 4 min., come to a trail on the right leading sharply back to the campground. As you continue walking this area, you will probably see tents and a paved campground loop to your right.

6) Now stroll for 55 min. through Lodgepole Pine with Common Juniper underneath, soon passing a trail to Sprague Lake on your right. When you reach the junction with the Storm Pass Trail, go left. (Going right here would take you to Bierstadt Lake Trailhead on Bear Lake Road.)

7) Begin climbing shallow switchbacks. Along a more level area, pass the high point of the circuit after about 40 min.

8) Descend about 6 min. to the junction with the Wind River Trail and turn left (the other way will take you to Storm Pass).

9) For 51 min., walk gently downhill with the Wind River on your right to complete the circuit per se at the junction with the access trail.

East Portal seen from the Wind River Circuit.

The course of the Wind River varies from open meadow, old ponds backed up by leaking beaver and earthen dams, thick patches of willow, and open brook. This is a nice place to find riparian wildflowers. Eventually, you come to a side trail leading to the last backcountry campsite, Wind River Bluff. Beyond this, the route runs fairly high above the river, passing outcrops of smooth, red rocks. A little farther on, past the hitching post for horses, look across the river for an orange rock formation, which Liz dubbed Three Chimneys.

10) Take the right fork at the access trail and continue for 18 min., passing the small cement dam, the trailhead sign, the reservoir, and the dam, heading down the road until you reach the circle. If you are using the alternative access route, do not turn right on the access trail; continue straight for 6 min. and go right at the trail intersection, which will take you back to the county park.

Clockwise walking time is the same overall, but individual segments differ from the clockwise circuit because the elevation gains are in different

Rock formation along the Wind River Trail.

places. The access trail, segments (1) and (10), is, of course, the same regardless of which direction the circuit per se is walked. **(9)** At the junction with the access trail from East Portal, turn left and walk 1 hr., 22 min. along the Wind River; **(8)** turn right on the Storm Pass Trail and climb for about 10 min. to reach the high point; **(7)** descend for 27 min. until you come to a junction, where you go right; **(6)** walk for 42 min., passing a trail to Sprague Lake and then a trail to Glacier Basin Campground, both on your left; **(5)** continue for 5 min., arriving at a trail junction where going straight will take you to the YMCA livery; **(4)** turn right and walk 15 min. to another trail junction; **(3)** turn right, heading downhill for 6 min. until you reach an intersection; and **(2)** finally, go right and descend for 6 min. until you reach the access trail leading to the East Portal.

OUR HIKING NOTES: We walked this circuit in early August. The formula time is 4 hr., 9 min.; our time was 3 hr., 44 min., including some bird-watching along the way. Aside from some backpackers hiking out from their sites, and a few groups of equestrians on plodding horses, we saw only one person: a runner with a water camel on his back. He passed us on Storm Pass Trail within 50 ft. of a park sign warning people not to run alone in the woods, which might stimulate pursuit by a Mountain Lion.

Habitats traversed: Lodgepole Pines predominate, in some places sheltering Common Juniper beneath. Less extensive are Ponderosa Pines and Douglas-firs (in more open places) and Quaking Aspen groves. There is open hillside near the East Portal, and riparian ecology, including alders and willows, along the Wind River. **Wildflowers noted:** A white parsley, a coneflower with green center, a small yellow composite, a purple aster, a ragwort *(Senecio),* a white daisy *(Erigeron),* a yellow composite with sparse, very ragged ray flowers, Heartleaf Arnica, Pearly-everlasting, Mountain Harebell, Fremont Geranium, Richardson Geranium, Common Fireweed, and Scarlet Paintbrush. **Other plants found:** Yellow Rabbitbrush (a shrub), Bush-cranberry (a shrub), and ferns.

Birds seen or heard: Broad-tailed Hummingbird, Say's Phoebe, Olive-sided Flycatcher, Warbling Vireo, Clark's Nutcracker, Violet-green Swallow, Mountain Chickadee, Red-breasted Nuthatch, Brown Creeper, Rock Wren, Green-tailed Towhee, Chipping Sparrow, Pine Siskin, and a species of goldfinch. **Mammals encountered:** Golden-mantled Ground Squirrel and Red Squirrel. **Other animals:** An orange butterfly.

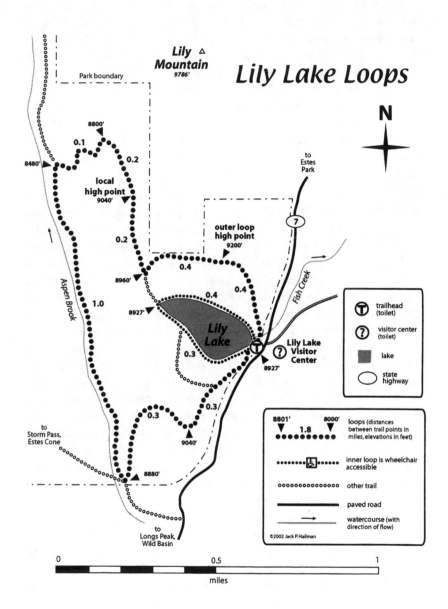

Lily △
Mountain
9786'

Lily Lake Loops

Park boundary

N

8800'

0.1

0.2

8480'

local
high point
9040'

to
Estes
Park

7

outer loop
high point
9200'

0.2

8960'

0.4

Aspen Brook

1.0

8927'

0.4

0.4

Fish Creek

Lily
Lake

to
Storm Pass,
Estes Cone

0.3

0.3

9040'

0.3/

8927'

Lily Lake
Visitor
Center

8927'

T   trailhead
    (toilet)

?   visitor center
    (toilet)

    lake

    state
    highway

0.3

8880'

to
Longs Peak,
Wild Basin

8801'   8000'
         1.8   loops (distances
                            between trail points in
                            miles, elevations in feet)

         &   inner loop is wheelchair
               accessible

ooooooooooooo   other trail

               paved road

               watercourse (with
               direction of flow)

©2002 Jack P. Hailman

0   0.5   1

miles

50

LILY LAKE LOOPS

FORMULA TIMES: 21 minutes for the inner loop; 2 hours, 22 minutes for the outer loop.

HIKING ELEVATIONS: 8927 feet on the inner loop (flat); 8480 to 9200 feet on the outer loop.

EXERTION RATINGS: 1.0 (stroll), inner loop; 6.8 (easy), outer loop.

FEATURES: Inner loop features a quiet lake with two species of ducks and exemplary trees; outer loop offers vistas overlooking the lake and valley, and a pleasant walk along Aspen Brook.

ACCESS POINT: Lily Lake Trailhead.

SEASONS: The small inner loop is popular year-round. Snowshoers and cross-country skiers climb the section of the outer loop directly north of the lake, where snows may linger well into spring. We need seasonal information on the long leg of the outer loop (much of it along Aspen Brook), so please write us with your experiences.

SUMMARY:

Route	Distance (mi.)	Total Elevation Gain (ft.)	Time (hr.:min.)	Exertion Rating
Inner Loop	0.7	flat	0:21	1.0
Outer Loop	2.9	913	2:22	6.8

FINDING THE ACCESS POINT: From the junction of US 34 and US 36 in Estes Park, drive 0.4 mi. east on US 36 and go right, uphill, on Colorado state route 7. Follow CO 7 south for 6.5 mi. to the Lily Lake Trailhead on the west side of the road, opposite the Lily Lake Visitor Center on the east side. There is a parking lot on either side of the highway. There are **outhouses** at the trailhead and flush **toilets** in the visitor center (open only during business hours, which may vary by season). There is **no water** source other than the restroom sinks in the visitor center. Remember to treat or filter any water you take from Lily Lake or Aspen Brook.

TRAIL DESCRIPTIONS:

Inner loop is a flat, level, wide trail accessible to wheelchairs. The route, which hugs the shore of Lily Lake, is easy in either direction.

Outer loop (counterclockwise): This circuit, which climbs to vantage points overlooking Lily Lake and then drops into the Aspen Brook Valley, is more of a hiking trail than the inner loop. The circuit can be walked

Ruins of an old cabin near Aspen Brook along the Lily Lake Outer Loop.

equally easily in either direction; we chose counterclockwise, putting the steepest climb behind us early on.

1) From the Lily Lake Trailhead, turn right (north) and walk for 3 min. Just before the bridge, make a right (not marked), leaving the inner loop. Your new route crosses the stream draining Lily Lake, but the stream is small and often dry. Climb gradually for about 25 more minutes to the trail's high point, passing several outcrops overlooking the lake (these provide good photo opportunities). In the distance, beyond Lily Lake, are Estes Cone and Longs Peak.

2) From the high point, descend for about 12 min. to reach a junction. To the left is a connector trail back to Lily Lake; to the right is the continuation of the outer loop.

3) Turn right and walk for about 11 min. to the local high point. Along this stretch, several faint trails lead off to the left to rock outcrops overlooking the Aspen Brook Valley. Do not try to shortcut by descending from any of these viewpoints.

4) In another 6 min. or so, the trail's gentle descent quickly steepens. To the left, you can see down into the valley. Notice on this leg the charred stumps from an old fire.

5) Continue downhill, partly on switchbacks. The suggested formula time of 3 min. probably underestimates the actual descent time. Pass several isolated cairns. When you reach the double cairns (one on each side of the trail), you know you are down, although you are still above Aspen Brook.

6) At the T-junction by the double cairns, turn left (south), following the trail upstream for 54 min. to the only trail intersection along this stretch of the loop. As you head south, you will see a hitching post and the ruins of two old log cabins on the other side of Aspen Brook. An old toll road once descended from here to the area now occupied by the YMCA complex. Soon, the trail enters the woods and runs close to the brook for the remainder of this segment.

7) At the trail intersection, turning right would take you across a handsome bridge and up Estes Cone on a fairly new trail. Continuing straight would take you out of RMNP just before the trail emerges on CO 7. Turning left keeps you on the outer loop. Turn left and climb for 19 min. amid Lodgepole Pines before emerging into an open area, an old dump site.

8) The route hugs the western edge of the open area, following the unpaved road back to the trailhead, which you will reach in another 9 min.

Clockwise walking time on the outer loop is the same overall, but individual segments differ from the counterclockwise circuit because the elevation gains are in different places. **(8)** From the trailhead, turn left and walk south for 16 min. along the unpaved road leaving the lower end of the parking lot; **(7)** enter the woods and descend for 9 min.; **(6)** turn right at the bridge and walk for 30 min., emerging from the woods and eventually reaching the double cairns; **(5)** climb the east side of the valley in 22 min.; **(4)** walk south, arriving at the local high point in 20 min.; **(3)** continue for 6 min. to reach the trail junction with the shortcut to Lily Lake; **(2)** turn left and climb to the trail's high point in 26 min.; and finally **(1)** descend to the Lily Lake Trailhead in 12 min.

OUR HIKING NOTES: The formula time for the inner loop is 21 min., but we have taken half an hour or longer, stopping to look at birds and photo-

Longs Peak (background) and Estes Cone (right) from Lily Lake Outer Loop.

graph trees. The outer loop's formula time is 2 hr., 22 min., but we walked it in almost exactly 2 hr. during early August.

Encounter with a tiger. Along Aspen Brook, we spotted a nearly black Tiger Salamander. Tiger Salamanders, the world's largest terrestrial salamander, love dark, damp places, but this one was out on the trail, perhaps having emerged during the hailstorm we experienced about half an hour earlier. The salamander was very sluggish and perhaps unwell, although it showed no visible sign of injury. This is the only salamander we have ever encountered while walking trails in Rocky Mountain National Park.

Habitats traversed: The inner loop, which stays close to the lake's edge, is wooded on the southeast side but otherwise mainly open. The outer loop features rock outcrops and Lodgepole Pine woods above the lake, open areas and sparsely wooded slopes, a small meadow in the valley, and riparian habitat along Aspen Brook. **Wildflowers noted:** Rose hips, a yucca, a thistle, a tufted goldenrod or ragwort with berries, a white parsley, Aspen Daisy, Black-eyed Susan, Blanketflower, Cutleaf Daisy, Hairy Golden Aster, various composites, Yarrow, a wallflower, Mountain Harebell, a lupine, Fremont Geranium, Common Fireweed, a buckwheat, a currant in berry, and Scarlet Paintbrush. **Other plants found:** We found some nice mosses along Aspen Brook. **Trees and shrubs:** The inner loop is a good place to see typical Rocky Mountain trees, as nice specimens of Douglas-fir, Blue Spruce, Ponderosa Pine, Limber Pine, and Quaking Aspen grow right along the trail, and willows of at least one species are found by the water. Also found here are Common Juniper and Shrubby Cinquefoil.

Birds seen or heard: Mallard (on Lily Lake), Ring-necked Duck (on the lake), Northern Flicker, Say's Phoebe, Steller's Jay, Common Raven (especially near Lily Mountain), Violet-green Swallow, American Robin, Chipping Sparrow, Savannah Sparrow, and Dark-eyed Junco. **Mammals encountered:** Least Chipmunk, Golden-mantled Ground Squirrel, Red Squirrel, an aquatic mammal on the lake (perhaps American Beaver or Muskrat), Long-tailed Weasel (in the visitor center parking lot), and Mule Deer. **Insects:** In a dry area, a grasshopper flashed yellow wings as it flushed near our feet, then did the usual trick—folding its wings and dropping into the vegetation, vanishing suddenly. Butterflies can be annoyingly difficult to identify at a glance, but we got a nice look at a Weidemeyer's Admiral—a black butterfly with a prominent white stripe and a white spot on the front part of the forewing between the stripe and the base of the wing.

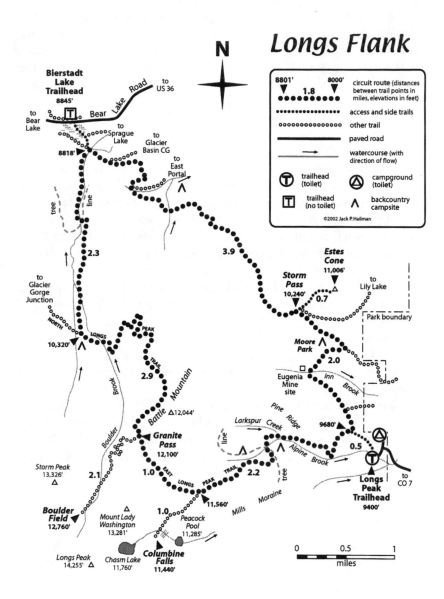

Longs Flank

N

Bierstadt Lake Trailhead 8845'

to US 36

Bear Lake Road

to Bear Lake

to Sprague Lake

to Glacier Basin CG

8818'

to East Portal

tree line

2.3

3.9

Estes Cone 11,006'

Storm Pass 10,240'

to Lily Lake

0.7

Park boundary

to Glacier Gorge Junction

NORTH

LONGS

PEAK

TRAIL

Moore Park

2.0

10,320'

Boulder Brook

2.9

Battle Mountain

Eugenia Mine site

Inn Brook

△12,044'

Pine Ridge

Larkspur Creek

line

9680'

Granite Pass 12,100'

Alpine Brook

0.5

Storm Peak 13,326' △

2.1

1.0

EAST

LONGS

PEAK

TRAIL

2.2

tree line

⊛

Ⓣ

to CO 7

Boulder Field 12,760'

△ Mount Lady Washington 13,281'

11,560'

Mills Moraine

Longs Peak Trailhead 9400'

1.0

Peacock Pool 11,285'

Longs Peak 14,255' △

Chasm Lake 11,760'

Columbine Falls 11,440'

| 0 | 0.5 | 1 |
miles

56

LONGS FLANK CIRCUIT

FORMULA TIMES: 11 hours, 46 minutes for the circuit, including out and back on the access trail, to 17 hours, 7 minutes with all optional side trips. Actually, two of the three side trips can be extended to create an even longer hike. This circuit probably could not be completed in a single day except by young adults in superb physical condition and well acclimated to high altitudes (see **Trail Description** for comments).

HIKING ELEVATIONS: 8818 to 12,100 feet (to 12,760 feet on the side trip to the Boulder Field).

EXERTION RATINGS: 36.7 (extremely strenuous) for the circuit, including the access trail from the Longs Peak Trailhead, to a maximum of 53.9 (off the scale) with all optional side trips. These exertion ratings would be for a continuous day hike, but as this is too long a circuit to be done in one day, the ratings have limited planning usefulness.

FEATURES: This circuit has almost everything. The trip provides spectacular mountain views; habitats varying from deep forest to open tundra; rushing creeks; a historic site; and even more.

ACCESS POINTS: Longs Peak Trailhead (East Side of the park). It is possible to access this circuit from Bierstadt Lake Trailhead on Bear Lake Road as well.

SEASONS: Summer is very popular, as is autumn, with its golden yellow aspen foliage. Winter hiking is not recommended, as the Lodgepole Pine forests hold deep snows late into spring and the more open leg down from Granite Pass is often dangerously icy.

SUMMARY:

Route	Distance (mi.)	Total Elevation Gain (ft.)	Time (hr.:min.)	Exertion Rating
Circuit, including access trail	15.3	4122	11:46	36.7
Roundtrip to Columbine Falls*	2.0	120	1:07	3.3
Roundtrip to Boulder Field*	4.2	660	2:46	9.4
Roundtrip to Estes Cone summit	1.4	766	1:28	4.6
Totals	22.9	5668	17:07	53.9

*These optional side trips can be extended beyond the end of the trail.

FINDING THE ACCESS POINT: From the junction of US 34 and US 36 in Estes Park, drive 0.4 mi. east on US 36, and go right, uphill, on Colorado state route 7. Drive south on CO 7 for 9.1 mi. and turn right on Longs

Peak Road at the sign. Drive 1.0 mi. to the end of the road, where you will come to a T-junction. Turn left (right will take you to the campground) and enter the parking lot by the ranger station and Longs Peak Trailhead. The parking lot is usually full by dawn, so you may have to park on the side of Longs Peak Road, facing downhill. There are flush **toilets** and drinking **water** near the ranger station.

TRAIL DESCRIPTION (clockwise): we describe this circuit clockwise from Longs Peak Trailhead, but it can be done in either direction—from there or from Bierstadt Lake Trailhead on Bear Lake Road. In any case, the basic circuit entails about 12 hr. of walking (formula time)—much of it on steep, high-altitude trails—which therefore must be spread out over two or more days.

Suggested options for hiking this circuit. At least two options exist for tackling this multiday hike without two vehicles at your disposal. The obvious choice is to make a backpacking trip of it. There are numerous overnighting possibilities, which you can choose from by referring to the backcountry campsites indicated on the accompanying map. Also, as you plan, seek the advice of the knowledgeable people in the backcountry office located downhill from the park headquarters building on US 36 east of the Beaver Meadows Entrance Station. A less obvious option would be to camp at Glacier Basin or Moraine Park Campgrounds off Bear Lake Road. Secure a permit from the backcountry office to leave your car overnight at Longs Peak Ranger Station. Hike from there down to the Bierstadt Lake Trailhead and take the shuttle bus from there to your campground to spend the night. The next day, reverse the process, taking the shuttle bus to Bierstadt Lake Trailhead and walking up to the Longs Peak ranger station to retrieve your vehicle. If you try this, we suggest walking clockwise (covering Granite Pass on the first day) to get through open, high-country tundra as early in the day as possible. The uphill leg on the second day would then be completely below tree line.

1) From the Longs Peak Trailhead near the ranger station, walk uphill for 32 min. to reach the East Longs Peak Trail. Unless you are on the trail within a few hours after midnight, the hoards assaulting Longs Peak will be way ahead of you on the way to Granite Pass.

2) Take the left fork at East Longs Peak Trail (the right fork goes to Storm Pass), continuing to climb for nearly 3 hr. (2:59) before reaching a junction with the trail leaving left to Columbine Falls and Chasm Lake. On the way, reach tundra shortly after crossing Alpine Brook.

2a) The optional side trip to **Columbine Falls** is quite rewarding. The trail crosses **Roaring Fork** above the falls, and it is an easy scramble down to **Peacock Pool**, named for its resemblance to the eye spots in the tail of a Peacock. The trail does not go all the way to **Chasm Lake**, ending instead by an old ranger station, which now houses RMNP mountain rescue equipment. As this spot is below Chasm Lake, you will need to clamber up about 300 ft. over rock to reach the lake, but the extra effort is worth it to behold this beautiful setting. The formula time for the roundtrip to the end of the trail is 1 hr., 7 min.; if you continue to Chasm Lake, you will need to allow an extra hour.

3) Continue to climb for 1 hr., 2 min. before reaching **Granite Pass** at 12,100 ft. Approaching Granite Pass, the trail up Longs Peak leaves to the left, but the pass itself (the highest point on the circuit) is about 0.2 mi. past the trail junction.

3a) The optional side trip to the **Boulder Field** takes you to one of the most famous places in Rocky Mountain National Park. *Here, boulders the size of small houses litter the landscape, and it was here on a cold September night in 1884 that Carrie Welton froze to death, becoming the first of nearly 60 known fatalities on Longs Peak. From the Boulder Field in 1970, on his first visit to Rocky Mountain National Park, Jack climbed the north face of Longs Peak, where on one famous stretch, hikers had to pull themselves up on cables anchored in the rocks along the edge of the precipitous east face. Park officials removed the cables in 1973, leaving only one nontechnical route to the summit. This unforgettable route runs through the* **Keyhole**—*a notch through which you must pass before negotiating a frighteningly narrow ledge called (what else?) the* **Narrows**. *Left of the Keyhole is a stone hut erected in memory of Agnes Vaille, who in January 1925 made the first winter ascent of Longs Peak but died of exposure during a storm, as did Herbert Sortland, one of the men who set out to rescue her. The mountain continues to take its toll; a few summers ago a man was blown off the Narrows in high winds, falling hundreds of feet to his death in front of his horrified wife.* Climb this mountain; it is truly a lot of fun. But please do it only in good weather in the summer and start down from the summit by noon. The roundtrip to the end of the trail has a formula time of 2 hr., 46 min., but if you continue on through the Boulder Field to the Keyhole or farther, allow hours of extra time.

4) From the junction near Granite Pass, follow the trail for 1 hr., 27 min. over tundra to reach the intersection with the trail to Glacier Gorge Junction. On the way, cross the actual pass, about 0.2 mi. past the trail to Longs Peak. It's downhill from this point for the next 5.0 mi. Here, as elsewhere above tree line, expect to be beseeched by Yellow-bellied Marmots (but please resist the urge to feed them). Descend, encountering some switchbacks, cross Boulder Brook, and arrive at a trail junction after losing more than 1500 ft. of altitude. The trail to the left goes to Glacier Gorge Junction.

5) At the trail intersection, go right, following Boulder Brook downhill for a little over an hour (1 hr., 9 min.) in sparsely treed low forest, crossing the brook and leaving the tundra, eventually arriving at a trail junction.

6) Trails in this area crisscross one another and can be confusing. At this junction (the lowest point on the circuit, at 8818 ft.), the trail leading straight ahead is an access route to Bierstadt Lake Trailhead on Bear Lake Road. The trail to the left goes up to Prospect Canyon on the way to Glacier Gorge Junction. Our circuit goes right, following the trail that leads up to Storm Pass. Spend the next 3 hr., 22 min. hiking mostly uphill. On the left, you will pass a trail for Glacier Basin Campground and one for East Portal before beginning the long walk that takes you up to the pass. **Storm Pass** is not nearly as high as Granite Pass, but it is the local high point on this second half of the circuit. Here there is an immense cairn, to which Liz ceremoniously added a small stone. Here, too, is the start of a fairly new trail to Lily Lake.

6a) The optional climb to the top of **Estes Cone,** the most perfectly cone-shaped mountain in RMNP, is quite popular as part of an out-and-back day trip from Longs Peak Trailhead. From Storm Pass, it takes about an hour and a half (1 hr., 28 min.) roundtrip. The way is not really a trail, but rather a steep route marked by cairns. *The slow going provides an opportunity to make friends with Limber Pine, which covers the slope.* Near the top, the forest gives way to open rock requiring a little climbing; keep circling right (counterclockwise) on the rocky face before ascending to the very top, with its spectacular views. *Estes Cone, like Estes Park, was named for Joel Estes (1806–1875), the region's first settler, although he did not stay long. The cone itself is not a volcano as the name might suggest, but rather an erosional feature of coincidentally symmetric shape.*

---

7) From here, walk mostly downhill for an hour. After approximately 30 min., arrive at a junction. Turn sharply right (straight ahead would take you out of the park). Continue, passing through lovely **Moore Park** and then the site of the **Eugenia Mine** at Inn Brook (which you cross on a log bridge), before eventually arriving at the junction with the access trail to Longs Peak Trailhead. *Between Inn Brook and the access trail, look for some impressively large hunks of white quartz lying along the trail. Eugenia*

Yellow-bellied Marmots are almost sure to be encountered near Granite Pass.

was the only mining operation that we're aware of on RMNP's eastern side, which on the whole is devoid of commercially useful deposits. If you walk uphill from the cabin ruins, you can see some rusty machinery bits and tailings from this 1905 operation. The origins of the names Moore Park and Eugenia Mine are unknown. Inn Brook is presumably so named because it burbled by the famous Longs Peak Inn run by Enos Mills.

8) Complete the circuit by walking downhill for 15 min. on the access trail to Longs Peak Trailhead.

Counterclockwise walking time is the same overall, but individual segments differ from the clockwise circuit because the elevation gains are in different places. From Longs Peak Trailhead counterclockwise: **(8)** walk 32 min. up the access trail; **(7)** turn right and climb 1 hr., 34 min. to Storm Pass; **(6)** descend 1 hr., 57 min. to the circuit's low point; **(5)** turn left at the trail junction and continue 2 hr., 39 min. uphill along Boulder Brook, soon emerging onto tundra before reaching the trail leaving right for Glacier Gorge Junction; **(4)** begin 3 hr., 14 min. of hard uphill climbing, gaining more than 1500 ft. of elevation to cross Granite Pass, then descending 0.2 mi. to reach the trail leaving right for the Boulder Field and Longs Peak; **(3)** walk 30 min. to the junction with the trail leaving

Artifacts at site of Eugenia Mine on Longs Flank Circuit.

right for Columbine Falls; **(2)** continue straight, descending 1 hr., 6 min. to the access trail; and **(1)** turn right, walking 15 min. down the access trail to Longs Peak Trailhead. The optional side trips to Estes Cone, Boulder Field, and Columbine Falls, based on out-and-back roundtrips, are the same as in the clockwise description.

Hiking the circuit from Bierstadt Lake Trailhead on Bear Lake Road. First, walk the 0.3 mi. from the trailhead across Bear Lake Road to the junction where the trail to Storm Pass goes off to the left. Then, if walking the circuit **clockwise,** follow legs 6, 7 (skip 8 and 1), 2, 3, 4 and 5 in the main description. If walking **counterclockwise,** follow legs 5, 4, 3, 2 (skip 1 and 8), 7, and 6.

OUR HIKING NOTES: We have never walked this circuit as a continuous multiday trip. Nevertheless, the segment hikes on which we jotted our notes all took place in early to mid-August. As with the other circuits in this book, the plants and animals encountered were therefore representative of a particular time of year.

About tall mountains and appetite. At 14,255 ft., Longs Peak is the highest mountain in RMNP, but Colorado boasts many others that are higher, including the tallest, Mt. Elbert, at 14,443 ft. A little higher it may be, but Elbert is a far easier hike; just ask Liz, who seemed to prance up it. One piece of lore about Longs is that by the time people reach the summit, they've lost their appetite. That's only partly true: Jack ate both his lunch and that of another hiker who could not face food.

Habitats traversed: This circuit includes almost everything: bare rock, open tundra, sparsely wooded slopes (above the tree line of USGS maps), mixed coniferous montane forest, primarily Lodgepole Pine woods, montane meadow, and riparian stream courses. Probably all species of coniferous trees found in RMNP occur along this route, although our notes fail to mention Engelmann Spruce specifically. **Wildflowers noted:** Nodding Onion, a golden aster, a purple aster, a ragwort, two different yellow composites, Aspen Daisy, Yarrow, chiming-bells (at stream crossings), Mountain Harebell, a small-flowered lupine, a gentian, Monument-plant, Common Fireweed, Bracted Alumroot, and Scarlet Paintbrush. **Other plants found:** Little clumps of true mosses, and Common Juniper and Shrubby Cinquefoil (shrubs).

Birds seen or heard (species marked with an asterisk were seen only on the high tundra): *White-tailed Ptarmigan (female with about 12 young), Broad-tailed Hummingbird, Northern Flicker, Hairy Woodpecker, Gray Jay, Steller's Jay, Common Raven, Mountain Chickadee, Red-breasted Nuthatch, Golden-crowned Kinglet, Ruby-crowned Kinglet, American Robin, *American Pipit, Yellow-rumped Warbler, Chipping Sparrow, and *Brown-capped Rosy Finch. **Mammals encountered** (species marked with an asterisk were seen only on the high tundra): *Pika, Snowshoe Rabbit, Least Chipmunk, *Yellow-bellied Marmot, Golden-mantled Ground Squirrel, Red Squirrel, and Coyote.

Wild Basin Loops

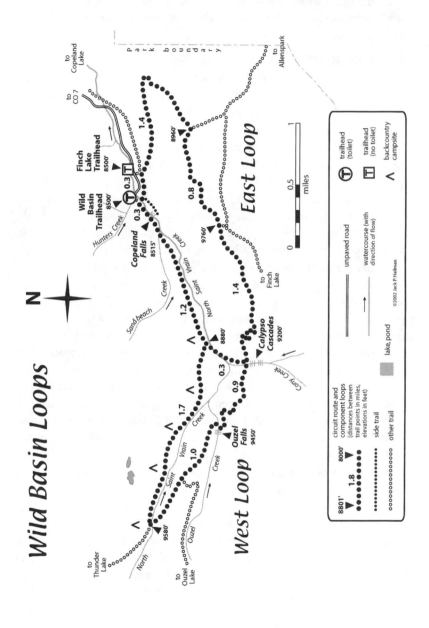

N

to Copeland Lake

to CO 7

Finch Lake Trailhead 8500'

Wild Basin Trailhead 8500'

0.3

0.3

0.3

Hunters Creek

Copeland Falls 8515'

1.4

8960'

0.8

9760'

1.4

Sand beach

North Saint Vrain Creek

1.2

8880'

0.3

Calypso Cascades 9200'

Cony Creek

East Loop

to Finch Lake

P a r k   b o u n d a r y

to Allenspark

1.7

0.3

0.9

1.0

Saint Vrain Creek

Ouzel Creek

Ouzel Falls 9450'

West Loop

North Saint Vrain Creek

9580'

to Thunder Lake

to Ouzel Lake

©2002 Jack P. Hailman

miles

0   0.5   1

8801' ▲
1.8 ●●●●●   circuit route and component loops (distances between trail points in miles, elevations in feet)

8000' ▲

●●●●●●   side trail

oooooooooooo   other trail

unpaved road

watercourse (with direction of flow)

lake, pond

Ⓣ trailhead (toilet)

T trailhead (no toilet)

∧ backcountry campsite

WILD BASIN LOOPS

FORMULA TIMES: 6 hours, 8 minutes for the entire circuit; 4 hours, 7 minutes for the East Loop only. **Note:** the West Loop cannot be walked on its own unless you access it from the 1.5-mile north leg of the East Loop.

HIKING ELEVATIONS: 8500 to 9760 feet. (The highest and lowest points of the entire circuit are both on the East Loop.)

EXERTION RATINGS: 18.0 (moderate) for the entire circuit, 12.0 (moderately easy) for the East Loop only.

FEATURES: Three waterfalls (Calypso Cascades, Ouzel Falls, and Copeland Falls), lush forest, solitude.

ACCESS POINTS: Wild Basin Trailhead or Finch Lake Trailhead (East Side of the park, south of Estes Park).

SEASONS: Year-round; winter activities are very popular here. Note that at these elevations, snow typically does not remain all winter, as it does at elevations above 10,000 ft.

SUMMARY:

Route	Distance (mi.)	Total Elevation Gain (ft.)	Time (hr.:min.)	Exertion Rating
East Loop only	5.7	1260	4:07	12.0
Entire circuit	9.0	1640	6:08	18.0

FINDING THE ACCESS POINT: From the junction of US 34 and US 36 in Estes Park, drive 0.4 mi. east on US 36 and go right, uphill, on Colorado state route 7. Drive south on CO 7 for 12.9 mi. and turn right on the paved road leading to Wild Basin. At 0.4 mi. from CO 7, the paved road turns left (south) just before the Wild Basin Entrance Station; the road to Wild Basin continues westward as an unpaved road. Go 0.8 mi. past the entrance station to the Finch Lake Trailhead **(no toilets, no water)**, continue 0.2 mi. past that to the "Horse Trail," and 0.1 mi. beyond that to the end of the road at the Wild Basin Trailhead, ranger station, and picnic area. There are **outhouses** here, and a **water** spigot at the ranger station.

TRAIL DESCRIPTION (clockwise from Wild Basin Trailhead): The circuit can be walked in either direction; we recommend clockwise to get the major elevation gain over with early on. Also, if you walk the circuit in this direction, you can enjoy a mainly downhill stretch on your way to the waterfalls. We recommend starting from the Wild Basin Trailhead, which has **water, toilets,** and a larger parking lot. Another advantage of this departure point is that you put the least enjoyable part of the circuit—the short walk along the road—behind you first. The following description is for the entire circuit, incorporating specific instructions for the East Loop. *The habitat is coniferous forest (some of it burned) and creek valleys.*

1) From the Wild Basin Trailhead, walk back along the road for 0.1 mi., cross the creek on the road bridge, turn right onto the horse trail that parallels the road, and continue for 0.2 mi., reaching the Finch Lake Trailhead 9 min. after you started out.

2) At the Finch Lake Trailhead (with parking lot), cross North Saint Vrain Creek and walk uphill for about 1 hr., 10 min. to a junction with a trail heading southeast for the Allenspark area.

3) Keep right (west) at the trail junction and continue uphill for 1 hr., 12 min. to a second junction, with trails leaving east for Allenspark and southwest for Finch Lake. This is the highest point on the circuit.

4) At the junction, keep right and descend for 42 min., crossing a creek and then dropping down on switchbacks to arrive at the **Calypso Cascades** trail junction. *Calypso Cascades was named by botanist William Cooper, who found numerous Fairyslippers* (Calypso bulbosa, *a lovely orchid*) *here.* **4a)** At the junction, the trail on the right, which follows Cony Creek downhill, is the route of the East Loop. Those hiking the East Loop only will follow this trail 0.3 mi. downhill for a short 9 min. to meet the outer circuit, picking up the trail description at leg (8), following. *Cony Creek is named for the Pika, an alpine relative of rabbits (known colloquially as coneys).*

5) Continue on the outer circuit by crossing Cony Creek and walking uphill for 42 min. to reach **Ouzel Falls.** Take a few extra minutes to cross the bridge to enjoy the scenery. About 100 yards farther on, find a rocky overlook from which you can see Longs Peak and Mt. Meeker to the northwest, as well as Wild Basin and, way off to the east, the Great Plains. Ouzel *is a colloquial name for the American Dipper, which takes the ultimate dip by walking completely underwater along mountain creekbeds as it forages. A book on bird names states that the origin is unknown and presumably derives either from the bird's habit of teetering ("dipping") while standing or from its subaquatic behavior.*

6) From Ouzel Falls, continue past the aforementioned rocky overlook and walk the next mile in 38 min., crossing North Saint Vrain Creek to a junction with the trail to Thunder Lake. On the way pass the trail to Ouzel Lake, which the hiker will encounter on the left. This is the westernmost point of the outer circuit. *Three smaller creeks unite to form Saint Vrain Creek, which flows out onto the plains to join the Platte River. The Saint Vrain brothers ran a store in the vicinity of where the Saint Vrain Creek flows into the Platte River.*

7) Now turn eastward (right), walking downhill for 51 min. in the North Saint Vrain Creek Valley to meet the cross-trail from Calypso Cascades.

8) With the East Loop and the overall circuit united again, continue down the North Saint Vrain Creek Valley for 36 min. to cross Sandbeach Creek and arrive at **Copeland Falls**. *These falls were named for John B. Copeland, a pioneer here in the 1860s.*

9) From Copeland Falls it is a short 9-min. walk back to the Wild Basin Ranger Station and picnic grounds.

Counterclockwise walking time is the same overall, but individual segments differ from the clockwise circuit because the elevation gains are in different places: **(9)** from the Wild Basin Ranger Station, walk about 10 min. to Copeland Falls; **(8)** continue 58 min. to the trail junction where the East Loop leaves left for 9 min. to Calypso Cascades, rejoining the outer circuit at leg (4); **(7)** head up the North St. Vrain Creek valley for 1 hr., 33 min. to the junction with the trail to Thunder Lake; **(6)** turn left and walk 30 min. to Ouzel Falls; **(5)** arrive 27 min. later at Calypso Cascades, where the East Loop rejoins the circuit; **(4)** hike 1 hr., 16 min. uphill to the junction with the trail to Finch Lake; **(3)** descend 24 min. to the junction with the trail to Allenspark; **(2)** continue 42 min. back to the Finch Lake Trailhead, and **(1)** walk 9 min., first on the horse trail, then on the road, back to the Wild Basin Trailhead.

OUR HIKING NOTES: We took no plant notes. The animals were recorded in mid-August.

Habitats traversed: Coniferous forest (some of it burned) and creek valleys.

Birds seen or heard: Downy Woodpecker, Hairy Woodpecker, Gray Jay, Steller's Jay, Mountain Chickadee, Red-breasted Nuthatch, Brown Creeper, Golden-crowned Kinglet, Ruby-crowned Kinglet, American Dipper, and Dark-eyed Junco. **Mammals encountered:** Least(?) Chipmunk, Golden-mantled Ground Squirrel, and Red Squirrel.

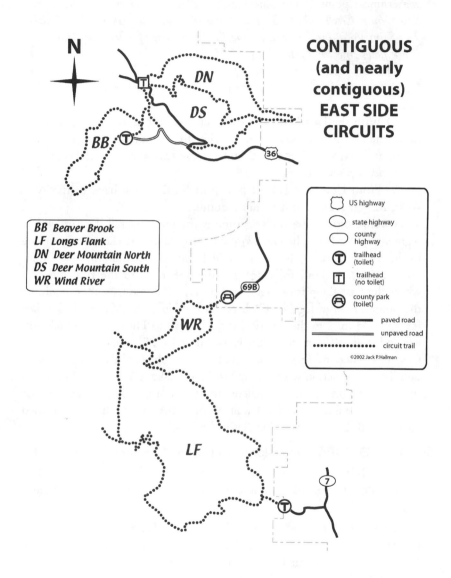

N

CONTIGUOUS
(and nearly contiguous)
EAST SIDE CIRCUITS

DN

DS

BB

36

BB Beaver Brook
LF Longs Flank
DN Deer Mountain North
DS Deer Mountain South
WR Wind River

⬡ US highway

⬭ state highway

⬭ county highway

Ⓣ trailhead (toilet)

🖳 trailhead (no toilet)

Ⓐ county park (toilet)

—— paved road

══ unpaved road

•••••••••• circuit trail

©2002 Jack P. Hailman

69B

WR

7

LF

Ⓣ

COMBINING EAST SIDE CIRCUITS

Gluttons for punishment may have noticed that two East Side circuits have a trail segment in common and therefore could be combined for an even longer circuit hike. The Wind River and Longs Flank Circuits are contiguous, but combining them may have limited appeal, as Longs Flank is already one of the two longest circuits in the book. Nevertheless, the several backcountry campsites along the Wind River Trail make it, if not the whole Wind River Circuit, attractive. (A more interesting extension of Longs Flank might be to combine it with the contiguous Boulder Brook Circuit accessed from Bear Lake Road. In a similar vein, Wind River could be combined with the Glacier Basin Loops Circuit. These possibilities are discussed at the end of the section on circuits accessed from Bear Lake Road.)

An easy-to-overlook possibility is to combine the Beaver Brook Circuit with the Deer Mountain Loops (South Loop or entire circuit). These are nearly contiguous, connected by a short trail shown in the maps of both accounts. The unpaved road leading to the Beaver Meadows Trailhead also connects the two circuits.

Bear Lake in snow, at the end of Bear Lake Road offering access to more circuit hikes than either the East or West Side.

Circuit Hikes From Access Points Along Bear Lake Road

INTRODUCTION TO BEAR LAKE ROAD CIRCUITS

Nearly half the circuits in this book are accessed from Bear Lake Road, the only major dead-end road in the park. Heading south from US 36 just east of the Beaver Meadows Entrance Station, it is readily accessible from the Estes Park area. Two circuits are accessed via the side road that leads past the Moraine Park Campground; the remainder of the access points lie on or just off Bear Lake Road itself.

The two most popular campgrounds in Rocky Mountain National Park are located off Bear Lake Road. Each provides the opportunity to hike at least two circuits virtually from your campsite. From Moraine Park Campground, you can leave the Cub Lake Trailhead for both the Moraine Park and Cub Lake Circuits. From the Glacier Basin Campground, you can hike the Glacier Basin Loops Circuit, the Wind River Circuit (an East Side circuit described earlier), or, by crossing the highway to the shuttle bus lot, the Bierstadt Moraine Loops. In fact, the two campgrounds are connected by the Moraine Park shuttle bus, so you can ride between campgrounds and hike the trails from either one without having to drive your vehicle. Finally, there is the Bear Lake shuttle bus, which picks up where the Moraine Park shuttle leaves off and stops at all of the access points (except the Sprague Lake Picnic Area) between the shuttle bus lot and Bear Lake.

The 11 accounts in this section are ordered geographically by access point from north to south. Several places serve as the primary or secondary access point for two or more circuits. For example, the Cub Lake Trailhead can be the jumping off place for both the Cub Lake and Moraine Park Circuits, Sprague Lake picnic grounds for both the Sprague Lake Circuit and Glacier Basin Loops, Glacier Gorge Junction Trailhead for both the Alpine Lakes and Boulder Brook Circuits, and Bear Lake Trailhead for the Bear Lake, Mount Wuh, and Tundra & Glaciers Circuits.

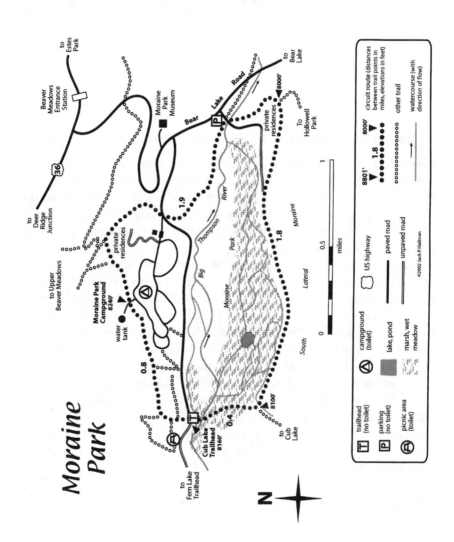

Moraine Park

Beaver Meadows Entrance Station

to Deer Ridge Junction

36

to Estes Park

to Upper Beaver Meadows

Moraine Park Museum

Bear **Lake** **Road**

private residences

water tank

Moraine Park Campground 8240'

private residences

P

to Bear Lake

To Hollowell Park

8000'

Big Thompson River

South Lateral Moraine

Moraine Park

1.9

0.8

Cub Lake Trailhead 8160'

to Fern Lake Trailhead

0.4

8100'

1.8

to Cub Lake

N

trailhead (no toilet)	8801' ▼	circuit route (distances between trail points in miles, elevations in feet)
P parking (no toilet)	1.8	
picnic area (toilet)	●●●●●●●●●●	other trail
campground (toilet)	ooooooooooo	unpaved road
lake, pond		
marsh, wet meadow	⟶	watercourse (with direction of flow)

8000' ▼

US highway

paved road

©2002 Jack P. Hailman

0   0.5   1

miles

MORAINE PARK CIRCUIT

FORMULA TIME: 2 hours, 41 minutes (but take much longer to enjoy the natural history).

HIKING ELEVATIONS: 8000 to 8240 feet.

EXERTION RATING: 7.5 (easy).

FEATURES: Natural history in one of the most visited and beloved areas in Rocky Mountain National Park. This is a great place to see birds, as well as many mammals and wildflowers. This is also a good walk for identifying a variety of trees.

ACCESS POINTS: Cub Lake Trailhead (off Bear Lake Road). The circuit could also be walked from a tiny parking lot just off Bear Lake Road itself (see map), or from Moraine Park Campground for those camping there.

SEASONS: Summer and fall are best. Despite the relatively low elevation, Moraine Park can be quite windy, creating blowing and drifting snow in winter. The snow that remains becomes hard-packed and icy.

SUMMARY:

Route	Distance (mi.)	Total Elevation Gain (ft.)	Time (hr.:min.)	Exertion Rating
Circuit	4.9	240	2:41	7.5

FINDING THE ACCESS POINT: From US 36, 0.3 mi. west of the Beaver Meadows Entrance Station, turn left onto Bear Lake Road. Drive 1.3 mi. and take the first right, which leads to Moraine Park Campground and two trailheads. From Bear Lake Road, drive 1.8 mi. (keeping left at the entrance road to the campground) to reach the Cub Lake Trailhead, which has a small parking area. There is additional parking at the stables area, which you will pass just before reaching the trailhead, and also at the small picnic grounds 0.2 mi. beyond the trailhead. The Moraine Park Shuttle Bus stops at both the trailhead and the picnic area. The Cub Lake Trailhead is marked with a large sign. The trail begins with a bridge that crosses a channel of the Big Thompson River within a few feet of the road. There are **toilets** at the picnic area but not at the trailhead itself; **no drinking water** is available. Remember to treat or filter any water you take from the Big Thompson River or other natural sources.

TRAIL DESCRIPTION (counterclockwise): We recommend walking this circuit counterclockwise in the morning so as to pass through Moraine

Upper Moraine Park sandwiched between dark, pine-laden lateral moraines.

Park early on, when the birds are singing and the mammals are active. Save the leg-stretching segment north around the campground for last.

Moraine Park is named for the lateral moraines that flank its north and south sides. The last major continental glaciation, the Wisconsinian, reached its maximum extent about 15,000 years ago. During this time, three episodes of montane glaciation, known as the Pinedale Glaciations, occurred in the Rockies. Probably all three episodes thrust an ice tongue (the Thompson Glacier) down the path where the Big Thompson River now flows through Moraine Park. As it crept downhill toward the east, it plowed up rocks and soil, pushing them to the side, much as a snowplow pushes snow. Those hills of jumbled rock today still outline the edges of the long-since-melted glacier.

1) From Cub Lake Trailhead, walk south across the west end of **Moraine Park** for 12 min. until you reach a trail junction. On the way, pass through wet thickets. **Note:** Twelve minutes is the actual walking time, but we encourage you to take much longer and enjoy the natural history along the way.

2) At the junction, take the left fork (right goes southeast to Cub Lake) and walk for 54 min. along the southern edge of Moraine Park, at the base of the **South Lateral Moraine.** For the most part, the trail stays just inside the coniferous woods. *This is a great place to see Wyoming Ground Squirrels running between their burrows at the edge of the wet meadow.* Do not follow the fishing paths at the water's edge, which soon peter out; instead, stay on the main trail, which runs above the wet meadow. Pass the western terminus of an unpaved road at the meadow's edge and climb through woods onto the moraine shoulder to arrive at another trail junction.

3) At the junction, take the left fork (the right leads to Hollowell Park) and walk 1 hr., 11 min. to Moraine Park Campground. On the way, the trail descends north from the moraine, passes between private residences, and strikes out across the meadow for the small road bridge over the Big Thompson River. (On the other side of the bridge is a small parking area just off Bear Lake Road; the circuit could be hiked from here, but the parking is usually taken by fly-fishing enthusiasts.) Turn left after crossing the bridge, walk through the meadow *(note a huge Douglas-fir standing by itself to the left of the trail),* and emerge on the paved road just east of the campground entrance. (From here you could shortcut the circuit by turning left and walking back on the road to the Cub Lake Trailhead.) Cross the road and ascend through fairly open Ponderosa parkland. There is a maze of old paths and horse trails in this area, but if you keep left at the junctions, you cannot get lost; the worst that will happen is that you'll end up in the campground instead of passing north of it. If you manage to find the correct trails, you will eventually come to a water tank above the campground, just to the right of the trail.

4) From the water tank, walk 24 min. back to the Cub Lake Trailhead. Again, there are many unmarked trails in the area, so you might come out at the stables east of the trailhead or (as we did) arrive at the picnic area west of the trailhead. In either case, it is a short walk along the road to the trailhead.

Clockwise walking time is the same overall, but individual segments differ slightly from the counterclockwise circuit because the elevation gains

Golden-mantled Ground Squirrel, denizen of Moraine Park and many other places.

are in different places. **(4)** From Cub Lake Trailhead, ascend the trail across the road to the north and take the second trail to the right, passing north of the campground and reaching the water tank in 29 min. **(3)** From the water tank, follow the trail eastward, turning south (right) at a junction past the area of scattered private residences. The trail descends through Ponderosa parkland, crosses the paved road, heads southeast through the meadow, crosses the small bridge over the Big Thompson, heads more southerly, passes between residences, and climbs the moraine shoulder to a trail junction. Make certain you cross the small bridge instead of heading toward Bear Lake Road along the river. Walking time is 57 min. **(2)** Take the right fork, walk 1 hr. on the south side of Moraine Park. **(1)** At the trail junction, go right and walk 16 min. back to Cub Lake Trailhead.

OUR HIKING NOTES: The formula time is 2 hr., 41 min., but we were so absorbed in the natural history of this hike that our time was a leisurely 4 hr., 2 min. in mid-July. Near the private residences at the southeast corner of the circuit, we watched a pair of Mountain Bluebirds feeding their three fledglings.

Habitats traversed: Meadows and ponds along the Big Thompson River, Ponderosa parkland. This is one of the best hikes in Rocky Mountain National Park for viewing a diversity of trees: willows, Thinleaf Alder, aspen, junipers, Ponderosa and Lodgepole Pine, Douglas-fir, and even Blue Spruce. **Wildflowers noted:** Blanketflower, Salsify, Miners-candle, a wallflower, Mountain Harebell, Yellow Stonecrop, a loco (a.k.a. locoweed), Golden Banner, Fremont Geranium, Blue Flax, Sulphurflower, a larkspur, a penstemon, and Scarlet Paintbrush. **Other plants found:** Common Juniper and Shrubby Cinquefoil (shrubs), and Plains Pricklypear (not in flower).

Birds seen or heard: Broad-tailed Hummingbird, Rufous Hummingbird, Hairy Woodpecker, Northern Flicker, Western Wood Pewee, Warbling Vireo, Black-billed Magpie, American Crow, Common Raven, Violet-green Swallow, Mountain Chickadee, Red-breasted Nuthatch, Pygmy Nuthatch, House Wren, Mountain Bluebird, American Robin, Yellow-rumped Warbler, Western Tanager, Song Sparrow, Dark-eyed Junco, Red Crossbill, and Pine Siskin. **Mammals encountered:** Least Chipmunk, Wyoming Ground Squirrel, Golden-mantled Ground Squirrel, Red Squirrel, and Mule Deer. **Insects:** Butterflies, including the Western Tiger Swallowtail and Anicia Checkerspot.

Cub Lake

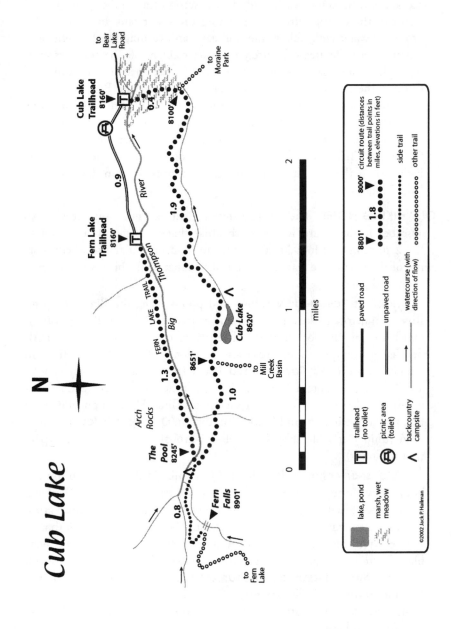

N

to Bear Lake Road

Cub Lake Trailhead
8160'

to Moraine Park

8100'

0.4

0.9

Thompson River

Fern Lake Trailhead
8160'

1.9

FERN LAKE TRAIL

Big Thompson

Cub Lake
8620'

to Mill Creek Basin

Arch Rocks

1.3

8651'

1.0

The Pool
8245'

0.8

Fern Falls
8901'

to Fern Lake

©2002 Jack P. Hallman

Legend

- lake, pond
- marsh, wet meadow

- ⊞ trailhead (no toilet)
- 🅿 picnic area (toilet)
- ⋀ backcountry campsite

8801' ► ●●●●● 8000' ►   circuit route (distances between trail points in miles, elevations in feet)

1.8 ●●●●●●●●●   side trail

ooooooooooooooooo   other trail

—— paved road

═══ unpaved road

→ watercourse (with direction of flow)

miles

0   1   2

CUB LAKE CIRCUIT

FORMULA TIMES: 3 hours, 18 minutes for the circuit; 4 hours, 45 minutes with side trip to Fern Falls.

HIKING ELEVATIONS: 8100 to 8651 feet (to 8901 feet on the side trip to Fern Falls).

EXERTION RATINGS: 9.2 (easy) for the circuit to 13.4 (moderately easy) with the side trip to Fern Falls.

FEATURES: Wildflowers, birds, mountain lake, The Pool on the Big Thompson River, geology; waterfall on the side trip.

ACCESS POINTS: Fern Lake Trailhead or Cub Lake Trailhead (off Bear Lake Road).

SEASONS: The trail is nice in summer and great in fall when the aspens, willows, and cottonwoods turn color. In winter, drifting snows can pose problems.

SUMMARY:

Route	Distance (mi.)	Total Elevation Gain (ft.)	Time (hr.:min.)	Exertion Rating
Basic circuit	5.5	551	3:18	9.2
Roundtrip to Fern Falls	1.6	656	1:27	4.2
Totals	7.1	1207	4:45	13.4

FINDING THE ACCESS POINT: From US 36, 0.3 mi. west of the Beaver Meadows Entrance Station, turn left onto Bear Lake Road. Drive 1.3 mi. and take the first right, which leads to Moraine Park Campground and two trailheads. From the Bear Lake Road intersection, drive 1.8 mi. (keeping left at the entrance road to the campground) to pass the Cub Lake Trailhead, with its small parking area. From here, the road continues unpaved for another 0.9 mi. to the Fern Lake Trailhead, passing a small picnic area 0.2 mi. after the pavement ceases. The 0.7-mi. stretch from the picnic area to the Fern Lake Trailhead is narrow and cannot accommodate trailers or large vehicles. Parking in small lots along this road and at Fern Lake Trailhead is very limited; there is additional parking at the picnic area, Cub Lake Trailhead, and even farther east in the stables area that you passed before reaching Cub Lake Trailhead. The Moraine Park Shuttle Bus does not go down the narrow road to Fern Lake Trailhead, turning around instead at the picnic area. There are **outhouses** at the picnic area but not at either trailhead. **No drinking water** is available at any of these places. Remember to treat or filter any water you take from the Big Thompson River or other natural sources.

TRAIL DESCRIPTION (clockwise from Fern Lake Trailhead): We recommend walking the circuit clockwise in the morning so as to traverse the wet thickets at the west end of Moraine Park early in the day, when the birds are singing and the mammals are active. Furthermore, by leaving your car at Fern Lake Trailhead, you put the 0.9-mi. walk on the unpaved road behind you at the start.

1) From the Fern Lake Trailhead, walk for 27 min. along the unpaved road, past the picnic area to the Cub Lake Trailhead. (Our actual time would have been faster than the formula time, but we stopped to enjoy the birds along the road.)

2) From Cub Lake Trailhead, walk south for 12 min. to a trail junction. This is a pleasant walk through the thickets at the western end of **Moraine Park**. In addition to spotting many birds, you may also see Wyoming Ground Squirrels at their burrows by the meadow's edge, where the soil is drier.

3) At the trail junction, take the right fork (left heads along the south side of Moraine Park) and walk uphill for 1 hr., 30 min., passing **Cub Lake** before reaching a trail junction. *Since Bear Lake was named for a bear once observed there, you might guess Cub Lake's name had a similar origin, but Abner Sprague dubbed it Cub Lake simply because it was small.* This is a nice walk along the creek draining Cub Lake. The route passes a number of beaver ponds. Less than 10 min. after leaving Moraine Park, watch for a large boulder on the right that has split in twain; you could take a picture of your hiking companion looking in from the other side of the crack. *The Cub Lake basin was scoured into the rock by the Thompson Glacier during the Pinedale montane glaciations, which peaked about 15,000 years ago. Basins like this fill with water when the glacier has receded, forming what is appropriately called a rock-basin lake. Cub Lake is virtually choked with Yellow Pondlilies.* The trail ascends above the north side of the lake, passing through an old burn area (popular among land birds) before reaching a trail junction.

4) At the junction, go right (left leads to Mill Creek Basin) and walk mainly downhill for 30 min. to **The Pool**. About midway, vistas open up to the north, offering good views of the steep rock face known as **The Arches**. Shortly after re-entering the woods, arrive at a trail junction and turn right onto the Fern Lake Trail (left leads to Fern Falls). Beyond this is a

Mallard (female shown) is a common species on Cub Lake and other lakes in the region.

bridge so substantial that you could drive a Sherman tank across it; the bridge, which spans the Big Thompson River, overlooks The Pool (left) at the base of a scenic waterfall. This is a good area to look for Colorado Columbine, Colorado's state flower.

4a) From the trail junction, the left fork leads to **Fern Falls,** a roundtrip of about 1 hr., 27 min. Cross a creek and ascend with roaring waters on both sides, then continue uphill on a switchback to reach the base of Fern Falls.

5) From the bridge at The Pool, walk for 39 min. along the Big Thompson to reach the Fern Lake Trailhead. This is another excellent stretch for bird-watching and enjoying natural history.

Counterclockwise walking time is the same overall, but individual segments differ from the clockwise circuit because the elevation gains are

Golden Banner, one of many wildflowers found on the Cub Lake Circuit.

in different places. **(5)** From Fern Lake Trailhead, walk 44 min. along the Big Thompson River to The Pool above the bridge; **(4)** take the left fork at the junction and ascend for 54 min. to the junction with the Cub Lake Trail; **(3)** go left onto the Cub Lake Trail and walk for 57 min., descending past Cub Lake and hiking along the creek that drains it; **(2)** at the trail junction, turn left and cross the western end of Moraine Park, walking for 16 min. to reach Cub Lake Trailhead; **(1)** go left on the unpaved road and walk for 27 min., past the picnic area, to Fern Lake Trailhead. **Side-trip time** to Fern Falls, based on an out-and-back roundtrip, is the same as in the main description.

OUR HIKING NOTES: The formula time for the circuit plus side trip is 4 hr., 45 min.; our time with full packs was 4 hr., 53 min. in mid-July.

Along the way. At the western end of Moraine Park, we watched small, fluorescent-blue dragonflies or damselflies darting about. Several beaver ponds on the creek draining Cub Lake sported Mallards, including one female with ducklings. By another pond we watched a cow Elk browsing. The Yellow Pondlilies on Cub Lake boasted a profusion of flowers when we visited in mid-July. *Pondlilies, also called water lilies, are not lilies at all—they are not even monocots. Their closest relatives are actually thought to be buttercups.* There were half a dozen Ring-necked Ducks on Cub Lake—gray-and-black males with two brown females.

Habitats traversed: River bottomlands and meadow, mixed forest. Find such trees as Rocky Mountain Juniper, Ponderosa and Lodgepole Pines, Blue Spruce, Douglas-fir, Thinleaf Alder, Quaking Aspen, and Mountain Maple. **Wildflowers noted:** A lily, a fleabane, Heartleaf Arnica (at water crossings), a wallflower, Plains Pricklypear (in flower), Mountain Harebell, Twinflower (technically a shrub), Yellow Stonecrop, Golden Banner, Yellow Pondlily, Colorado Columbine, Globeflower, a rose, two species of paintbrush, and a small blue penstemon. **Other plants and fungi found:** Common Juniper and Shrubby Cinquefoil (shrubs), ferns, and the beautiful but poisonous mushroom Fly Amanita.

Birds seen or heard: Mallard, Ring-necked Duck, Broad-tailed Hummingbird, Williamson's Sapsucker, Cordilleran Flycatcher, Gray Jay, Steller's Jay, Black-billed Magpie, American Crow, Mountain Chickadee, Red-breasted Nuthatch, House Wren (at nesting cavity), and American Dipper. **Mammals encountered:** Wyoming Ground Squirrel, Golden-mantled Ground Squirrel, Red Squirrel, Elk, and Mule Deer.

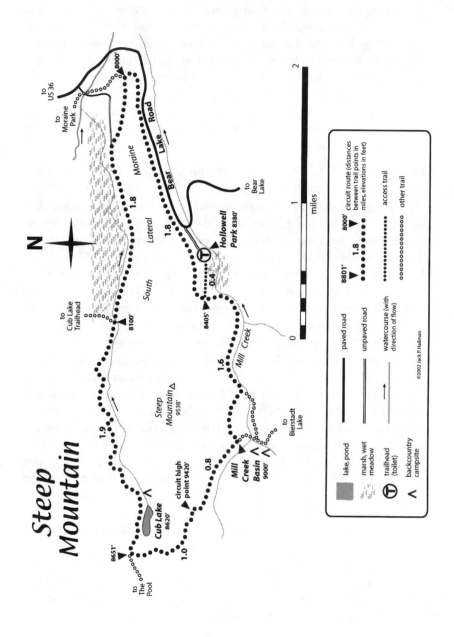

Steep Mountain

N

to US 36

to Moraine Park

to Cub Lake Trailhead

to The Pool

8651'

Cub Lake 8620'

circuit high point 9420'

Steep Mountain △ 9538'

Mill Creek Basin 9000'

to Bierstadt Lake

Mill Creek

8100'

8405'

Hollowell Park 8380'

8000'

Moraine

Bear Lake Road

South Lateral

to Bear Lake

1.9

1.0

0.8

1.6

0.4

1.8

1.8

miles

0   1   2

paved road

unpaved road

watercourse (with direction of flow)

trailhead (toilet)

backcountry campsite

lake, pond

marsh, wet meadow

8801' ▶   8000' ▶
       1.8   circuit route (distances
●●●●●●●●●   between trail points in
                        miles, elevations in feet)

●●●●●●●●●●●●●● access trail

ooooooooooooooo other trail

©2002 Jack P. Hailman

STEEP MOUNTAIN CIRCUIT

FORMULA TIME: 6 hours, 18 minutes, including roundtrip on the access trail.

HIKING ELEVATIONS: 8000 to 9420 feet.

EXERTION RATING: 18.1 (moderate), including out and back on the access trail.

FEATURES: The trail encircles Steep Mountain and the South Lateral Moraine that extends eastward from it, bordering Moraine Park on the south. The way boasts Cub Lake and varied habitat, including the Moraine Park wet meadows, all with interesting natural history. **Note:** this circuit overlaps several others: Moraine Park (along its south side), Cub Lake (from Moraine Park to Cub Lake), and Mount Wuh (Cub Lake to Mill Creek Basin).

ACCESS POINT: Mill Creek Basin Trailhead in Hollowell Park (off Bear Lake Road).

SEASONS: Typically, year-round, as the many aspen groves make for colorful fall hiking, and winter snows often do not last long.

SUMMARY:

Route	Distance (mi.)	Total Elevation Gain (ft.)	Time (hr.:min.)	Exertion Rating
Circuit, including access trail	9.7	1445	6:18	18.1

FINDING THE ACCESS POINT: From US 36, 0.3 mi. west of the Beaver Meadows Entrance Station, turn left onto Bear Lake Road and drive 3.7 mi. Turn right onto the unpaved road leading into Hollowell Park and drive 0.2 mi. to the picnic area. Mill Creek Basin Trailhead is at the end of the road. The Moraine Park Shuttle Bus does stop at Hollowell Park. There are **outhouses** but **no drinking water** at the trailhead. Remember to treat or filter any water you take from Mill Creek or other natural sources of water.

TRAIL DESCRIPTION (clockwise): The circuit can be walked in either direction: clockwise gets the major elevation gains over with near the beginning, counterclockwise delivers you to Moraine Park earlier in the day, when the birds are more active. We arbitrarily chose to describe the route clockwise.

1) From the picnic area in Hollowell Park, walk 14 min. up the access trail to the junction with the circuit trail. *The park is named for George C. Hollowell, an early settler who homesteaded here.*

2) Going left at the junction, walk 1 hr., 24 min., encountering some moderate elevation gain as you head to **Mill Creek Basin.** On the way, follow along Mill Creek passing a trail junction. (The trail to the left crosses a bridge and leads to Mill Creek Basin on a route that is flatter but slightly longer.) You eventually emerge on the north side of Mill Creek Basin. **Warning!** There is a lot of loose gravel on steep sections so it is easy to slip. *So many things are named for Enos Mills, the driving force behind the creation of Rocky Mountain National Park, that people sometimes carelessly refer to this creek as "Mills" Creek. Actually, it is named for the sawmill that was built along its banks in 1877.*

3) At Mill Creek Basin, the alternative trail rejoins at a junction. Turn right and climb through Lodgepole forest and then Ponderosa Pines for 49 min. to reach the circuit high point (9420 ft.) in a flat area on the col between Steep Mountain to the east and Mount Wuh to the west. *Here Steep Mountain is, in fact, not so steep—the summit is only about 100 ft. higher than the trail. When viewed from the trail on the north side, however, the mountain lives up to its name.*

4) Descend for 30 min. over a sometimes rough trail to the junction with the Cub Lake Trail. Through the trees, there are great views of **Cub Lake** as you descend 800 ft. to a junction, nearly at the level of the lake.

5) Turn right (east) onto the Cub Lake Trail and walk 57 min. to the southwestern edge of Moraine Park. As the trail skirts Cub Lake, notice the Yellow Pondlilies and look for ducks. The route then follows the stream draining the lake, offering an excellent stretch for observing natural history.

5a) Although not listed as a side trip because it is accessible from other places, **Cub Lake Trailhead** is a worthwhile diversion, requiring only 27 min. roundtrip. On the way, you can see many wildflowers, birds, mammals and other aspects of nature.

---

6) From the trail junction at the southwest corner of Moraine Park, go right (east) and walk for 54 min. along the south side of **Moraine Park,** another great stretch for enjoying natural history. The trail first hugs the base of the **South Lateral Moraine;** avoid the fishing paths that wander along the creekside and dead-end. At the end of an unpaved road, the trail angles toward the moraine and heads gently uphill to a trail junction.

The south side of the South Lateral Moraine is one of several places in the general vicinity of Moraine Park where hikers share a portion of the circuit with equestrians. When meeting a wrangler, the hiker should step quietly off the trail and allow all the group's horses to pass.

7) At the junction, go right and walk for 1 hr., 18 min. back to the access trail at Hollowell Park along a dry trail through Ponderosa parkland on the South Lateral Moraine.

8) To complete the hike, turn left (east) on the access trail and walk for 12 min.

Ponderosa Pine, one of many tree species found on the Steep Mountain Circuit.

Counterclockwise walking time is the same overall, but individual segments differ from the clockwise circuit because the elevation gains are in different places. **(8)** From the picnic area, walk 14 min. to the circuit trail; **(7)** go right and walk east on the south side of the South Lateral Moraine for 54 min. to a trail junction; **(6)** go left and walk the north side of the moraine along Moraine Park for 1 hr.; **(5)** at the trail junction at the southwest corner of Moraine Park, go left (west) on the Cub Lake Trail for 1 hr., 30 min., following the stream to Cub Lake and then ascending more steeply to the trail junction; **(4)** go left at the trail junction and climb for 1 hr., 16 min. to the circuit high point on the col between Steep Mountain and Mount Wuh; **(3)** descend for 24 min. to Mill Creek Basin and take the first trail leading left (east) or, alternatively, continue into the meadow, cross the bridge, and go left; **(2)** walk 48 min. (the time is the same using either route—the two soon converge) to Hollowell Park; and **(1)** return to the picnic area by walking the access trail for 12 min.

OUR HIKING NOTES: Our notes reveal that we have hiked this circuit only in pieces, as out-and-back walks or as parts of other circuits, in July and August.

Habitats traversed: Ponderosa parkland on the southern side of the South Lateral Moraine, wet meadows along the northern side, stream bottomlands between Moraine Park and Cub Lake, montane coniferous forest, and drier meadows at Mill Creek Basin and Hollowell Park. **Wildflowers noted:** Mountain Iris, a lily, a fleabane, Blanketflower, Heartleaf Arnica (at stream crossings), Salsify, chiming-bells (at stream crossings), Miners-candle, a wallflower, Plains Pricklypear (in flower), Mountain Harebell, Twinflower (technically a shrub), Yellow Stonecrop, a loco, Golden Banner, White Clover, Fremont Geranium, Blue Flax, Yellow Pondlily (on Cub Lake), Sulphurflower, a larkspur, Globeflower, a rose, a blue penstemon, and Scarlet Paintbrush. **Other plants and fungi found:** There were ferns along the Cub Lake Trail and some monstrous brown mushrooms in Mill Creek Basin, probably the King Bolete. **Trees and shrubs:** Most of RMNP's tree species (except those restricted to the subalpine zone) can be seen on this circuit, among them Rocky Mountain Juniper, Ponderosa and Lodgepole Pine, Douglas-fir, Blue Spruce, Quaking Aspen, and Thinleaf Alder. Shrubs included Common Juniper and Shrubby Cinquefoil.

Insects: Butterflies feeding on the flowers in Moraine Park included Arnica Checkerspot and Western Tiger Swallowtail. We also saw small blue dragonflies or damselflies.

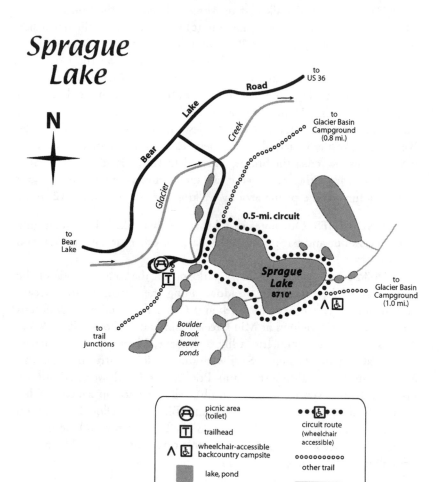

Sprague Lake

N

to
US 36

Lake **Road**

Bear

Creek

to
Glacier Basin
Campground
(0.8 mi.)

Glacier

0.5-mi. circuit

to
Bear
Lake

*Sprague
Lake*
8710'

to
Glacier Basin
Campground
(1.0 mi.)

to
trail
junctions

*Boulder
Brook
beaver
ponds*

🚻	picnic area (toilet)
T	trailhead
∧ ♿	wheelchair-accessible backcountry campsite
	lake, pond
→	watercourse (with direction of flow)

••♿•• circuit route (wheelchair accessible)

ooooooooooo other trail

━━━ paved road

©2002 Jack P. Hailman

90

SPRAGUE LAKE CIRCUIT

FORMULA TIME: 15 minutes (but take much longer to enjoy the scenery).

HIKING ELEVATIONS: 8710 feet (elevation of Sprague Lake).

EXERTION RATING: 0.7 (stroll).

FEATURES: Pleasant lakeside stroll, natural history. There is a nice board-walk across the marshy area on the southwestern side of the lake.

ACCESS POINT: Sprague Lake Picnic Area (off Bear Lake Road).

SEASONS: Good walking at all seasons, but do not venture onto the lake in winter, when winds create open areas that weaken the ice. There may be snowdrifts on the south side of the lake (which is in shadow in winter), however, making walking difficult. Also, the crust on the snow can give way, plunging the hiker up to the thighs in snow.

SUMMARY:

Route	Distance (mi.)	Total Elevation Gain (ft.)	Time (hr.:min.)	Exertion Rating
Circuit	0.5	flat	0:15	0.7

FINDING THE ACCESS POINT: From US 36, 0.3 mi. west of the Beaver Meadows Entrance Station, turn left onto Bear Lake Road. Drive 5.8 mi. and turn left (southeast) on the paved road into the Sprague Lake Picnic Grounds. (During 2003–2004, Bear Lake Road is scheduled to be rebuilt beyond the shuttle bus parking lot at mi. 5.1 and will not be open to private vehicles. The shuttle bus does not ordinarily stop at Sprague Lake, but perhaps during 2003–2004, it will make an extra stop here.) Sprague Lake lies to the east, accessible just where the entrance road swings right, into the parking loop. **Toilet facilities** are located in the middle of the loop. **No drinking water** is available. Remember to treat or filter any water you take from natural sources.

TRAIL DESCRIPTION: The trail may be walked in either direction. Walking time is the same because there is no elevation gain. The trail is paved, flat, and wide to accommodate wheelchairs. A trail-guide brochure may be purchased at park visitor centers. *The lake was named for Abner E. Sprague (1850–1943), one of the most prominent settlers of the Estes Park area. It was he who named Moraine Park; also Mills Lake for Enos Mills. Mills recipro-cated by naming this lake after Sprague.*

Beaver Dam alongside the trail at the outlet of Sprague Lake.

OUR HIKING NOTES: We have walked around this lake many times; our bird and mammal sightings come from mid-August.

Habitats traversed: Mixed woodlands surrounding the lake; some aquatic shallows on the west side; and open water.

Birds seen or heard: Mallards on the lake (often females with ducklings in summer), Spotted Sandpiper, Williamson's Sapsucker, Solitary Vireo, Gray Jay, Steller's Jay, American Crow, Violet-green Swallow, Mountain Chickadee, White-breasted Nuthatch, Brown Creeper, American Robin, Yellow-rumped Warbler, Dark-eyed Junco, and Redwing Blackbird. **Mammals encountered:** Snowshoe Hare, Golden-mantled Ground Squirrel, Red Squirrel, and American Beaver. Many years ago, one could see beaver at dusk on the lake and hear them slap their tails on the water's surface. The last time we dropped by (2002), there was a beaver dam across the stream feeding the lake, right along the boardwalk leading to the footpath. Most of the beaver work, though, begins upstream, near the picnic area.

Sprague Lake area of Glacial Basin seen from Bierstadt Moraine.

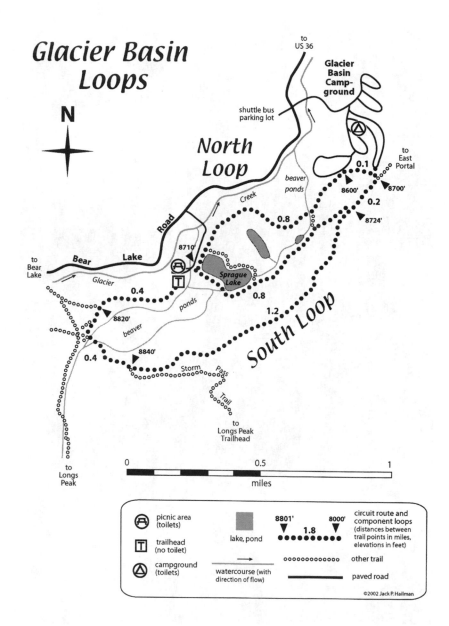

Glacier Basin Loops

N

to
US 36

Glacier Basin Camp-ground

shuttle bus
parking lot

North Loop

beaver ponds

Creek

Road

0.1

8600'

to East Portal

8700'

0.2

8724'

0.8

Bear   Lake

to
Bear
Lake

Glacier

8710'

0.4

ponds

beaver

Sprague Lake

0.8

1.2

South Loop

8820'

8840'

0.4

Storm   Pass

Trail

to
Longs Peak
Trailhead

to
Longs
Peak

0   0.5   1

miles

Symbol		
picnic area (toilets)	lake, pond	8801' ▼ 1.8 8000' ▼ ●●●●●●●●●●●	circuit route and component loops (distances between trail points in miles, elevations in feet)
trailhead (no toilet)		ooooooooooooo other trail
campground (toilets)	→ watercourse (with direction of flow)	──── paved road

©2002 Jack P. Hailman

GLACIER BASIN LOOPS

FORMULA TIMES: 1 hour, 47 minutes for the entire circuit; 1 hour, 4 minutes for the North Loop only; 1 hour, 32 minutes for the South Loop only.

HIKING ELEVATIONS: 8600 to 8840 feet.

EXERTION RATINGS: 5.1 (very easy) for the entire circuit; 3.1 (very easy) for the North Loop only; 4.4 (very easy) for the South Loop only.

FEATURES: Pleasant walking in the stream valley of Boulder Brook and Glacier Creek, where beavers have created several series of ponds. Sprague Lake is on the main circuit and on both loops.

ACCESS POINTS: Sprague Lake Trailhead in the Sprague Lake Picnic Area. The entire circuit or the North Loop alone can also be walked from Glacier Basin Campground, making them convenient hikes if you are camping there.

SEASONS: The hiking is good in summer and fall; snowshoeing and cross-country skiing dominate in winter. The Lodgepoles hold snow into spring, so hikers beware.

SUMMARY:

Route	Distance (mi.)	Total Elevation Gain (ft.)	Time (hr.:min.)	Exertion Rating
Entire circuit	3.1	240	1:47	5.1
North Loop only	1.9	124	1:04	3.1
South Loop only	2.8	130	1:32	4.4

FINDING THE ACCESS POINT: From US 36, 0.3 mi. west of the Beaver Meadows Entrance Station, turn left onto Bear Lake Road. Drive 5.8 mi. and turn left (southeast) on the paved road into the Sprague Lake Picnic Grounds. (During 2003–2004, Bear Lake Road is scheduled to be rebuilt above the shuttle bus parking lot at mile 5.1. Private vehicles will not be allowed beyond this point. The shuttle bus does not ordinarily stop at Sprague Lake, but perhaps during 2003–2004, it will make an extra stop here.) Sprague Lake lies to the east, accessible just where the entrance road swings right, into the parking loop. To begin southbound, go to the southeast corner of the picnic area, where you will see a trailhead sign. **Toilet facilities** are located in the middle of the loop. **No drinking water** is available. Remember to treat or filter any water you take from natural sources.

If the Sprague Lake access road is closed during the rebuilding of Bear Lake Road in 2003–2004, you can access the North Loop through the Glacier Basin Campground. Park in the shuttle bus parking lot at mile 5.1, cross Bear Lake Road on foot, and walk down the campground entrance road. Go right on the first campground road, and right again at the next opportunity. Access to the trail is midway down the left (east) fork of this southernmost campground loop. (Actually, there are several informal trails from the campground that lead to the Glacier Basin Loops; this is the formal one.)

TRAIL DESCRIPTION:

Entire circuit (clockwise from Sprague Lake): The circuit may be hiked in either direction from Sprague Lake; we describe it clockwise. *Glacier Basin was plowed by a montane glacier that moved down from the southwest, throwing up the Bierstadt lateral moraine across Bear Lake Road and creating the flat-bottomed basin through which Boulder Brook and Glacier Creek run.*

1) At the trailhead by Sprague Lake, take the left fork and walk 24 min. to Glacier Basin Campground. The trail first follows the paved foot highway around the lake but soon exits left, and after about 15 min. crosses a part of the Boulder Brook delta, a stream much impounded by beavers. *Beavers are mainly crepuscular (active at dawn and dusk), so your chances of seeing one on a day hike are slim; you will probably spot their dams and lodges.*

2) A short (9 min.) trail leads from one campground loop past another to meet the main trail south. It is not necessary to enter the campground, but note that **water** and **toilets** are available there.

3) From the main trail, walk 7 min. to meet a trail leaving right (southwest) for Sprague Lake.

4) Ignore this trail and continue south, walking 43 min. through Lodgepole Pine forest to the junction with the Storm Pass Trail, which leaves left (southeast) for the Longs Peak area.

5) At the junction, continue straight and walk about 12 min., crossing two branches of Boulder Brook, then passing two trail junctions that leave left, arriving at a third, which also leaves left.

6) From this third trail junction, continue on the main trail and walk about 12 min. back to the Sprague Lake Picnic Grounds.

Counterclockwise walking time is the same overall and almost the same for each segment because the way is so flat. **(6)** From the trailhead, walk southwest for 19 min. to the trail junction; **(5)** continue 13 min. and go left at the junction where the main trail continues to Storm Pass; **(4)** walk 36 min. to the junction where a trail leaves left to Sprague Lake; **(3)** continue straight for 6 min. to the next junction, where you turn left off the main trail and head toward the campground; **(2)** walk 3 min., passing one campground loop and reaching the second one; and **(1)** continue 31 min. back to Sprague Lake.

No formal side trips are listed, but you may walk the half-mile loop around Sprague Lake at the beginning or end of the circuit (see the Sprague Lake account).

North Loop (clockwise): This loop begins the same way the entire circuit does. Follow steps **(1)** through **(3)** in the main account. **(3a)** Follow the trail to Sprague Lake for about 24 min. back to the trailhead. Soon after leaving the main trail in **(3)**, pass a trail going right along the brook; at Sprague Lake meet the trail around the lake. The distances around the lake are the same in both directions.

Counterclockwise starts with **(3a)** for 25 min., then **(3)** through **(1)** in the counterclockwise directions for the entire circuit.

South Loop (clockwise): This loop ends the same way the entire circuit does. **(1a)** At the Sprague Lake Trailhead, take either the left (clockwise) or right (counterclockwise) loop halfway around Sprague Lake to find the connecting trail leaving on the east side and continue on it for the second half of this segment. Walking time from the start to the circuit trail is about 25 min. Then follow steps **(4)** through **(6)** in the main account to complete the loop.

Counterclockwise begins with legs **(6)** through **(4)** of the counterclockwise directions for the main account, then follows **(1a)** 24 min. back to the Sprague Lake access point.

OUR HIKING NOTES: The formula time for the entire circuit is 1 hr., 47 min.; we walked the circuit from Glacier Basin Campground with small children in 1 hr., 50 min. during early August, and took regrettably few notes.

Habitats traversed: Riparian areas and beaver ponds along Boulder Brook, open water of Sprague Lake, mixed forest in the basin, and primarily Lodgepole Pine forest along the main trail on the southeast side of the circuit.

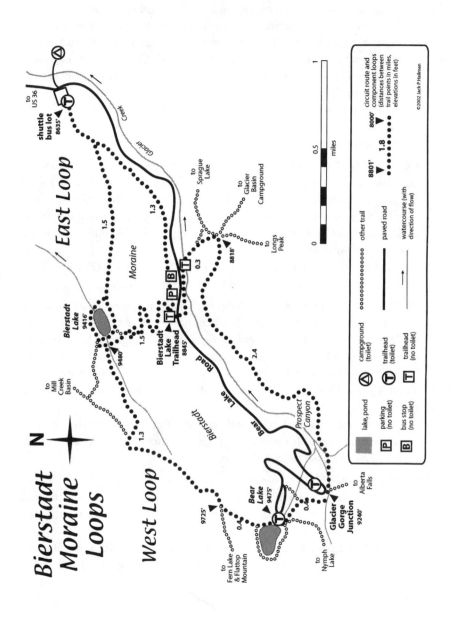

Bierstadt Moraine Loops

N

East Loop

West Loop

shuttle bus lot
8635'

to US 36

Glacier Creek

1.5

Moraine

1.3

to Sprague Lake

to Glacier Basin Campground

0.3

8818'

to Longs Peak

Bierstadt Lake
9416'

9460'

to Mill Creek Basin

1.5

Bierstadt Lake Trailhead
8845'

Bear Lake Road

Bierstadt

2.4

Prospect Canyon

Bear Lake
9475'

9725'

0.4

Glacier Gorge Junction
9240'

0.4

to Alberta Falls

to Nymph Lake

to Fern Lake & Flattop Mountain

Legend

- lake, pond
- P parking (no toilet)
- B bus stop (no toilet)
- ▲ campground (toilet)
- T trailhead (toilet)
- T trailhead (no toilet)

- ooooooooo other trail
- ▬▬▬ paved road
- — watercourse (with direction of flow)

0   0.5   1
miles

8801' ▶ •••••• 1.8 ▶ 8000' ▶
circuit route and component loops (distances between trail points in miles, elevations in feet)

©2002 Jack P.Hailman

BIERSTADT MORAINE LOOPS

FORMULA TIMES: 4 hours, 55 minutes for the entire circuit; 4 hours, 3 minutes for the West Loop only; 3 hours for the East Loop only.

HIKING ELEVATIONS: 8635 to 9725 feet.

EXERTION RATINGS: 14.4 (moderately easy) for the entire circuit; 12.0 (moderately easy) for the West Loop only; 8.7 (easy) for the East Loop only.

FEATURES: Bierstadt Moraine; Prospect Canyon on Glacier Creek; Bear and Bierstadt Lakes.

ACCESS POINTS: Bierstadt Lake Trailhead (on Bear Lake Road). The West Loop or entire circuit can also be hiked from Glacier Gorge Junction and Bear Lake Trailheads; the East Loop or entire circuit can also be walked from the shuttle bus parking lot on Bear Lake Road.

SEASONS: In summer, the open south face of Bierstadt Moraine can make for a hot climb from the trailhead, but most of the trail is well shaded. The West Loop is particularly good in fall when the aspens turn color. In winter, when there is adequate snow, the trail between Bear Lake and Bierstadt Lake is good on cross-country skis or snowshoes.

SUMMARY:

Route	Distance (mi.)	Total Elevation Gain (ft.)	Time (hr.:min.)	Exertion Rating
Entire circuit	7.6	1117	4:55	14.4
West Loop only	6.3	907	4:03	12.0
East Loop only	4.3	845	3:00	8.7

FINDING THE ACCESS POINT: All the possible access points are on Bear Lake Road. From US 36, 0.3 mi. west of the Beaver Meadows Entrance Station, turn left onto Bear Lake Road. Drive 6.8 mi. to the Bierstadt Lake Trailhead, where there is a small parking lot. The East Loop and the entire circuit can be walked counterclockwise by going back to the bus stop and following the trail that parallels Bear Lake Road. The West Loop and the entire circuit can be hiked clockwise by walking 0.1 mi. back along Bear Lake Road toward US 36 and crossing the road to find the Storm Pass Trailhead. There are **no toilets** and **no drinking water** at either of these trailheads. To walk the East Loop clockwise or the West Loop counterclockwise, ascend Bierstadt Moraine from the Bierstadt Lake Trailhead.

To access the West Loop from Glacier Gorge Junction, continue another 2.0 mi. up Bear Lake Road, and to access from Bear Lake, continue another 0.8 mi. past Glacier Gorge Junction. There are **outhouses** at both trailheads, those at Bear Lake temporarily replacing the rest building that was destroyed by arsonists in the winter of 2001–2002. **Drinking water** is **ordinarily not available** at either trailhead, but during the summer tourist season, RMNP employees truck water up to Bear Lake. Remember to treat or filter all water you take from natural sources.

During 2003–2004, Bear Lake Road will be rebuilt above the shuttle bus parking lot at mile 5.1. Private vehicles will not be allowed beyond this point, but the Bear Lake shuttle bus will continue to run at frequent intervals during extended hours. The Bierstadt Lake bus stop is at mile 6.6, so if you get off there, you will need to walk 0.2 mi. farther to reach Bierstadt Lake Trailhead. There is a trail of sorts paralleling the road, or you can walk the side of the road. The shuttle bus continues on, stopping at both Glacier Gorge Junction and Bear Lake.

TRAIL DESCRIPTION:

Entire Circuit (clockwise from Bierstadt Lake Trailhead): The circuit and both of its component loops can be walked in either direction. Nevertheless, you may wish to avoid the uphill climb from Bierstadt Lake Trailhead to the top of the moraine in summer because the long climb on switchbacks through open scattered aspens can be hot and dusty. (Actually, we've done it at least twice in August; it's really not bad if you get an early start.) The entire circuit avoids this segment (either direction), and the West Loop clockwise comes *down* it (not so bad), as does the East Loop counterclockwise. We arbitrarily describe the trail clockwise from the Bierstadt Lake Trailhead.

Albert Bierstadt (1830–1902) was a German-born American landscape painter whose romanticized works are credited as importantly aiding the establishment of some of our national parks. Perhaps his most famous painting is Domes of the Yosemite *(1864), but he also painted Longs Peak as seen from Moraine Park. Critics generally do not consider his works art, but decide for yourself. The Longs Peak painting hangs in Denver, but you can see a reproduction of it on a signboard in the parking lot of the Moraine Park Museum. We think it looks more like the Swiss Alps.*

1) From Bierstadt Lake Trailhead, walk east on the trail paralleling the road to a small parking lot and cross Bear Lake Road to descend into the Glacier Creek Valley. Cross the creek, pass a trail leaving left for Sprague

Lake, and arrive at a second trail junction (with a trail leaving for the Longs Peak area). Total walking time for this short segment is about 9 min.

2) Walk west and then southwest for about 1 hr., 37 min., no doubt wishing all along that Glacier Creek and Prospect Canyon were closer to the trail. Emerge just below Glacier Gorge Junction after crossing a tributary of Glacier Creek. **(2a)** Although not listed here as a side trip for this circuit, a trail leaving Glacier Gorge Junction goes 46 min. out and back to **Alberta Falls;** see the Alpine Lakes account.

3) From Glacier Gorge Junction, walk uphill for about 26 min. to **Bear Lake. (3a)** Although not listed here as a side trip for this circuit, a trail heads left to **Nymph Lake** (about 28 min. out and back) and beyond; see the Alpine Lakes account. **(3b)** It is also possible to loop around Bear Lake before continuing the ascent; see the Bear Lake account.

4) From Bear Lake, continue uphill for about 27 min. to the junction where a trail leaves west (left) for **Fern Lake** and Flattop Mountain. This is the high point of the circuit (9725 ft.).

5) From the trail junction, continue straight and walk about 39 min., passing a trail leaving left for Mill Creek Basin, to the trail junction near Bierstadt Lake. The trail going south (right) descends to the Bierstadt Lake Trailhead, completing the West Loop.

6) Keep left at the junction and pass another trail leaving west (left) for Mill Creek Basin. There is yet another trail (leaving right) to the shore of **Bierstadt Lake,** a spot popular with hikers from Bierstadt Lake Trailhead. Most of the ducks on the lake are cheeky Mallards, which beseech hikers for scraps; do not feed them, or any other animals in the park. The trail continues around the north side of the lake and then descends a long and admittedly less than exciting trek down the moraine's north side to the shuttle bus parking area. Allow 45 min.

7) From the shuttle bus parking area, walk west for about 52 min. on the unimproved trail paralleling Bear Lake Road to regain Bierstadt Lake Trailhead.

Counterclockwise walking time is the same overall, but individual segments differ from the clockwise circuit because the elevation gains are in different places: **(7)** from Bierstadt Lake Trailhead, walk east then northeast 39 min. to the shuttle bus parking lot; **(6)** continue 1 hr., 36 min., skirting Bierstadt Lake to the south and reaching a trail junction just beyond the end of the lake; **(5)** go straight, walking 54 min. to the junction with the trail to Fern Lake and Flattop Mountain; **(4)** at the junction, bear left and walk 12 min. to Bear Lake; **(3)** descend 12 min. to Glacier

This cheerful hiker allowed Jack to take the photo of him carrying his daughter on switchbacks of the south face of Bierstadt Moraine.

Gorge Junction, taking the trail leaving left for Glacier Basin; **(2)** continue 1 hr., 12 min. to the junction with the trail leaving for the Longs Peak area; and **(1)** bear left, walking 11 min. back to Bierstadt Lake Trailhead.

West Loop (clockwise): This loop, which we recommend doing clockwise, begins with steps **(1)** through **(5)** in main account for the complete circuit. Then **(5a)** descend the south face of Bierstadt Moraine on switchbacks for about 45 min., enjoying great views of the valley below and the mountains, including Longs Peak, to the south.

Counterclockwise, the route ascends for about 1 hr., 23 min., arriving at a trail junction near the western end of Bierstadt Lake. From here, follow steps **(5)** through **(1)** in the counterclockwise summary of the main account, entire circuit. Total time (either direction): 4:03.

East Loop (clockwise): The route ascends for about 1 hr., 23 min. to a trail junction near the western end of Bierstadt Lake. From here, follow steps **(6)** and **(7)** in the main account.

Counterclockwise (the best routing to avoid a hot ascent of the moraine slope), follow steps **(7)** and **(6)** in the counterclockwise summary of the main account. Then descend the south face of Bierstadt Moraine for about 45 min., enjoying great views of the valley below and the mountains, including Longs Peak, off to the south. Total time (either direction) is 3 hr.

OUR HIKING NOTES: Although our notes are sparse, we have walked various segments of these loops on many occasions, with markedly varied times. For example, many years ago in mid-August, we took 62 min. to ascend the moraine on switchbacks, but in early August 2002, we did it unrushed in 45 min. (The formula time is 1 hr., 23 min., which is clearly more than one really needs.)

Habitats traversed: Quite varied, from open aspen groves on the south flank of Bierstadt Moraine, through stream valley on Glacier Creek, and various coniferous forests. The East Loop, however, runs mainly through Lodgepole Pine forest. **Wildflowers and shrubs noted:** Common Juniper, Nodding Onion, Squawbush, a ragwort, a white daisy *(Erigeron)*, Aspen Daisy, Pearly-everlasting, some pussytoes, and Common Fireweed.

Birds seen or heard: Mallard (Bear and Bierstadt Lakes), Ring-necked Duck (Bierstadt Lake), Gray Jay, Steller's Jay, Clark's Nutcracker, Violet-green Swallow, Mountain Chickadee, Red-breasted Nuthatch, Hermit Thrush, and Dark-eyed Junco. **Mammals encountered:** Least Chipmunk, Golden-mantled Ground Squirrel, and Red Squirrel.

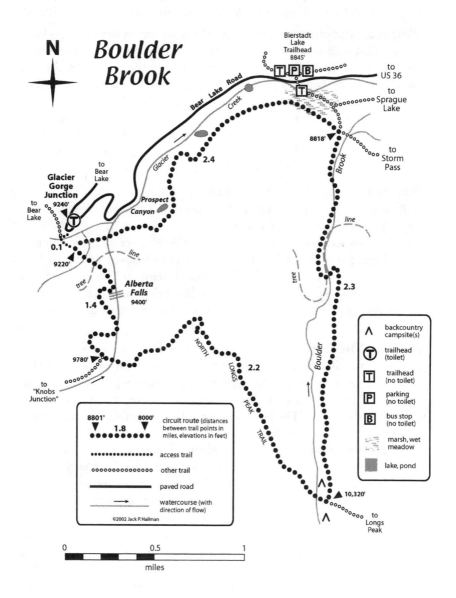

N

Boulder Brook

Bierstadt Lake Trailhead 8845'

T P B · · · · · · · · · · · to US 36

Bear Lake Road

T

to Sprague Lake

Creek

2.4

8818'

to Storm Pass

Glacier

to Bear Lake

Glacier Gorge Junction

to Bear Lake

9240'

T

Prospect Canyon

Brook

line

0.1

9220'

line

tree

tree

2.3

Alberta Falls 9400'

1.4

Boulder

9780'

to "Knobs Junction"

NORTH

2.2

LONGS

8801'   8000'
▼   1.8   ▼
• • • • • • • • •   circuit route (distances between trail points in miles, elevations in feet)

• • • • • • • • • • • • • •   access trail

○○○○○○○○○○○○○○○○○   other trail

━━━━━━━━━   paved road

→   watercourse (with direction of flow)

©2002 Jack P. Hailman

PEAK

TRAIL

∧   backcountry campsite(s)

Ⓣ   trailhead (toilet)

T   trailhead (no toilet)

P   parking (no toilet)

B   bus stop (no toilet)

marsh, wet meadow

lake, pond

∧   10,320'

∧   to Longs Peak

0   0.5   1

miles

BOULDER BROOK CIRCUIT

FORMULA TIME: 5 hours, 46 minutes (including roundtrip on the short access trail).

HIKING ELEVATIONS: 8818 to 10,320 feet.

EXERTION RATING: 17.2 (moderate).

FEATURES: Lovely canyon, long stretch above tree line at relatively low elevation, mountain vistas, Alberta Falls.

ACCESS POINTS: Glacier Gorge Junction Trailhead. (If the parking lot there is full, the circuit can be walked from Bear Lake via a short access trail.)

SEASONS: Summer and fall; in winter there is too much snow and ice on the steep portions of the trail.

SUMMARY:

Route	Distance (mi.)	Total Elevation Gain (ft.)	Time (hr.:min.)	Exertion Rating
Circuit, including access trail	8.5	1522	5:46	17.2

FINDING THE ACCESS POINT: From US 36, 0.3 mi. west of the Beaver Meadows Entrance Station, turn left onto Bear Lake Road. Drive 8.8 mi. to Glacier Gorge Junction, where there is a small parking lot. The lot usually fills before 8 A.M. The Glacier Gorge Junction Trailhead is across Bear Lake Road from the middle of the curve. **Outhouses** are located at the upper edge of the lot, There is **no drinking water.** Remember to treat or filter any water you take from natural sources.

If the Glacier Gorge Junction lot is full, drive an additional 0.8 mi. to the Bear Lake parking lot, which normally fills by about 8:30 A.M. in summer. Nevertheless, many people stay just long enough to see Bear Lake, so it is usually worthwhile to wait for a parking place to become available. The Bear Lake Trailhead is at the upper end of the parking lot. From here, you must walk 0.2 mi. down to the Glacier Gorge Junction Trailhead to access the circuit. **Drinking water** is **not ordinarily available,** but in the summer tourist season, park employees truck water up to Bear Lake. **Outhouses** at Bear Lake temporarily replace the rest building that was destroyed by arsonists in the winter of 2001–2002.

During 2003–2004, Bear Lake Road will be rebuilt above the shuttle bus parking lot at mile 5.1. Private vehicles will not be allowed beyond this point, but the Bear Lake Shuttle Bus will continue to run at frequent intervals during extended hours. The shuttle bus stops at both Glacier

Gorge Junction and Bear Lake. At the former, the bus stop is below the parking lot; at the latter, it is near the top of the large parking lot.

It is also possible, via a slightly longer access trail, to walk this circuit from the Storm Pass Trailhead, located across Bear Lake Road from the Bierstadt Lake Trailhead.

TRAIL DESCRIPTION (clockwise from Glacier Gorge Junction): This circuit can be hiked in either direction; clockwise has the advantage of ending with a 3.6-mi. downhill stretch instead of a 2.4-mi. uphill hike. *On this trail, tree line is below 10,000 ft., whereas on the other side of the Longs Peak–Mount Meeker massif, tree line is generally above 11,000 ft. Why the difference? At least two factors are involved. First, here in the Boulder Brook area, the slope is north-facing and subject to more severe winters; second, some of this area has never fully recovered from the forest fire of 1900. Although triggered by lightning, the fire raged far longer and covered far more territory than is usual for natural fires. Some evidence suggests that the fires were purposely kept going by resort employees in order to stimulate tourism. (For the official definition of tree line, see leg (3) in the following trail description.)*

1) From Glacier Gorge Junction, cross the road at the bend, head downhill to an intersection with the trail to Bear Lake, turn left on that trail, and walk to the first trail junction (3 min. total).

2) Go left at the trail junction and walk for 1 hr., 12 min., crossing Glacier Creek early on and ultimately arriving at a trail junction, the low point of the circuit.

3) Go right at the junction (left would take you to the Bierstadt Lake Trailhead; straight would take you to Storm Pass) and begin the 2 hr., 39 min. climb along Boulder Brook. At first, the brook is on your left, then you cross it on a log bridge. Not long thereafter, you cross it again. About halfway along this leg of the hike, cross the brook for a third time and break out above tree line before reaching the circuit high point. The route does not cross tundra or open rock; rather, on this trail, the area above tree line is characterized by stunted trees, shrubs, and small open areas. *So exactly what is "tree line" on USGS topographic maps (and maps derived from them)? The green overlay on these maps represents forest sufficiently tall and dense to hide an army division (no kidding: we inquired of USGS and that's the answer we received).*

4) From the junction at the top of the trail, go right on North Longs Peak Trail and walk for 1 hr., 6 min. to a trail junction. At the beginning of this leg, you will cross Boulder Brook; near the end, you will cross Glacier Creek. At the Glacier Creek crossing, take a few moments to

The Boulder Brook Circuit at one place passes along the base of a dramatic rock face.

walk downslope over the bare rocks and appreciate the full view; this is a great place to take photos.

5) From the trail junction, walk 42 min. downhill, passing popular **Alberta Falls** and re-entering the forest, crossing a couple of streams before reaching the trail junction that completes the circuit per se. *Abner Sprague, one of the area's most prominent early settlers, named the falls for his wife, Mary Alberta Sprague.*

6) Upon completing the circuit, go straight at the trail junction and turn right on the feeder trail to Glacier Gorge Junction Trailhead (4 min. total).

Counterclockwise walking time is the same overall, but individual segments differ from the clockwise circuit because the elevation gains are in different places. From Glacier Gorge Junction counterclockwise: **(6)** walk 3 min. on the access trail; **(5)** turn right and walk 1 hr., 16 min. uphill past Alberta Falls; **(4)** continue 1 hr., 38 min. uphill on North Longs Peak Trail to the circuit high point; **(3)** bear left at the junction with the trail to Longs Peak and descend 1 hr., 9 min. along Boulder Brook; **(2)** turn left at the trail junction where right would take you to Storm Pass, continuing 1 hr., 36 min. through Prospect Canyon to complete the circuit per se; and **(1)** turn right on the access trail back to Glacier Gorge Junction, walking an additional 4 min. to complete the hike.

OUR HIKING NOTES:

Habitats traversed: Coniferous and mixed forests on the slopes, some aspen groves, Lodgepole forest on the lowland section paralleling Glacier Creek, riparian brook edges, dwarf forest above tree line, and some open rock areas. Virtually all major tree species in RMNP are represented on this trail, excepting willows and alders. The hike provides good opportunities to see Subalpine Firs, with their purple upright cones. **Wildflowers noted:** Nodding Onion, a golden aster, a ragwort, Aspen Daisy, some pussytoes in flower, Yarrow, chiming-bells (stream crossings), Mountain Harebell, a gentian, Monument-plant, Common Fireweed, a cinquefoil or buttercup, and Scarlet Paintbrush. **Other plants found:** Common Juniper and Shrubby Cinquefoil (shrubs), and Twisted Stalk in berry.

Birds seen or heard: Hairy Woodpecker, Northern Flicker, Gray Jay, Steller's Jay, Clark's Nutcracker, Common Raven, Mountain Chickadee, Red-breasted Nuthatch, Ruby-crowned Kinglet, American Robin, Yellow-rumped Warbler, Chipping Sparrow, and Dark-eyed Junco. **Mammals encountered:** Snowshoe Hare (a.k.a. Snowshoe Rabbit, Varying Hare), Least Chipmunk, Golden-mantled Ground Squirrel, Red Squirrel, and Coyote.

Bridge over Glacier Creek on the Boulder Brook Circuit.

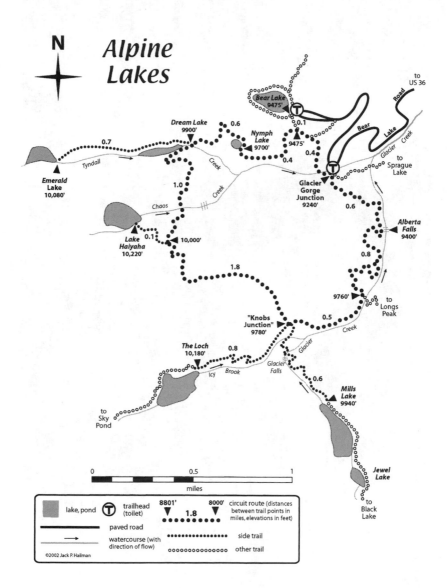

Alpine Lakes

N

Bear Lake
9475'

to
US 36

Dream Lake
9900'   0.6

Nymph
Lake
9700'

9475'

0.1

Bear   Lake

Glacier   Creek

0.7   0.4

0.4

to
Sprague
Lake

Tyndall   Creek

Emerald
Lake
10,080'

1.0   Creek

Glacier
Gorge
Junction
9240'   0.6

Alberta
Falls
9400'

Chaos

0.8

0.1   10,000'

Lake
Haiyaha
10,220'

1.8   9760'

to
Longs
Peak

"Knobs
Junction"
9780'   0.5

Glacier   Creek

The Loch
10,180'   0.8

Icy   Brook

Glacier
Falls

0.6

Mills
Lake
9940'

to
Sky
Pond

Jewel
Lake

to
Black
Lake

Legend

lake, pond	trailhead (toilet)	8801' ▼ 1.8 ▼ 8000'	circuit route (distances between trail points in miles, elevations in feet)	
	paved road			
→	watercourse (with direction of flow)	••••••••••••••	side trail	
©2002 Jack P. Hailman		oooooooooooooo	other trail	

0   0.5   1

miles

110

ALPINE LAKES CIRCUIT

FORMULA TIMES: 3 hours, 49 minutes for the circuit; 6 hours, 58 minutes with all four side trips. **Note:** side trips can be extended beyond Lake Haiyaha, The Loch, and Mills Lake to make even longer hikes.

HIKING ELEVATIONS: 9240 to 10,000 feet (to 10,080 feet on the side trip to Emerald Lake; to 10,180 feet on the side trip to The Loch; to 10,220 feet on the side trip to Lake Haiyaha).

EXERTION RATINGS: 11.4 (moderately easy) to 21.0 (moderately strenuous) with all four side trips.

FEATURES: Alpine scenery, wildflowers, and animals; lakes (Nymph, Dream); Alberta Falls; optional side trips to four more alpine lakes (Emerald, Haiyaha, The Loch, Mills). This is arguably the best circuit day hike in all of Rocky Mountain National Park; expect to encounter other hikers everywhere.

ACCESS POINTS: Glacier Gorge Junction Trailhead or Bear Lake Trailhead (on Bear Lake Road).

SEASONS: This is a wonderful circuit in summer and fall. It also offers good cross-country skiing and snowshoeing in winter, with some caveats. Heavy snows tend to accumulate on several stretches of the hiking trails, so winter routes offer unsigned alternatives, mainly following drainages. Skiers and snowshoers should check with rangers. Spring hikers also need to beware of lingering heavy snowbanks.

SUMMARY:

Route	Distance (mi.)	Total Elevation Gain (ft.)	Time (hr.:min.)	Exertion Rating
Circuit	6.1	760	3:49	11.4
Roundtrip to Emerald Lake	1.4	180	0:53	2.7
Roundtrip to Lake Haiyaha	0.2	220	0:19	1.0
Roundtrip to The Loch	1.6	400	1:12	3.7
Roundtrip to Mills Lake	1.2	160	0:46	2.3
Totals	10.5	1720	6:58	21.0

FINDING THE ACCESS POINTS: From US 36, 0.3 mi. west of the Beaver Meadows Entrance Station, turn left onto Bear Lake Road. Drive 8.8 mi. to Glacier Gorge Junction, where there is a small parking lot. The lot usually fills before 8 A.M. The Glacier Gorge Junction Trailhead is across Bear Lake Road from the middle of the curve. **Outhouses** are located at the upper edge of the lot. There is **no drinking water**. Remember to treat or filter any water you take from natural sources.

If the Glacier Gorge Junction lot is full, drive an additional 0.8 mi. uphill to the Bear Lake parking lot, which normally fills by about 8:30 A.M. in summer. Nevertheless, many people stay just long enough to see Bear Lake, so it is usually worthwhile to wait for a parking place to become available. The Bear Lake Trailhead is at the upper end of the parking lot. **Drinking water** is **not ordinarily available,** but during the summer tourist season, park employees truck water up to Bear Lake. **Outhouses** at Bear Lake temporarily replace the rest building that was destroyed by arsonists in the winter of 2001–2002.

During 2003–2004, Bear Lake Road will be rebuilt above the shuttle bus parking lot at mile 5.1. Private vehicles will not be allowed beyond this point, but the Bear Lake Shuttle Bus will continue to run at frequent intervals during extended hours. The shuttle bus stops at both Glacier Gorge Junction and Bear Lake. At the former, the bus stop is below the parking lot; at the latter, it is near the top of the large parking lot.

TRAIL DESCRIPTION (counterclockwise from Glacier Gorge Junction): We have hiked the circuit in both directions and marginally prefer the counterclockwise circuit, which spreads out the elevation gain more evenly. Furthermore, if you do the route counterclockwise from Glacier Gorge Junction, you avoid walking uphill on the last leg.

1) From Glacier Gorge Junction, walk uphill about 26 min. to the trail junction near Bear Lake. The lake is less than 0.1 mi. to the right. At this highly popular place, Least Chipmunks, Golden-mantled Ground Squirrels, Gray Jays, Steller's Jays, and Clark's Nutcrackers may all seek handouts; do not feed the animals.

2) From the trail junction, walk uphill about 26 min. on an easy, manicured, largely paved trail to **Nymph Lake,** which is covered in pondlilies in summer. Here you will find benches to sit on. *The lake was apparently named for the Yellow Pondlily (family Nymphaeacae) that adorns it. In fact, the scientific name for the genus of this species was formerly* Nymphaea, *although this genus has been combined with* Nuphar, *which name has priority because it is older.*

3) The trail circles the east and north sides of Nymph Lake and continues uphill for about 30 min. to a junction near Tyndall Creek.

3a) You can take the right fork (you'll actually be heading straight) a short distance to reach the shore of linear **Dream Lake** on your way to Emerald Lake. Dream Lake sits in Tyndall Gorge between the ridges of Flattop Mountain and Hallett Peak. *Dream Lake's origin is different from those of most other lakes in the* *region. When a glacier melts back, it leaves behind the huge load of rock and earth formerly embedded in the ice. Occasionally, a large chunk of ice does not melt as quickly as the main mass so is left behind, buried under the glacial till. When the ice chunk finally melts, the overlying till slumps to form a depression known as a kettle hole. If a kettle hole subsequently fills with water, it is appropriately called a kettle-hole lake. Dream Lake is one example, although its long, skinny basin is unusual; kettle-hole lakes are typically much rounder.*

Emerald Lake, 0.7 mi. farther up the trail from Dream Lake, is indeed a gem. The trail is narrow and rugged, and it has some annoyingly steep spots, but we think it a worthy side trip, even though it takes almost an hour out and back. The lake is a favorite of many hikers because of its stunning beauty and isolated setting. *Unlike Dream Lake, Emerald Lake is a tarn: a water-filled depression in solid rock scoured out by a glacier. Emerald Lake was supposedly named for its color; you decide whether it does indeed look green.*

4) From the trail junction at Tyndall Creek near Dream Lake, cross Tyndall Creek on a bridge, ascend, enjoying good views of the lake through the trees, and walk about 36 min. to a junction with the trail leaving right for Lake Haiyaha. The forest is often open along this stretch, providing good views of lower elevations.

4a) Lake Haiyaha is a short side trip (19 min. out and back). The lake is a scenic place for a lunch stop. Haiyaha *is supposedly a Native American word for rock or boulder, but no source we consulted could identify the source language.* Anyway, the lake is lined with massive boulders.

5) From the trail junction, walk nearly an hour (about 54 min.)—the longest leg of the circuit—downhill over an unmaintained but perfectly adequate trail to "Knobs Junction," as we have come to call it because it sits between two hills of rocks known as the **Glacier Knobs**. On the way, cross several streams and rocky open areas. From "Knobs Junction," two worthwhile side trips are possible.

5a) The rightmost trail leaving southwest ascends on two long switchbacks, following above Icy Brook to **The Loch.** Allow 1 hr., 12 min. out and back. *This body of water was originally named for a Mr. Locke, but the name was later changed to the Scottish word for lake.* If you are a glutton for punishment, or are captivated by Loch Vale, you can continue up the valley of Icy Brook to Timberline Falls (1.3 mi.), Lake of Glass (1.5 mi.), and Sky Pond (1.9 mi. from The Loch). About halfway to Sky Pond, a trail leaves right for Andrews Tarn, the lake below Andrews Glacier. This is the homeward route of the Tundra & Glaciers Circuit.

5b) The middle trail leads south to **Mills Lake.** On the way, walk through forest (including some Quaking Aspens), passing near a small waterfall, where you will be required to cross open rock surfaces (follow the cairns). Allow 46 min. out and back. *Early settler Abner Sprague named this lake for Enos Abijah Mills (1870–1922), a self-taught naturalist who more than any other person was responsible for the creation of Rocky Mountain National Park. Watch in the stream below Mills Lake for an American Dipper foraging underwater.* The trail through Glacier Gorge continues all the way to Black Lake (2.0 mi. beyond the bottom of Mills Lake), passing Jewel Lake just above Mills Lake, and Ribbon Falls just before Black Lake.

6) From "Knobs Junction," head east and walk about 15 min. to the junction with the trail leaving right for the Longs Peak area.

7) Go straight at the junction and continue downhill for about 24 min. to **Alberta Falls** on Glacier Creek. Expect to see plenty of people, as this is an easy hike from Glacier Gorge Junction and the most accessible waterfall in RMNP after Chasm Falls on the Old Fall River Road. *Abner Sprague, one of the area's most prominent early settlers, named the falls for his wife, Mary Alberta Sprague.*

8) To complete the circuit, walk another 18 min. or so downhill to Glacier Gorge Junction.

Clockwise walking time is the same overall, but individual segments differ from the counterclockwise circuit because the elevation gains are in different places. From Glacier Gorge Junction clockwise: **(8)** ascend 28 min. to Alberta Falls; **(7)** continue 46 min. to the trail junction where a trail leaves left for Longs Peak; **(6)** walk 16 min. to "Knobs Junction"; **(5)** bear right and continue 1 hr., 7 min. to the trail junction where a trail leaves left to Lake Haiyaha; **(4)** walk 30 min. to Dream Lake; **(3)** descend 18 min. to Nymph Lake; **(2)** continue downhill 12 min. to Bear Lake; and **(1)** walk 12 min. to Glacier Gorge Junction. **Side-trip times,** based on roundtrips, are the same as in the main description.

OUR HIKING NOTES: The formula walking time for this hike, including three side trips (Emerald Lake omitted), is 6 hr., 5 min. On the one outing that we timed, we hiked it in 6 hr., 30 min., including a 20-min. lunch stop, making the walking time 6 hr., 10 min.—so close to the formula time that we don't expect anyone to believe it! Our best bird and mammal notes come from a trip in mid-June. Our notes from hikes in early and mid-August were sparse because we were showing the area to friends. The plants were all noted down in August. Animals were encountered in both June and August unless otherwise noted.

Clark's Nutcracker is likely to be encountered on the Alpine Lakes Circuit and other high altitude hikes.

Habitats traversed: Montane coniferous forest and some open rocky areas, with creeks and lakeshores. **Wildflowers and fungi noted:** Heartleaf Arnica, Pearly-everlasting, Yarrow, Tall Chiming-bells (by stream), Yellow Pondlily, Scarlet Paintbrush, and the lovely but poisonous mushroom Fly Amanita. **Trees and shrubs:** Limber Pine, Lodgepole Pine, Engelmann Spruce, Blue Spruce, Douglas-fir, and Subalpine Fir, with low-spreading Common Juniper (a shrub). There are scattered groves of Quaking Aspen.

Birds seen or heard: Broad-tailed Hummingbird, Gray Jay, Steller's Jay (August only), Clark's Nutcracker, Black-billed Magpie (June only), American Crow (June only), Common Raven, Violet-green Swallow (June only), Rough-winged Swallow (June only), Barn Swallow (June only), Mountain Chickadee, Red-breasted Nuthatch, Brown Creeper (August only), Ruby-crowned Kinglet, American Dipper, Mountain Bluebird (June only), Hermit Thrush (June only), American Robin, a pipit (June only), Yellow-rumped Warbler, Wilson's Warbler, White-crowned Sparrow (August only), Dark-eyed Junco, and Red Crossbill. **Mammals encountered:** Least Chipmunk, Yellow-bellied Marmot, Golden-mantled Ground Squirrel, Red Squirrel, Mule Deer, and Bighorn Sheep. **Amphibians:** Northern Chorus Frog (singing near Alberta Falls).

Bear Lake

to Bierstadt Lake

N

0.6-mi. circuit

Bear Lake 9475'

parking lot

Lake Road

Bear

to Nymph Lake

to Glacier Gorge Junction

to US 36

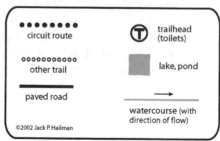

•••••••••
circuit route

ooooooooooo
other trail

———
paved road

Ⓣ trailhead (toilets)

lake, pond

→
watercourse (with direction of flow)

©2002 Jack P. Hailman

BEAR LAKE CIRCUIT

FORMULA TIME: 18 minutes (but take much longer to enjoy the scenery, plants, and animals).

HIKING ELEVATIONS: 9475 feet (elevation of Bear Lake).

EXERTION RATING: 0.9 (stroll).

FEATURES: Pleasant lakeside stroll, natural history. This is one of the loveliest subalpine spots reachable by public road in all of North America, and once you have been there yourself, you will recognize photographs of Bear Lake in all sorts of magazines and books about the Rocky Mountains.

ACCESS POINT: Bear Lake Trailhead (end of Bear Lake Road).

SEASONS: All seasons, but snow on the trail does get packed down and icy, so be careful. Perhaps Bear Lake is at its most photogenic when snow falls while the aspens are still golden.

SUMMARY:

Route	Distance (mi.)	Total Elevation Gain (ft.)	Time (hr.:min.)	Exertion Rating
Circuit	0.6	flat	0:18	0.9

FINDING THE ACCESS POINT: From US 36, 0.3 mi. west of the Beaver Meadows Entrance Station, turn left onto Bear Lake Road. Drive 9.6 mi. to its terminus at the Bear Lake parking lot. Bear Lake is at the upper end of the lot, which normally fills by about 8:30 A.M. in summer. Nevertheless, many people stay just long enough to see Bear Lake, so it is usually worthwhile to wait for a parking place to become available. **Drinking water is not ordinarily available,** but during the summer tourist season, park employees truck water up to Bear Lake. **Outhouses** at Bear Lake temporarily replace the rest building that was destroyed by arsonists in the winter of 2001–2002.

During 2003–2004, Bear Lake Road will be rebuilt above the shuttle bus parking lot at mile 5.1. Private vehicles will not be allowed beyond this point, but the Bear Lake Shuttle Bus will continue to run at frequent intervals during extended hours. The shuttle bus stops at Bear Lake, near the top of the large parking lot.

TRAIL DESCRIPTION: The trail may be walked clockwise or counterclockwise. The time is the same either way because there is no elevation gain. For some distance in both directions from the trailhead, the way is paved and wide to accommodate wheelchairs. You will undoubtedly be beseeched for handouts by both mammals and birds; do not feed the animals. The

Chipmunks are among the several species of mammals and birds that beseech visitors to Bear Lake.

circuit can be walked in less than 20 min., but stroll it leisurely to enjoy the alpine scenery and natural history. A brochure about the trail may be obtained at RMNP visitor centers and may be on sale at the trailhead when the small trailer is staffed by volunteers.

Bear Lake's origin is different from all other lakes in the region except Dream Lake (a mile away by trail; closer as the raven flies). When a glacier melts back, it leaves behind the huge load of rock and earth formerly embedded in the ice. Occasionally, a large chunk of ice does not melt as quickly as the main mass so is left behind, buried under the glacial till. When the ice chunk finally melts, the overlying till slumps to form a depression known as a kettle hole. If a kettle hole subsequently fills with water, it is appropriately called a kettle-hole lake. Bear Lake is an archetypical example because its basin is truly kettle-shaped.

OUR HIKING NOTES: We've been by and around Bear Lake so many times in the summer that we've neglected to take specific notes. But don't mistake our sparse notes for contempt bred by familiarity: we continue to stand in awe of this lovely place.

Habitats traversed: Mixed coniferous forest surrounding the lake. By the trail, you can see most of the high-elevation conifers, including Lodgepole Pine (more characteristic of lower altitudes in RMNP) and the shrub Common Juniper. Look also for Mountain Maple. **Wildflowers noted:** At the far end of the lake, cross a small stream where Tall Chiming-bells grow. (At this same spot, we've also seen Cutthroat Trout spawning in mid-July.)

Birds seen or heard: Mallards (on the lake), Gray Jay, Steller's Jay, Clark's Nutcracker, Common Raven, Mountain Chickadee, and Dark-eyed Junco. **Mammals encountered:** Least Chipmunk, Golden-mantled Ground Squirrel, and Red Squirrel.

Bear Lake with Hallett Peak in the background.

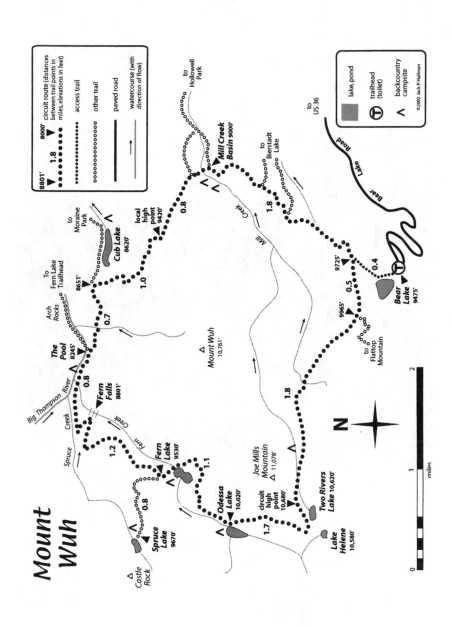

Mount Wuh

Legend:

8801' ▲ ... 8000' ▲ circuit route (distances between trail points in miles, elevations in feet)
1.8

●●●●● access trail
○○○○○ other trail
▬▬▬ paved road
→ watercourse (with direction of flow)

lake, pond
Ⓣ trailhead (toilet)
∨ backcountry campsite
©2002 Jack P. Hallman

Map labels:

Castle Rock △
Spruce Lake 9670'
Fern Lake 9530'
Odessa Lake 10,020'
Two Rivers Lake 10,620'
Lake Helene 10,580'
Joe Mills Mountain △ 11,078'
circuit high point 10,680'
The Pool 8245'
Fern Falls 8801'
Arch Rocks
To Fern Lake Trailhead
8651'
Cub Lake 8620'
local high point 9420'
Mill Creek Basin 9000'
Mount Wuh △ 10,761'
9725'
9965'
Bear Lake 9475'
to Moraine Park
to Hollowell Park
to Bierstadt Lake
to Flattop Mountain
to US 36

Big Thompson River
Spruce Creek
Fern Creek
Mill Creek
Bear Lake Road

Distances: 0.7, 0.8, 1.2, 0.8, 1.1, 1.7, 1.8, 1.8, 0.5, 0.4, 1.8, 0.8, 1.0, 1.0

N

0 ——— 1 ——— 2 miles

MOUNT WUH CIRCUIT

FORMULA TIME: 9 hours, 12 minutes for the circuit, including roundtrip access from Bear Lake.

HIKING ELEVATIONS: 8245 to 10,680 feet.

EXERTION RATING: 27.4 (very strenuous).

FEATURES: High alpine scenery, tundra mammals, alpine lakes, a waterfall, The Pool on the Big Thompson River; a highly varied but exhaustingly long hike.

ACCESS POINT: Bear Lake Trailhead, at the end of Bear Lake Road. You must climb 0.4 mile from Bear Lake to reach the circuit. (You could also hike the 1.3 miles in from the Fern Lake Trailhead to access this circuit, but the extra time required would make this a very long day hike indeed.

SEASONS: Summer and fall are very nice, but be warned that snow may last well into summer at the highest elevations. The circuit should not be attempted in winter and late spring because of the deep and often unstable icy snow between Odessa Lake and Lake Helene, where elevations exceed 10,000 ft.

SUMMARY:

Route	Distance (mi.)	Total Elevation Gain (ft.)	Time (hr.:min.)	Exertion Rating
Circuit, including access trail	12.2	3105	9:12	27.4

FINDING THE ACCESS POINT: From US 36, 0.3 mi. west of the Beaver Meadows Entrance Station, turn left onto Bear Lake Road. Drive 9.6 mi. to its terminus at the Bear Lake parking lot. Bear Lake is at the upper end of the lot, which typically fills by about 8:30 A.M. in summer. Nevertheless, many people stay just long enough to see Bear Lake, so it is usually worthwhile to wait for a parking place to become available. **Drinking water is not ordinarily available,** but during the summer tourist season, park employees truck water up to Bear Lake. **Outhouses** at Bear Lake temporarily replace the rest building that was destroyed by arsonists in the winter of 2001–2002.

During 2003–2004, Bear Lake Road will be rebuilt above the shuttle bus parking lot at mile 5.1. Private vehicles will not be allowed beyond this point, but the Bear Lake Shuttle Bus will continue to run at frequent intervals during extended hours. The shuttle bus stops at Bear Lake, near the top of the large parking lot.

TRAIL DESCRIPTION (counterclockwise): The circuit can be walked in either direction. We describe it counterclockwise because that is the direction we took; however, there is much to be said for doing the circuit clockwise, as that way takes you past the highest elevations before midday thunderstorms begin building. (On the other hand, this direction covers the most interesting parts of the hike early on, leaving a long and less absorbing haul to complete the circuit.) The route encircles Mt. Wuh, but that heavily forested mountain is not an obvious feature of the scenery. *Wuh,* originally transcribed *woo,* means "Grizzly Bear" in the Arapaho language.

1) From the parking lot, walk uphill toward Bear Lake and take the trail leaving right (counterclockwise around Bear Lake); shortly thereafter, arrive at a junction where the trail ascending to the circuit route leaves right. Walking time for this leg is 27 min.

2) For the counterclockwise circuit, go right at this junction, the direction of Bierstadt Lake, and walk downhill for 54 min., passing through mainly Lodgepole Pine to reach **Mill Creek Basin.** Along the way, pass two trails leaving right for Bierstadt Lake, and then the spur leading left and across Mill Creek to the Upper Mill Creek Basin backcountry campsite.

3) At Mill Creek Basin, ignore the trail leaving right for Hollowell Park and continue on. After crossing Mill Creek, pass through the basin meadow (the trail may be wet in spots), pass another trail leaving right for Hollowell Park, and ascend through mainly Lodgepole forest to reach a local high point on the trail in about 49 min.

4) From the local high point, which is nearly level ground with many Ponderosa Pines, descend on a sometimes steep trail to reach Cub Lake Trail in about 30 min. You will see **Cub Lake** 800 ft. below you, first to the north and finally to the east as you descend and approach the trail junction. (See the Cub Lake Circuit account.)

5) On the Cub Lake Trail, descend for 21 min. to **The Pool,** a whirling body of water on the Big Thompson River where the river has cut through rocks. *Go to the substantial bridge that spans the river and look upstream before returning a few steps to the trail junction. Once, while we were chatting here with other hikers, an American Dipper flew up- and downriver several times, passing under the bridge. This is the only bird in North America that forages by walking underwater in streams—a truly extraordinary habit.*

6) From the trail junction just before the bridge, head west and ascend for about 57 min. to reach **Fern Falls.** About 10 min. after leaving The Pool, cross Fern Creek on a half-log bridge with handrail. This creek, flowing down from Fern Falls, empties into the Big Thompson River just downstream. You now ascend between Fern Creek to the south and Spruce Creek to the north. (Spruce Creek also empties into the Big Thompson in this area.) It is truly unusual to hear waters rushing past on both sides of you as you walk a trail. After leaving Fern Creek, the trail switches back up to the base of the falls.

7) From Fern Falls, follow switchbacks that lead away from the creek and then toward it again. Overall, ascend for 1 hr., 20 min. (we took only 1 hr., 1 min. with full backpacks) to reach the trail junction below Fern Lake. The trail to the right takes you to **Spruce Lake** and the Fern Lake backcountry campsites. You could divert here to Spruce Lake, which we did with a roundtrip time of 1 hr., 23 min., but in all honesty there is nothing on this side trip—scenery, plants, or animals—that you won't find on the main circuit.

8) From the trail junction below Fern Lake, ascend for 1 hr., 2 min. to reach a point above the bottom of **Odessa Lake** (elevation, 10,020 ft.). On this leg, you will pass the Fern Lake ranger cabin (not routinely manned) on your right, then cross the outlet of lovely **Fern Lake** on half-log bridges. From the end of Fern Lake, look southwest for a magnificent view of Little Matterhorn (on the right, closer) and Notchtop Mountain. The Continental Divide runs along the top of the latter. As you ascend, crossing a talus slope, you can look back down at Fern Lake for most of the way. Notice the crustose lichens on boulders. Before reaching Odessa Lake, arrive at a junction; the right fork crosses the creek and proceeds up the gorge to a backcountry campsite. (If you want to go to the shore of Odessa Lake, you must take this trail and return on it.) The main trail continues to ascend; you are actually above Lake Odessa by the time you reach the trail point opposite its lower end. *Fern and Odessa are rock-basin lakes created by a montane glacier. In this case, the same glacier excavated both basins, leaving behind a typical (if short) chain of rock-basin lakes. Businessman W. J. Worman named the lake for his daughter Odessa.*

9) From Odessa Lake, ascend for an additional 1 hr., 31 min. to reach the high point on the circuit. This is a wonderful stretch of trail, opening into tundra, with spectacular views to the west. Here a Yellow-bellied Marmot spotted us and came lumbering down the trail, apparently in hopes of a handout. We resisted; please do the same. *A close cousin of* *the Woodchuck of eastern United States, this large and beautiful rodent ranges to lower altitudes but is far commoner above tree line, so you are likely to encounter it only on the highest circuits in this book.* As you near the end of this leg, the trail turns sharply right above **Lake Helene** and climbs more gently to the high point of the circuit (10,680 ft.), from which you can see vaguely rectangular **Two Rivers Lake** below. *Lake Helene was named for the daughter of a Denver lawyer; neither father nor daughter had any special connection with this region of the park.*

10) From the high point, descend for 54 min. to reach a junction with the trail leaving right to Flattop Mountain. The snow tends to linger longest in this stretch, and in mid-July of an admittedly snowy year, we had to traverse a long snowbank. If you encounter the same, be careful: it is possible to miss the trail on the other side if you stray too far downhill.

11) Ignore the trail to Flattop Mountain and continue about 15 min. to the next junction.

12) At this junction, go right and descend the access trail to Bear Lake in 12 min.

Clockwise walking time is the same overall, but individual segments differ from the counterclockwise circuit because the elevation gains are in different places. From the Bear Lake parking lot, **(12)** walk uphill to Bear Lake, bear right (counterclockwise) around the lake, turn right at the first trail junction, and ascend to the circuit in 27 min.; **(11)** go left at the junction with the circuit route and ascend for 29 min. to reach the trail leaving left for Flattop Mountain; **(10)** pass the trail and continue ascending, perhaps crossing snowbanks into July, to reach the high point on the circuit in about 1 hr., 37 min. (Two Rivers Lake is just below the trail); **(9)** begin descending, turning north as the trail bears sharply right, and cross areas of near-tundra to reach a point opposite the lower end of Odessa Lake in 51 min.; **(8)** continue descending for 33 min., passing the trail to Odessa Lake backcountry campsites, crossing the outlet of Fern Lake near the ranger cabin, and reaching the junction with the trail to Spruce Lake; **(7)** descend for another 36 min. to reach the base of Fern Falls; **(6)** descend for an additional 24 min., walking between Spruce and Fern Creeks, crossing the latter, and arriving at The Pool on the Big Thompson River; **(5)** go right at the trail junction (the bridge over the river is just a few steps down the left fork) and ascend for 45 min. to reach the Cub Lake Trail leaving left; **(4)** continue ascending above Cub Lake for 1 hr., 16 min. to reach fairly level ground, which is a local high point on the circuit; **(3)** then descend for 24 min., passing a trail leaving left for Hollowell

Park, crossing the bridge over Mill Creek, and arriving at Mill Creek Basin, where another trail to Hollowell Park leaves left; **(2)** go right at the junction and ascend for 1 hr., 38 min., soon passing the spur to Upper Mill Creek backcountry site on the right, then later two trails leaving left for Bierstadt Lake, before finally arriving at the access trail leading down to Bear Lake; **(1)** go left at the junction and descend for 12 min. to reach Bear Lake and retrace your steps to the parking lot. **Side-trip time** to Spruce Lake is the same as in the main account.

OUR HIKING NOTES: The formula time for the circuit per se is 9 hr., 12 min. We required 9 hr., 28 min., partly because we did the hike as a segment of a larger backpacking trip and were carrying full packs. The other factor holding us up was that even though it was mid-July, we had to traverse many snowbanks in the high country—and then we got socked with a three-hour drenching electrical storm. Hey, these things happen.

Habitats traversed: Highly varied, from river bottomlands through montane forest to open tundra. Every common tree species in Rocky Mountain National Park can probably be found somewhere on this circuit. **Wildflowers noted:** Mountain Iris, Spotted Coralroot, Fairybells, chiming-bells (at creek crossings), Miners-candle, a wallflower, Twinflower (technically a shrub), Golden Banner, White Clover, Colorado Columbine, Globeflower, Marsh-marigold, a rose, a small blue penstemon, Rosy Paintbrush, and Narrowleaf Paintbrush. **Other plants and fungi noted:** Common Juniper and Shrubby Cinquefoil (shrubs); King Bolete and the beautiful but poisonous Fly Amanita (mushrooms).

Birds seen or heard: Gray Jay, Steller's Jay, Clark's Nutcracker, Mountain Chickadee, Red-breasted Nuthatch, Brown Creeper, Golden-crowned Kinglet, Ruby-crowned Kinglet, American Dipper, Hermit Thrush, American Robin, Yellow-rumped Warbler, Dark-eyed Junco, Red Crossbill, and Pine Siskin. **Mammals encountered:** Least Chipmunk, Yellow-bellied Marmot (Odessa Lake–Two Rivers Lake area), Golden-mantled Ground Squirrel, Red Squirrel, and Southern Redback Vole.

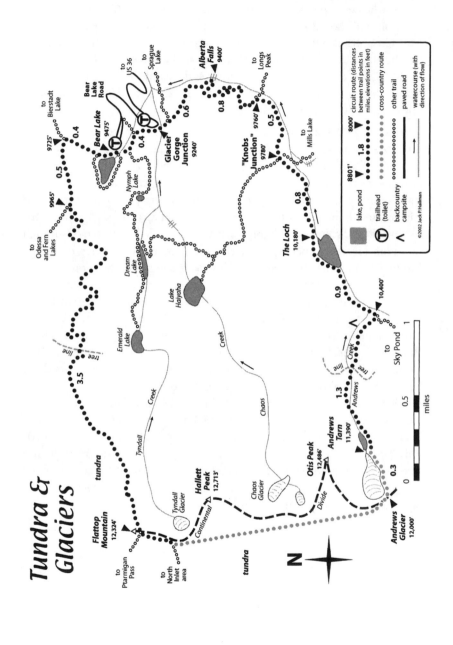

Tundra & Glaciers

Flattop Mountain 12,324'

to Ptarmigan Pass

to North Inlet area

Hallett Peak 12,713'

Tyndall Glacier

tundra

Tyndall *Creek*

tree line

3.5

to Odessa and Fern Lakes

9965'

Bear Lake 9475'

Bear Lake Road

to Bierstadt Lake

9725'

0.4

0.5

to US 36

Nymph Lake

Dream Lake

Emerald Lake

Lake Haiyaha

Continental Divide

Chaos Glacier

Otis Peak 12,486'

Chaos *Creek*

Andrews Tarn 11,390'

Andrews Glacier 12,000'

0.3

1.3

Andrews *Creek*

tree line

to Sky Pond

10,400'

0.9

The Loch 10,180'

0.8

"Knobs Junction" 9780'

0.5

9760'

to Mills Lake

0.8

Alberta Falls 9400'

to Longs Peak

0.6

Glacier Gorge Junction 9240'

0.4

Bear Lake 9475'

Sprague Lake

tundra

N

Legend:

8801' ▲ ●●●●● circuit route (distances between trail points in miles, elevations in feet) 8000' ▲

1.8 ●●●●●

○○○○○○ cross-country route

───── other trail

▲ backcountry campsite

■ lake, pond

⊤ trailhead (toilet)

watercourse (with direction of flow)

paved road

©2002 Jack P.Hailman

0   0.5   1
miles

TUNDRA & GLACIERS CIRCUIT

"MODIFIED" FORMULA TIME: 9 hours, 26 minutes

HIKING ELEVATIONS: 9240 to 12,324 feet. This is one of the two highest circuit hikes in this book, the other being the Continental Divide Circuit.

EXERTION RATING: 28.7 (very strenuous).

FEATURES: Glaciers (Tyndall, Chaos, Andrews), tundra hiking, spectacular views, alpine lakes (Bear Lake, Andrews Tarn, The Loch), Alberta Falls. This hike will require you to slide down snow on part of Andrews Glacier (no ice equipment necessary but previous experience negotiating snowfields desirable). We think this is the premier day hike in Rocky Mountain National Park, but it makes for a very long day indeed and should be attempted only by experienced hikers in good physical condition. **Warning!** In early spring, inquire about the condition of the snowpack at the base of Andrews Tarn (below the glacier) and how to negotiate it safely, if you should even attempt it at all. Toward late summer, conditions on the glacier itself become icier and crevasses open. Conditions vary from month to month and year to year; check with knowledgeable rangers before undertaking this hike.

ACCESS POINTS: Glacier Gorge Junction Trailhead or Bear Lake Trailhead (on Bear Lake Road).

SEASONS: Summer only, and then only if rangers affirm that the deep snows below Andrews Tarn are negotiable and the glacier has not begun to develop crevasses. The window of opportunity can be narrow in some years.

SUMMARY:

Route	Distance (mi.)	Total Elevation Gain (ft.)	Time (hr.:min.)	Exertion Rating
Circuit	12.0	3084	9:26	28.7

FINDING THE ACCESS POINT: From US 36, 0.3 mi. west of the Beaver Meadows Entrance Station, turn left on Bear Lake Road and drive 8.8 mi. to Glacier Gorge Junction, where there is a small parking lot. The lot usually fills before 8 A.M. The Glacier Gorge Junction Trailhead is across Bear Lake Road from the middle of the curve. **Outhouses** are located at the upper edge of the lot. There is **no drinking water**. Remember to treat or filter any water you take from natural sources.

If the Glacier Gorge Junction lot is full, drive an additional 0.8 mi. to the Bear Lake parking lot, which normally fills by about 8:30 A.M. in summer. Nevertheless, many people stay just long enough to see Bear Lake, so it is usually worthwhile to wait for a parking place to become available. The Bear Lake Trailhead is at the upper end of the parking lot. **Drinking water** is **not ordinarily available,** but during the summer tourist season, park employees truck water up to Bear Lake. **Outhouses** at Bear Lake temporarily replace the rest building that was destroyed by arsonists in the winter of 2001–2002.

During 2003–2004, Bear Lake Road will be rebuilt above the shuttle bus parking lot at mile 5.1. Private vehicles will not be allowed beyond this point, but the Bear Lake Shuttle Bus will continue to run at frequent intervals over extended hours. The shuttle bus stops at both Glacier Gorge Junction and Bear Lake. At the former, the bus stop is below the parking lot; at the latter, it is near the top of the large parking lot. **Note:** As of 2002, the shuttle bus began running at 7 A.M. and is projected to begin even earlier in subsequent years. We recommend beginning this circuit as early in the morning as possible so that you are certain to complete the hike before nightfall. **Warning!** Once you leave Bear Lake, no reliable natural water is available until you reach Andrews Tarn (three-quarters of the way into the hike), so carry an ample supply. If snow is available for melting, the water it yields should also be filtered or treated; it is not certainly known whether snowfields can harbor *Giardia.*

TRAIL DESCRIPTION (counterclockwise from Glacier Gorge Junction): This circuit should be done counterclockwise because clockwise would require ascending Andrews Glacier. We recommend starting from Glacier Gorge Junction; beginning at Bear Lake would require an uphill leg at the end of the hike. The leg is short, but no one wants to conclude such a long day by slogging uphill. **Repeat warning!** Glacier conditions vary from month to month and year to year; check with knowledgeable rangers as to current conditions at Andrews Glacier and the snowpack below Andrews Tarn before attempting this hike. Remember that the glacier becomes icier and crevasses open by late summer.

1) From Glacier Gorge Junction, walk uphill about 26 min. to the trail junction near **Bear Lake,** passing on the way first the trail leaving left for Nymph Lake and then the trail leading left for a clockwise loop around Bear Lake. Ducks on Bear Lake are usually Mallards. Least Chipmunks, Golden-mantled Ground Squirrels, Gray Jays, Steller's Jays, and Clark's Nutcrackers may all seek handouts; do not feed the animals.

2) At the trail junction, turn right and walk uphill, passing Bear Lake to your left, for about 27 min. to arrive at a junction with the trail leaving right for Bierstadt Lake.

3) Bear left and continue uphill for about 29 min. to the junction with a trail leaving right for Odessa and Fern Lakes.

4) Going left at the trail junction, begin the *very* long hike to **Flattop Mountain** (approximately 4 hr., 7 min.). Although the elevation gain is massive (nearly 2400 ft.), there are switchbacks, and the uphill climb is spread over 3.5 mi., so it is not as arduous as it would be over a shorter distance. About halfway along this segment, leave the coniferous forest and emerge onto open tundra. The trail peaks out on Flattop Mountain (12,324 ft.), the highest point on the circuit. Be of good cheer—it's all downhill from here.

The trail from Bear Lake to Flattop Mountain is an old route over the Continental Divide and can be seen on maps from around the turn of the twentieth century. As its name suggests, the mountain is surprisingly flat on top. The reason lies in its geologic past. The present-day Rockies are relatively new. Previous mountain ranges have stood here at least twice in geologically ancient times. As soon as mountains are pushed up, they begin eroding away, and if the process goes on long enough, they wear down to a nearly flat surface called a peneplain. *(Pene is "almost" in Latin.) When new mountains push up, remnants of the peneplain may survive as flat areas in the high country. The summits of Deer Mountain, Longs Peak, and Flattop Mountain are all thought to be remnants of ancient peneplains. Flattop Mountain's is by far the largest.*

5) From Flattop Mountain, walk about 1 hr. south across the tundra to the top of Andrews Glacier. As you cross the tundra, keep any eye out for alpine birds and mammals such as Brown-capped Rosy Finches, Water Pipits, White-tailed Ptarmigans, Bighorn Sheep, American Pikas, and Yellow-bellied Marmots. At first there is a southbound trail to follow, but it soon leaves right for the North Inlet area. From here, you will be making your own way across the tundra to the top of Andrews Glacier. If you walk the curving Continental Divide, you traverse the summits of **Hallett** and **Otis Peaks** on the way, and can look down on **Tyndall Glacier** and, about a half hour later, the two parts of **Chaos Glacier. Warning!** Under no circumstances should you attempt to descend via Tyndall or Chaos Glacier. Signs (unless they've been vandalized) will warn you of this. When Jack made the hike, routes across the tundra were marked by cairns, but it may be useful to follow a compass line slightly east of south in order to walk an efficient, straight route. If you are in a group, it is wise for the group to spread out to prevent trampling a new, unnecessary path into the fragile tundra. *Hallett Peak is named for William L. Hallett, one of Colorado's early climbers; Otis Peak for Dr. Edward Osgood Otis, who climbed here in the 1880s; and Tyndall Glacier for the great English physicist John Tyndall (1820–1893), who also took an interest in glacial phenomena.*

6) The most difficult part of this hike is descending **Andrews Glacier.** *The glacier was named by Abner Sprague for his brother-in-law, Edwin B. Andrews.* We walked down it most of the way (no crampons or ice axes needed), staying to the right (south) of center. Near the bottom, there was a wonderful place to slide down on the snow without risk of hitting boulders. Keeping right, we were able to walk alongside the lowest part of the glacier, off the snow (but remember, conditions change, so don't count on this). Above all, take no risks in descending the glacier; go very slowly and be certain of your footing at all times. We have allowed 30 min. for descent of the glacier because of the need to go slowly, whereas the calculated formula time is merely 9 min.

What, exactly, is a glacier? It is, of course, a large body of ice, but there are two distinct types of glacier: continental glaciers and montane glaciers. Continental glaciers are enormous shields of ice that form over vast areas, such as those that covered northern North America during the Pleistocene Epoch. Montane glaciers, which form high in the mountains, are much smaller, and discrete. A montane glacier begins forming when the winter's snowfall is not completely melted by the summer's heat, leaving behind a snowfield that persists through the summer. The snow then compacts under its own weight, in several phases distinguished by geologists, and slowly turns to ice. When the ice mass is large enough to begin flowing downhill, it becomes a glacier, by definition. Small glaciers are distinguished from snowfields by their terminal moraines (lips of till along their leading edge).

7) Andrews Tarn lies at the foot of the glacier. *Tarn is a Scandinavian word for a small mountain lake fed by a glacier.* Walk about 39 min., twice crossing Andrews Creek on bridges, to the junction with the trail leaving right for Sky Pond. Look directly south to see a spectacular rock spire called the **Sharkstooth. Warning!** In early spring, there may be deep snowpack below Andrews Tarn. Before setting out on the circuit, find out from knowledgeable rangers how best to negotiate the snowpack (if you should even attempt it).

8) At the trail junction, bear left and walk about 27 min. to the foot of **The Loch.** *Loch is a Scottish word for lake, but this one was originally named for a Mr. Locke, later corrupted.*

9) From The Loch, descend on two complete switchbacks, walking for 24 min. to reach "Knobs Junction," as we call it because it sits between two hills of rocks known as the **Glacier Knobs**. From here you could make a side trip to Mills Lake, but you will be much too tired and pressed for time even to think about it. Nevertheless, if you are a glutton for punishment, turn to the Alpine Lakes Circuit account for a description of the side trip to Mills Lake.

10) From "Knobs Junction," walk about 15 min. to the junction with the trail leaving right for the Longs Peak area.

11) At the trail junction, continue straight and head downhill for about 24 min. to **Alberta Falls** on Glacier Creek. Expect to see lots of people, as this is an easy hike from Glacier Gorge Junction and the most accessible waterfall in RMNP after Chasm Falls on the Old Fall River Road. *Abner Sprague, one of the area's most prominent early settlers, named the falls for his wife, Mary Alberta Sprague.*

12) To complete the circuit, walk another 18 min. or so downhill to Glacier Gorge Junction.

OUR HIKING NOTES: Jack did this circuit on a ranger-led hike in mid-August. He was dropped off at Bear Lake and finished the hike at Glacier Gorge Junction, which shortens the modified formula time to 9 hr.; his actual time (excluding the lunch stop) was 8 hr., 30 min. The following warning is worth repeating yet again: glacier conditions vary from month to month and year to year; check with knowledgeable rangers as to current conditions at Andrews Glacier before attempting this hike.

Habitats traversed: Roughly the first and last quarters of the hike pass through subalpine coniferous forests; the middle half emerges above tree line and includes a tundra walk from Flattop Mountain to Andrews Glacier.

Birds seen or heard: The usual assortment of coniferous forest birds (Jack did not keep a complete list), including Gray Jay, Steller's Jay, and Clark's Nutcracker; on the tundra, Common Raven and Water Pipit. **Mammals encountered:** American Pika (tundra), Least Chipmunk, Yellow-bellied Marmot, Golden-mantled Ground Squirrel, and Red Squirrel (coniferous forest).

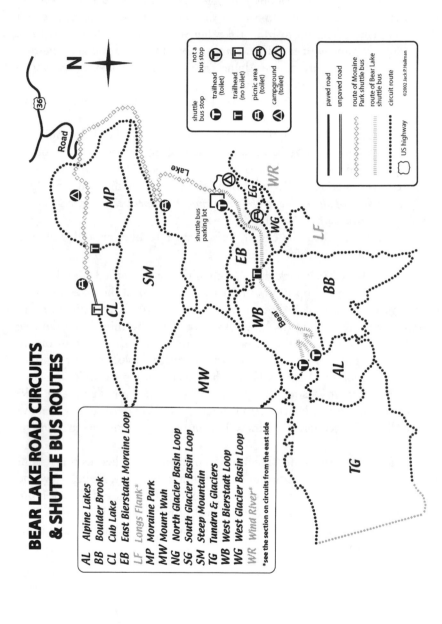

BEAR LAKE ROAD CIRCUITS & SHUTTLE BUS ROUTES

AL Alpine Lakes
BB Boulder Brook
CL Cub Lake
EB East Bierstadt Moraine Loop
LF Longs Flank*
MP Moraine Park
MW Mount Wuh
NG North Glacier Basin Loop
SG South Glacier Basin Loop
SM Steep Mountain
TG Tundra & Glaciers
WB West Bierstadt Loop
WG West Glacier Basin Loop
WR Wind River*

*see the section on circuits from the east side

Legend:

shuttle
bus stop — T

not a
bus stop — T

trailhead
(toilet) — T

trailhead
(no toilet) — T

picnic area
(toilet) — P

campground
(toilet) — ▲

paved road

unpaved road

route of Moraine
Park shuttle bus

route of Bear Lake
shuttle bus

circuit route

US highway

©2002 Jack P.Hailman

COMBINING BEAR LAKE ROAD CIRCUITS AND USING THE SHUTTLE BUS TO COMPLETE A CIRCUIT

The accompanying map shows that many Bear Lake Road circuits share trail segments and therefore could be combined into a longer circuit. For example, it is possible to combine Glacier Basin Loops with Wind River (an East Side circuit) and Boulder Brook with Longs Flank (also an East Side circuit). The possibilities for combining two (or more) Bear Lake Road circuits are legion, but beware of taking on more than you are up to. The Mount Wuh and Tundra & Glaciers Circuits are already so long that it isn't feasible to combine either with another circuit, except as a multiday backpacking trip.

In summer, shuttle buses run on two routes. The Moraine Park shuttle runs from the end of the paved road near the Cub Lake Trailhead to the lot at Glacier Basin, and the Bear Lake shuttle operates between the shuttle bus parking lot and Bear Lake. You can use the buses to complete a myriad of hikes involving no retracing of steps. The accompanying map shows the bus routes and the access points that are also bus stops. An attractive strategy is to park your car near a bus stop at low elevation, let the bus do most of the climbing, and then hike mainly downhill back to your vehicle. (You could also hike uphill and take the bus back, but we seem to be among the few who have done things that way.) **Note:** Buses, especially on the Bear Lake route, are often crowded to capacity. Do not count on being able to take the first bus you see.

Bus service varies seasonally and from year to year, so be sure to check current park information for details. Generally, both routes operate daily from early June to mid-September. Beginning May 1, 2003, Bear Lake shuttle buses will run every half hour, from 5 A.M. to 10 P.M. **Note:** During the rebuilding of Bear Lake Road above Sprague Lake in 2003–2004, the road will not be open to private vehicles between May 1 and October 31. Winter travel on the gravel roadbed will be allowed to Bear Lake from November 1, 2003, to April 30, 2004.

Tonahutu Creek, on one of the many scenic circuits on the West Side of Rocky Mountain National Park.

Circuit Hikes From Access Points on the West Side

INTRODUCTION TO WEST SIDE CIRCUITS

"West is best," according to some enthusiasts. Despite the popularity of the park's East Side, which is easily accessible from Estes Park and much of the northern Front Range, some of the most rewarding hikes can be found on Rocky's West Side.

The seven accounts in this section are ordered geographically by access point from north to south along US 34. The Grand Ditch Circuit is accessible only from the Colorado River Trailhead, but the Red Mountain Circuit can be hiked from four other points as well. The Green Mountain Trailhead serves both the Big Meadows and Green Mountain Circuits, although both can be hiked from alternative access points (we chose to describe Green Mountain from one of them). The Kawuneeche Valley Loops, the imposing Continental Divide Circuit, and the unique Shadow Shore Circuit all have but one direct access point.

Those staying in Timber Creek Campground, the park's only West Side campground, might enjoy doing a circuit hike that begins near their campsite. If so, the Red Mountain Circuit leaves right from the campground.

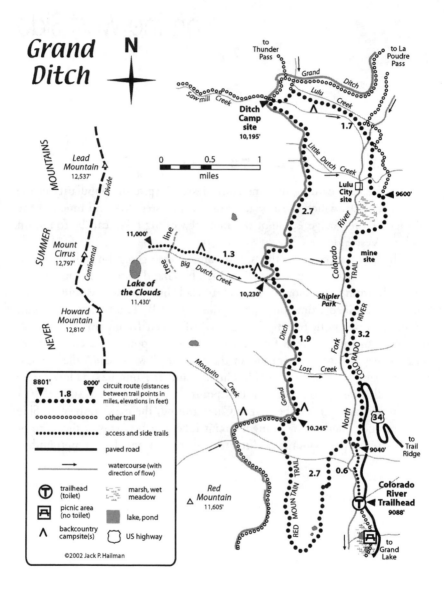

Grand Ditch

N

to Thunder Pass

to La Poudre Pass

Grand Ditch

Sawmill Creek

Lulu Creek

Ditch Camp site
10,195'

1.7

Little Dutch Creek

MOUNTAINS

Lead Mountain
12,537'

0   0.5   1
miles

Lulu City site

9600'

Divide

SUMMER

Mount Cirrus
12,797'

Continental

11,000'

tree line

1.3

Big Dutch Creek

Lake of the Clouds
11,430'

10,230'

Colorado River

mine site

COLORADO TRAIL

Shipler Park

NEVER

Howard Mountain
12,810'

Ditch

1.9

Fork

3.2

COLORADO RIVER

Lost Creek

8801'   8000'

1.8   circuit route (distances between trail points in miles, elevations in feet)

○○○○○○○○○○○○○○○○   other trail

●●●●●●●●●●●   access and side trails

━━━━━   paved road

→   watercourse (with direction of flow)

Ⓣ   trailhead (toilet)

🅿   picnic area (no toilet)

∧   backcountry campsite(s)

marsh, wet meadow

lake, pond

US highway

©2002 Jack P. Hailman

Mosquito Creek

10,245'

North

34

9040'

to Trail Ridge

RED MOUNTAIN TRAIL

2.7   **0.6**

Red Mountain
11,605'

Colorado River Trailhead
9088'

to Grand Lake

GRAND DITCH CIRCUIT

FORMULA TIMES: 7 hours, 57 minutes for the circuit; 10 hours, 1 minute including the side trip to the end of the trail below Lake of the Clouds.

HIKING ELEVATIONS: 9040 to 10,245 feet (to 11,000 feet on the side trip, which could be extended to 11,430 feet if you climb the boulder field below Lake of the Clouds).

EXERTION RATINGS: 23.8 (strenuous) for the circuit to 30.3 (very strenuous) with the optional side trip to Lake of the Clouds.

FEATURES: Grand Ditch (a late-nineteenth-century diversion channel carrying water east of the Rockies), Ditch Camp site, old mining remnants (Lulu City site, mine, site of Shipler cabins), views of the Never Summer Mountains and the valley of the North Fork of the Colorado River.

ACCESS POINTS: Colorado River Trailhead (West Side of the park).

SEASONS: Summer and fall offer wonderful views; cross-country skiing and snowshoeing in winter should be restricted to the trail along the Colorado River as climbing to the Grand Ditch is too dangerous.

SUMMARY: Side-trip time is to the end of the trail below Lake of the Clouds; climbing the boulder field another 430 ft. or so requires considerable additional time.

Route	Distance (mi.)	Total Elevation Gain (ft.)	Time (hr.:min.)	Exertion Rating
Circuit, including access trail	13.4	1253	7:57	23.8
Roundtrip to below the lake	2.6	770	2:04	6.5
Totals	16.0	2023	10:01	30.3

FINDING THE ACCESS POINT: From the Grand Lake Entrance Station, drive 9.6 mi. north on US 34, passing Timber Creek Campground and then two picnic grounds on the left. If coming from the eastern side of the park over Trail Ridge Road, drive southwest from the Alpine Visitor Center for 10.8 mi., passing the Lake Irene Picnic Area and descending the switchbacks until you bottom out in the valley. In either case, watch for a signed side road leaving west from the highway, leading to the Colorado River Trailhead parking areas. The access trail begins beyond the north end of the parking lot. There is an **outhouse** at the north end, but **no drinking water.** Remember to treat or filter any water you take from natural sources.

TRAIL DESCRIPTION (clockwise): This is a long but otherwise easy hike, which can be done in either direction. We describe it clockwise merely because that is the direction we hiked it.

1) From the trailhead, walk north along the North Fork of the Colorado River for about 18 min. to a trail junction. Here the circuit part of the hike begins.

2) At the junction, turn left and head west on Red Mountain Trail, climbing for about 2 hr., 33 min. until you reach the **Grand Ditch.** Along the way, twice cross Opposition Creek. Most of the circuit's elevation gain occurs on this stretch; once you reach the Grand Ditch, it's almost all downhill from there (unless you take the side trip to Lake of the Clouds).

3) Begin the long walk on the unpaved maintenance road hugging the Grand Ditch. *Construction of the Grand Ditch began in the late 1880s. Designed to divert water to the Loveland area east of the Rockies, this environmental eyesore is still in use so do not be surprised if you meet a maintenance vehicle during your hike.* After about 57 min., arrive at the trail leaving left for Lake of the Clouds.

3a) A side trip to the **Lake of the Clouds** area requires at least 2 hr. out and back, so it will not be feasible unless you get an early start or are overnight backpacking on the circuit. During summer, a bridge crosses the Grand Ditch and leads to the trail; in fall, if the bridge is not in place, you must ford the ditch, which carries little water at that time of year. After passing a small lake, the trail emerges onto the tundra and essentially ends below Lake of the Clouds. Climbing the boulder field to the lake will extend the side trip considerably beyond the formula time.

---

4) From the trail to Lake of the Clouds, it is another 1 hr., 21 min. to the junction with the Ditch Camp Trail. **Ditch Camp** *is the site of a construction camp occupied during the building of the Grand Ditch.*

5) As you approach the junction, veer away from the Grand Ditch and cross Sawmill Creek. Turn right at the trail junction and follow along the south side of Lulu Creek (the trail leaving north to Thunder Pass eventually leads out of Rocky Mountain National Park). From the Grand Ditch, walk about 51 min., passing current trail junctions and older trails, crossing the North Fork of the Colorado River, and passing near the site of **Lulu City** before arriving at the final junction. *Lulu City was a short-lived (and therefore typical) mining town, boasting a population of 500 in 1879. All the structures have long since been removed, and there is nothing left to see* *except a pretty spot in the valley. Two women named Lulu once lived here-abouts; the argument continues as to which one the town was named for.*

6) On the last leg of the circuit per se, walk about 1 hr., 36 min. down the Colorado River Trail. An old mine is visible on the east slope above the trail. Later on, the trail traverses **Shipler Park,** where two cabins erected by a miner survived remarkably well into modern times. *The first was built by Joseph L. Shipler in 1876.*

7) Last, continue south on the access trail for 21 min. to arrive back at the Colorado River Trailhead.

Counterclockwise walking time is the same overall, but individual segments differ from the clockwise circuit because the elevation gains are in different places: **(7)** from the Colorado River Trailhead walk north for 18 min. to a trail junction; **(6)** from the junction continue north for 2 hr., 10 min. to a trail junction, in the vicinity of the Lulu City site; **(5)** at the trail junction, keep left and ascend northwest for 1 hr., 27 min. to the Grand Ditch, **(4)** head south along the east side of the ditch for 1 hr., 23 min. to the junction with the trail for Lake of the Clouds; **(3)** continue south along the ditch for another 58 min. to the junction with Red Mountain Trail; **(2)** walk downhill on Red Mountain Trail for 1 hr., 21 min. to the North Fork of the Colorado River and the junction with the Colorado River Trail; and **(1)** head south along the river for 21 min. to the trailhead. **Side-trip time,** based on an out-and-back roundtrip, is the same as in the main description.

OUR HIKING NOTES: We did this circuit clockwise as a family backpacking trip, camping at a backcountry site near Ditch Camp. The formula time for the circuit (excluding the access trail) is 7 hr., 57 min.; our total walking time was 6 hr., 45 min. (with full backpacks), including a short lunch stop on the first day.

Habitats traversed: River bottom, coniferous and mixed forest, open areas along the Grand Ditch.

The Never Summer Mountains lived up to their name on our early August trip. We began the day wearing sunscreen and shorts, donning windbreakers before noon; by 1:15 P.M. it started to rain, the rain later turning to sleet. At 3 P.M. we set up camp, and before dinner snow began falling, which continued into the night.

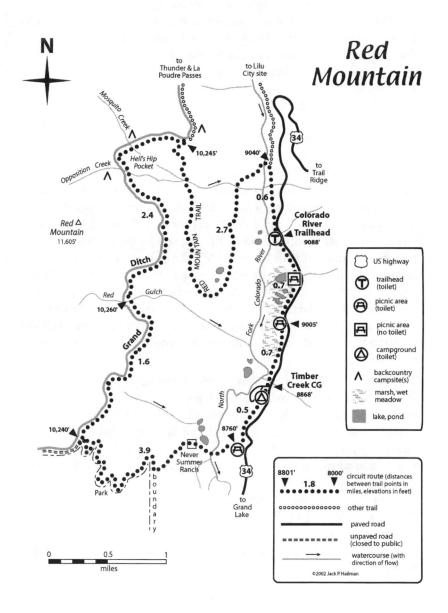

Red Mountain

N

to Thunder & La Poudre Passes

to Lilu City site

Mosquito Creek

Λ

▼ 10,245'

Hell's Hip Pocket

Opposition Creek Λ

9040' ▼

0.6

Red △
Mountain
11,605'

2.4

RED MOUNTAIN TRAIL

2.7

Colorado River Trailhead 9088'
Ⓣ

Ditch

Red *Gulch*

▼ 10,260'

0.7

Ⓐ ▼ 9005'

Colorado River
North Fork

Grand

1.6

0.7

Timber Creek CG 8868'
Ⓐ

0.5

▼ 10,240'

8760' ▼

Ⓐ

3.9

Never Summer Ranch

34

Park

b o u n d a r y

to Grand Lake

0   0.5   1
miles

Ⓗ	US highway
Ⓣ	trailhead (toilet)
Ⓐ	picnic area (toilet)
🄱	picnic area (no toilet)
Ⓐ	campground (toilet)
Λ	backcountry campsite(s)
	marsh, wet meadow
	lake, pond

8801' ▼   8000' ▼
• 1.8 •••••• circuit route (distances between trail points in miles, elevations in feet)

ooooooooooooo other trail

━━━━━━ paved road

= = = = = = unpaved road (closed to public)

→ watercourse (with direction of flow)

©2002 Jack P. Hailman

to Trail Ridge

RED MOUNTAIN CIRCUIT

FORMULA TIME: 8 hours, 6 minutes.

HIKING ELEVATIONS: 8760 to 10,260 feet.

EXERTION RATING: 24.1 (strenuous).

FEATURES: Great wildlife viewing, wonderful views of the valley of the North Fork of the Colorado River.

ACCESS POINTS: Colorado River Trailhead (West Side of the park); also, Timber Creek Campground and three picnic areas (see accompanying map).

SEASONS: Like the Grand Ditch Circuit, this circuit offers wonderful views in summer and fall. Cross-country skiing or snowshoeing up to the Grand Ditch in winter could be dangerous and certainly would be extremely demanding physically.

SUMMARY:

Route	Distance (mi.)	Total Elevation Gain (ft.)	Time (hr.:min.)	Exertion Rating
Circuit	13.1	1548	8:06	24.1

FINDING THE ACCESS POINTS: From the Grand Lake Entrance Station, drive 9.6 mi. north on US 34, passing Timber Creek Campground and then two picnic grounds on the left. If coming from the eastern side of the park over Trail Ridge Road, drive southwest from the Alpine Visitor Center for 10.8 mi., passing the Lake Irene Picnic Grounds and descending the switchbacks until you bottom out in the valley. In either case, watch for a signed side road leaving west from the highway, leading to the Colorado River Trailhead parking areas. The access points for this hike are the south and north ends of the parking lot (clockwise and counterclockwise circuit, respectively). There is an **outhouse** at the north end, but **no drinking water.** Remember to treat or filter any water you take from natural sources.

From north to south, other possible access points (see accompanying map) south of the Colorado River Trailhead are a small picnic area **(no water, no toilets),** a larger picnic area **(no water, outhouse),** Timber Creek Campground **(water, toilets),** and the picnic area at the parking lot for tours of Never Summer Ranch **(no water, toilets).** The campground is 5.3 mi. north of the Grand Lake Entrance Station and 12.4 mi. southwest from the Alpine Visitor Center on Trail Ridge Road.

TRAIL DESCRIPTION (clockwise from Colorado River Trailhead): This circuit may be walked in either direction from any of the access points.

We describe it clockwise from the Colorado River Trailhead, which is the direction we walked it.

1) From the Colorado River Trailhead parking lot, locate the unmarked trail leaving from the south end and walk south for 21 min. past a small picnic area (no toilets or water) to a second, larger picnic area (with toilets). Try not to fret about whether you are or are not on *the* trail. In general, the route stays fairly close to the highway, and by midway through this leg, the river marshes tend to pin you against the highway embankment. You might even have to retreat up onto the road for short distances when the water is high.

2) From the larger picnic area, continue south for another 21 min. to the entrance road of the Timber Creek Campground. (Water and toilets can be found here.)

3) The last leg paralleling the highway is a 15-min. walk to a picnic area and parking lot for tours of the Never Summer Ranch.

4) From the parking lot, head west on the old road to the ranch, crossing the North Fork of the Colorado River. When you reach the buildings of the **Never Summer Ranch,** continue straight ahead uphill between buildings (or follow the road curving left, rising, and curving right again) to regain the old road, where you go right. It may sound confusing, but actually if you just plow ahead blithely, you'll discover that there is only one way for a vehicle to ascend the mountain, and you want to begin the long trek on that road. Ascend on switchbacks. Shortly after you leave the ranch, the road becomes the park boundary. The way is long, as is the formula time—3 hr., 26 min. from the parking lot. In this case, the formula time must exaggerate the climb, because it took us a little less than 2 hr. from the parking lot. The grade is shallow enough for the vehicles that are used to inspect and maintain the Grand Ditch.

5) At the **Grand Ditch,** turn right on the maintenance road and walk for 49 min. to **Red Gulch,** the reputed high point of the circuit. Assuming that water does not flow uphill, the ditch itself must be slightly lower here than where you first encountered it (or else the topographic maps are slightly off). *Construction on the Grand Ditch began in the 1880s. Designed to divert water to the Loveland area east of the Rockies, this environmental eyesore is still in use, so do not be surprised if you meet a maintenance vehicle during your hike.*

6) From Red Gulch, continue walking the maintenance road for 1 hr., 12 min., enjoying the great views, until you reach the Red Mountain Trail, the first trail you come to that leads down the mountain.

Along Grand Ditch.

7) At the trail junction, turn right (left would take you up to Thunder Pass) and descend on the Red Mountain Trail for 1 hr., 21 min., crossing a creek (not a bad lunch spot) and describing a huge U-shape before recrossing the same creek nearly an hour later. The formula time underestimates the actual time (it took us 1 hr., 50 min.) because of some elevation changes that were not figured into the calculations. Eventually you reach a substantial bridge over the North Fork of the Colorado River. Just beyond it is the junction with the Colorado River Trail.

8) Turn right (south) on the trail, walking 21 min. to the Colorado River Trailhead.

Counterclockwise walking time is the same overall, but individual segments differ from the clockwise circuit because the elevation gains are in different places. From the Colorado River Trailhead counterclockwise: **(8)** walk 18 min. north to the Red Mountain Trail; **(7)** turn left and ascend 2 hr., 33 min. to the Grand Ditch; **(6)** turn left and head south 1 hr., 13 min. on the maintenance road to Red Gulch; **(5)** continue 48 min. south to the access road from Never Summer Ranch; **(4)** descend 1 hr., 57 min., passing through Never Summer Ranch to the picnic area and parking lot at the highway; **(3)** turn left and head north 21 min., paralleling the road to Timber Creek Campground; **(2)** continue north 29 min. more to the picnic area; and **(1)** walk an additional 26 min., passing the small picnic area and completing the circuit at the Colorado River Trailhead.

Other access points. From the small picnic area south of the Colorado River Trailhead, begin the trail description at leg **(1)** in the main account; from the larger picnic area south of that, begin at leg **(2)**; from Timber Creek Campground, begin at leg **(3)**; and from the picnic and parking area for Never Summer Ranch, begin at leg **(4)**.

OUR HIKING NOTES: The formula time for this hike is 8 hr., 6 min. We hiked it from our campsite at Timber Creek in 7 hr., 3 min., including short rests and a lunch stop. This circuit, which we did in early August, was our premier "mammal hike" in the park. Simply listing the species wouldn't do justice to the experience, so we have chosen to describe three mammal highlights and even share a bird story.

The herd. We would never, ever intentionally walk into the middle of an Elk herd, yet that is exactly what we did by accident. Walking south through aspen woodlands between Timber Creek Campground and the parking lot for the Never Summer Ranch, we were suddenly startled by two cow Elk that bolted from close by on the left. It was early morning, and perhaps we were not quite awake yet, because we usually spot wildlife some ways off. Now fully alert, we saw immediately that there were also Elk foraging on our right, but we kept walking slowly, fearful of turning around, stopping, or otherwise changing our pace or direction lest we stampede the herd. Then we passed a young bull in velvet on our left and didn't breathe again until a ways down the trail. In actuality, the huge animals paid little attention to us, but we never knowingly tempt fate where wildlife is concerned. Elk-human encounters are increasing in the park, mainly because people get too close when bulls are rounding up cows.

Roughhousing. We soon passed more Elk as we followed the gravel road across the marshes and bridge over the North Fork of the Colorado, but what captured our attention next was two Golden-mantled Ground Squirrels vigorously wrestling near a Never Summer Ranch building. They were probably juveniles at play, although they looked no different from adults. Marc Bekoff, a well-known biologist at the University of Colorado in Boulder and one of the world's few experts on mammalian play, discovered that canids (*e.g.*, wolves, coyotes, and domestic dogs) have a special postural signal that means "This is play; I'm not really trying to harm you." If the ground squirrels have a similar signal, we couldn't detect it in the rough and tumble spectacle before our eyes. More recently, Bekoff and colleagues have made a strong case that some play in animals involves entering a situation that threatens great harm in order to practice getting out of it—which is partly why first one individual and then the other seems to get the upper hand. That alternating dominance is what we think we were seeing in the wrestling ground squirrels.

A coincidence. As we began ascending above the Never Summer Ranch, a remarkable coincidence occurred. The previous day, while looking at wildlife displays in the Kawuneeche Visitor Center, Liz had asked Jack about martens, and he had replied in his wisest field biologist's voice that we should never expect to see one of these secretive cousins of weasels. After all, we had never seen one before during decades of camping and hiking in RMNP. Yet what should be coming straight at us on the primitive road up to the Grand Ditch but a beautiful American Marten (a.k.a. Pine Marten). Without breaking stride, it left the road about 20 ft. in front of us, detoured around us about 10 ft. away, returned to the road, and then continued on its way as unconcernedly as it had approached.

The hummingbird. We weren't expecting any other fascinating animal encounters on this hike, yet an extraordinary incident of avian behavior caught our attention just before we completed the long circuit. A Broad-tailed Hummingbird—from its plumage, doubtless a youngster—was repeatedly trying to penetrate a red patch that it had found. Unlike a red flower, this patch dodged to avoid the hummingbird's efforts each time, for the patch was on the head of a surely quite puzzled Red-breasted Sapsucker.

Habitats traversed: River bottom with alder groves, meadow, coniferous forest, and open area along the Grand Ditch. **Wildflowers noted:** A yellow composite with gray leaves, another yellow composite, an aster with few ray flowers, Aspen Daisy, Common Dandelion, Cow Parsnip, Diffuse Knapweed, Pearly-everlasting, some pussytoes, Yarrow, chimingbells, Mountain Harebell, a gentian, Common Fireweed, a dock, Star Pyrola, a larkspur, a raspberry, a paintbrush, and an unidentified white five-petaled flower. **Trees and shrubs found:** Quaking Aspen, Limber Pine, Blue Spruce, Thinleaf Alder (trees); Common Juniper, Mountain Maple, and Shrubby Cinquefoil (shrubs).

Birds seen or heard: Sharp-shinned Hawk, Wilson's Snipe, Broad-tailed Hummingbird, Red-breasted Sapsucker, Northern Flicker, Gray Jay, Steller's Jay, Clark's Nutcracker, American Crow, Violet-green Swallow, Hermit Thrush, American Robin, Yellow-rumped Warbler, Chipping Sparrow, Song Sparrow, Dark-eyed Junco, Red-winged Blackbird, and Pine Siskin. **Mammals encountered:** Snowshoe Hare, Least Chipmunk, Golden-mantled Ground Squirrel, Red Squirrel, American Marten, and Elk.

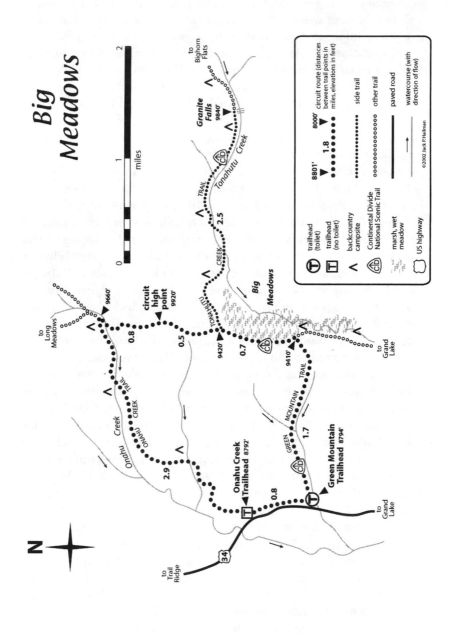

Big
Meadows

miles

0   1   2

N

to
Trail
Ridge

to
Grand
Lake

34

**Green Mountain
Trailhead** 8794'

0.8

GREEN

MOUNTAIN

TRAIL

1.7

9410'

**Onahu Creek
Trailhead** 8792'

2.9

ONAHU   CREEK   TRAIL

Onahu Creek

0.8

**circuit
high
point**
9920'

9660'

to
Long
Meadows

0.5

9420'

0.7

TONAHUTU

CREEK

TRAIL

2.5

*Big
Meadows*

to
Grand
Lake

Tonahutu Creek

9840'

*Granite
Falls*

to
Bighorn
Flats

Legend:

trailhead (toilet)	circuit route (distances between trail points in miles, elevations in feet)
trailhead (no toilet)	8801' 8000'
backcountry campsite	1.8
Continental Divide National Scenic Trail	side trail
	other trail
marsh, wet meadow	paved road
US highway	watercourse (with direction of flow)

©2002 Jack P. Hailman

BIG MEADOWS CIRCUIT

FORMULA TIMES: 4 hours, 50 minutes for the circuit; 7 hours, 45 minutes with optional side trip to Granite Falls.

HIKING ELEVATIONS: 8792 to 9920 feet.

EXERTION RATINGS: 14.3 (moderately easy) for the circuit to 22.7 (strenuous) with the side trip to Granite Falls.

FEATURES: Big Meadows (largest high meadow in the park), good montane leg-stretcher with easy grades; Granite Falls on a (long) side trip.

ACCESS POINTS: Green Mountain Trailhead or Onahu Creek Trailhead (West Side of the park).

SEASONS: Year-round. Hiking is especially good in early fall when the foliage is colorful and late spring when the wildflowers appear. Big Meadows itself is a particularly nice area for winter cross-country skiing and snowshoeing.

SUMMARY:

Route	Distance (mi.)	Total Elevation Gain (ft.)	Time (hr.:min.)	Exertion Rating
Circuit	7.4	1128	4:50	14.3
Roundtrip to Granite Falls	5.0	420	2:55	8.4
Totals	12.4	1548	7:45	22.7

FINDING THE ACCESS POINT: From the Grand Lake Entrance Station, drive north on US 34 for 2.7 mi. to the Green Mountain Trailhead or 3.3 mi. to the Onahu Creek Trailhead. If you are coming from the Alpine Visitor Center on Trail Ridge Road, drive southwest 17.7 and 17.1 mi., respectively. The trails heading up the mountain leave next to the trailhead signs in both cases. The trail connecting the two trailheads begins at the north end of the Green Mountain Trailhead parking lot and the south end of the Onahu Creek Trailhead parking lot. There is an **outhouse** but **no water** at the Green Mountain Trailhead; there is **no outhouse** and **no water** at the Onahu Trailhead. Remember to treat or filter all water you take from natural sources.

TRAIL DESCRIPTION (clockwise from Green Mountain Trailhead): We recommend a clockwise hike from Green Mountain Trailhead. Leaving from this trailhead makes toilets available at the beginning and end of the hike. Also, the clockwise route takes you through the least interesting parts of the circuit (especially the long stretch parallel with the road) first.

On some legs, our walking times seemed to deviate more noticeably than usual from formula times, sometimes proving faster and other times slower. The trail description notes some of these discrepancies.

1) Find the trail at the north end of the Green Mountain Trailhead lot and walk 24 min. to Onahu Creek Trailhead, paralleling the road through Lodgepole Pine forest.

2) From Onahu Creek Trailhead, ascend through largely Lodgepole Pine and then mixed coniferous forest for 2 hr., 19 min. to the upper bridge on Onahu Creek. (This stretch took us only 1 hr., 41 min.) The trail parallels the road briefly in open terrain, then heads more to the northeast into Lodgepole forest with Quaking Aspens at its edge. After 20 min. or so, cross an unnamed tributary of Onahu Creek on a wooden bridge. About 45 min. later, cross the lower bridge over Onahu Creek; the sound of rushing waters will greet you long before you reach the creek. The trail now stays north of the creek until arriving at the upper bridge. *This creek used to be known rather unimaginatively as Fish Creek. In 1914, however, the elderly Arapahos brought here to recall from their childhood names for local geographical features said they called this creek onahu (O-na-HU), which means "warms himself," in honor of one of their horses, which was in the habit of coming near the campfire at night. The horse died here near the creek.*

3) Cross the upper bridge over Onahu Creek and ascend for about 40 min. to reach a level area about 0.3 mi. long. The exact high point on the circuit (about 9920 ft.) is somewhere on this fairly level stretch.

4) From the high point, cross the remainder of the level area and descend to **Big Meadows** in about 15 min. (this part of the journey took us longer, 31 min.), reaching a junction with the Tonahutu Creek Trail on your left. From here to the end of the circuit, the route becomes part of the Continental Divide National Scenic Trail. *The remarkable National Trails System Act of 1968 promoted the development of national scenic trails with federal support. The Continental Divide National Scenic Trail is one of eight, the first and most famous being the Appalachian Trail. The Continental Divide Trail was designated a national scenic trail on November 10, 1976. When completed, it will be approximately 3260 mi. long, running through Montana, Idaho, Wyoming, Colorado, and New Mexico.*

4a) The Tonahutu Creek Trail leads to **Granite Falls**. The trail runs along **Tonahutu Creek,** and although the elevation gain is negligible, the 5.0-mi. roundtrip consumes nearly 3 hr. of walking time.

Moose cow with calves. Because Moose are by far the largest animals in Rocky Mountain National Park, they are very dangerous—especially bulls and cows with calves.

5) From the trail junction, continue south along the western edge of Big Meadows for about 21 min. to the Green Mountain Trail junction. About 15 min. into this leg, pass the remains of an old cabin between the trail and Big Meadows; shortly thereafter, pass similar remains on the other side of the trail.

6) Go right (west) at the junction and descend Green Mountain Trail for 51 min. (it took us 40 min.—we were running from mosquitoes) to the Green Mountain Trailhead. The route follows a creek most of the way. Note the old beaver ponds that have created small open areas. In one of these we saw a nearly black cow Moose with her brown calf.

Counterclockwise walking time is the same overall, but individual segments differ from the clockwise circuit because the elevation gains are

149

Big Meadows, skirted on the Big Meadows, Green Mountain, and Continental Divide Circuits.

in different places. **(6)** From Green Mountain Trailhead, ascend for 1 hr., 28 min. to the trail junction at Big Meadows; **(5)** turn left and walk north along the western edge of Big Meadows for 22 min.; **(4)** at the Tonahutu Creek Trail junction, bear left and ascend for 45 min. to the circuit's high point; **(3)** continue north, descending for 24 min. to the upper bridge over Onahu Creek; **(2)** cross the bridge and turn left, following the creek, passing over it on another bridge, and descending to cross a tributary on a third bridge before arriving at the Onahu Creek Trailhead after about 1 hr., 27 min.; **(1)** find the trail at the south end of the parking lot and walk 24 min. back to the Green Mountain Trailhead. **Side trip:** the roundtrip time to Granite Falls is the same as in the main description.

From Onahu Creek Trailhead: clockwise, begin the main trail description from Green Mountain Trailhead with legs **(2)** through **(6)**, ending with leg **(1)**; counterclockwise, begin the counterclockwise description from Green Lake Trailhead with leg **(1)**, then follow legs **(6)** through **(2)**.

OUR HIKING NOTES: The formula time for the circuit is 4 hr., 50 min., but we actually walked it in 3 hr., 48 min. in mid-July. Mosquitoes hurried us along; bring plenty of insect repellent, especially for the Big Meadows area.

Habitats traversed: Lodgepole Pine forest with some Quaking Aspen at lower elevations, mixed coniferous forest with Douglas-fir and Engelmann Spruce at higher elevations, stream crossings with Thinleaf Alder, and alpine meadows. **Wildflowers noted:** Fairyslipper (an orchid), a purple aster, Cow Parsnip, Heartleaf Arnica (by stream crossings), chimingbells, a spurge, Fremont Geranium, Pinedrops, Yellow Pondlily, Shooting Star, and Colorado Columbine. **Other plants and fungi found:** Horsetail (especially along Green Mountain Trail), Shrubby Cinquefoil, a raspberry just coming into berry, and several kinds of brown mushrooms.

Birds seen or heard: Hairy Woodpecker, Gray Jay, Ruby-crowned Kinglet, Hermit Thrush, American Robin, Savannah Sparrow, and Dark-eyed Junco. **Mammals encountered:** A chipmunk species, Red Squirrel, Mule Deer, and Moose (cow with calf).

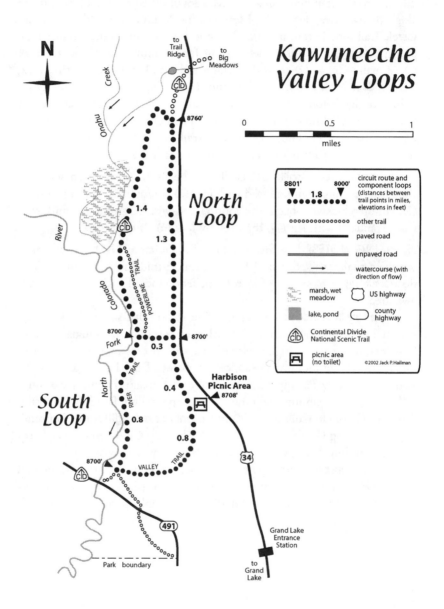

N

to
Trail
Ridge

to
Big
Meadows

Kawuneeche
Valley Loops

8760'

0   0.5   1
miles

North
Loop

1.4

1.3

circuit route and
component loops
(distances between
trail points in miles,
elevations in feet)

8801'   8000'
1.8

other trail

paved road

unpaved road

watercourse (with
direction of flow)

marsh, wet
meadow   US highway

lake, pond   county
highway

Continental Divide
National Scenic Trail

picnic area
(no toilet)   ©2002 Jack P. Hailman

8700'

0.3   8700'

**Harbison
Picnic Area**
8708'

0.4

South
Loop

0.8

0.8

8700'

VALLEY   TRAIL

34

491

Grand Lake
Entrance
Station

to
Grand
Lake

Park   boundary

KAWUNEECHE VALLEY LOOPS

FORMULA TIMES: 2 hours, 25 minutes for the entire circuit; 1 hour, 9 minutes for the South Loop only. (The North Loop cannot be walked separately from the access point.)

HIKING ELEVATIONS: 8700 to 8760 feet (to 8708 feet on the South Loop).

EXERTION RATINGS: 7.0 (easy) for the circuit; 3.3 (very easy) for the South Loop only.

FEATURES: Valley habitats, including route along the North Fork of the Colorado River.

ACCESS POINT: Harbison Picnic Area (West Side of the park).

SEASONS: Year-round, but the best time is probably during the fall foliage season.

SUMMARY:

Route	Distance (mi.)	Total Elevation Gain (ft.)	Time (hr.:min.)	Exertion Rating
Entire circuit	4.7	68	2:25	7.0
South Loop only	2.3	8	1:09	3.3

FINDING THE ACCESS POINT: From the Grand Lake Entrance Station, drive 0.8 mi. north on US 34 to the Harbison Picnic Area on the west (left) side of the road. If coming over Trail Ridge Road from the eastern side of the park, drive 19.6 mi. southwest on US 34 from the Alpine Visitor Center. To find the trail, walk about 100 ft. west into the woods, cutting through the picnic area. There are **no toilets** and **no water sources** here. Remember to treat or filter any water you take from the Colorado River or other natural sources.

TRAIL DESCRIPTIONS: The full circuit, as well as the South Loop individually, may be walked either clockwise or counterclockwise. Formula times for all segments are almost the same in either direction because there is so little elevation change on the trail. *In 1914, some elderly Arapahos were brought to the park and asked to remember from their childhood names for various features of the landscape. They called this valley* Cowoonache, *meaning "coyote."*

Entire circuit (clockwise):

1) From the picnic area, head into the woods to find the trail, turn left (south) on the Valley Trail, and walk for about 24 min. to a trail

junction. Along the way, the route will curve to the west. In early morning or late afternoon, if you look through the trees to your left, you may catch glimpses of Elk in the meadows. During the heat of the day, they may move into the shade of the woods, so stay alert.

2) From the trail junction, turn right and walk north on the River Trail along the North Fork of the Colorado River for about 24 min. to the junction with the connecting trail that runs east, dividing the north and south loops. The entire River Trail is supposed to be part of the Continental Divide National Scenic Trail (NST), but when we walked it in 2002, we could find no NST signs.

3) From the connecting trail, continue north for about 46 min., at first following along the river, then veering away from it to pass the marshes of Onahu Creek, and finally bearing sharply right before reaching a trail junction near the highway.

4) At the trail junction, turn right and walk south for about 39 min., paralleling the highway, to the connecting trail dividing the North and South Loops.

5) Continue south for another 12 min. to the Harbison Picnic Area.

Counterclockwise: (5) From the Harbison Picnic Area head into the woods to find the trail, turn right (north) on the Valley Trail, and walk for about 12 min. to a junction with the connecting trail; **(4)** continue north for 43 min. to another trail junction, with the River Trail, which is part of the Continental Divide National Scenic Trail; **(3)** go left, heading first a little northwesterly, then turning south, passing the Powerline Trail leaving left, and in 42 min. arrive at a junction with the connecting trail; **(2)** continue south on the River Trail for 24 min., reaching a junction with the Valley Trail; **(1)** go left on the Valley Trail and walk 24 min. back to the Harbison Picnic Area.

South Kawuneeche Loop (clockwise): Follow steps **(1)** and **(2)** in the preceding description. Then, **(2a)** turn right (east) on the connecting trail and walk 9 min. to the trail junction. From there return as in **(5)**.

Counterclockwise: (5) From the Harbison Picnic Area head into the woods to find the trail, turn right (north) on the Valley Trail, and walk for about 12 min. to a junction with the connecting trail; **(2a)** turn left and walk 9 min. to the junction with the River Trail; **(2)** turn left and walk south on the River Trail for 24 min., reaching a junction with the Valley Trail; **(1)** go left on the Valley Trail and walk 24 min. back to the Harbison Picnic Area.

The Colorado River along the Kawuneeche Valley Loops.

OUR HIKING NOTES: The formula time for the entire circuit is 2 hr., 25 min.; our walking time in mid-August with small children was 2 hr., 8 min., including stops to enjoy flowers.

Habitats traversed: Ponderosa Pine parkland, Lodgepole Pine stands, river bottomlands (North Fork of the Colorado River), and creek marsh (Onahu Creek). **Wildflowers noted:** A fleabane, a goldenrod, Common Dandelion, Salsify, some pussytoes, Mountain Harebell, Yellow Stonecrop, a lupine, White Clover, a gentian, Sulphurflower, and a nonshrubby cinquefoil. **Other plants and fungi found:** Common Juniper and Shrubby Cinquefoil (shrubs); Mushrooms galore.

Birds seen or heard: Belted Kingfisher, Northern Flicker, flycatcher *(Empidonax)*, Gray Jay, Steller's Jay, American Crow, Mountain Chickadee, Ruby-crowned Kinglet, Mountain Bluebird (in meadow by the picnic area), Chipping Sparrow, White-crowned Sparrow, and Dark-eyed Junco. **Mammals encountered:** Red Squirrel, Least Chipmunk, and Golden-mantled Ground Squirrel.

Green Mountain

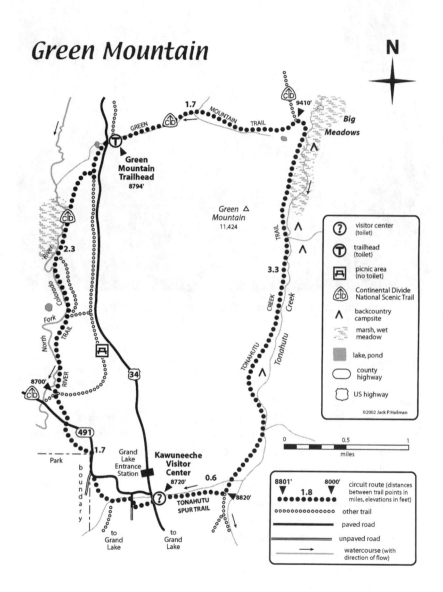

N

Big
Meadows

1.7

GREEN
MOUNTAIN TRAIL

9410'

Green
Mountain
Trailhead
8794'

Green △
Mountain
11,424

2.3

River

Colorado

North Fork

RIVER TRAIL

TRAIL

3.3

TONAHUTU

CREEK

Tonahutu

Creek

8700'

34

491

1.7

Park
boundary

Grand
Lake
Entrance
Station

Kawuneeche
Visitor
Center
8720'

0.6

TONAHUTU
SPUR TRAIL

8820'

to
Grand
Lake

to
Grand
Lake

?	visitor center (toilet)
T	trailhead (toilet)
🚻	picnic area (no toilet)
CD	Continental Divide National Scenic Trail
∧	backcountry campsite
	marsh, wet meadow
	lake, pond
	county highway
	US highway

©2002 Jack P. Hailman

0   0.5   1
miles

8801'   8000'
▼   1.8   ▼   circuit route (distances between trail points in miles, elevations in feet)
∘∘∘∘∘∘∘∘∘∘∘∘∘   other trail
━━━━━━   paved road
══════   unpaved road
→   watercourse (with direction of flow)

GREEN MOUNTAIN CIRCUIT

FORMULA TIME: 5 hours, 31 minutes

HIKING ELEVATIONS: 8700 to 9410 feet.

EXERTION RATING: 16.1 (moderate).

FEATURES: Largest montane meadow in the park, marshes of the North Fork of the Colorado River.

ACCESS POINTS: Kawuneeche Visitor Center or Green Mountain Trailhead (West Side of the park).

SEASONS: Year-round, but the best times are early fall when the foliage is colorful and late spring when the wildflowers bloom. Big Meadows itself is a particularly nice area for winter cross-country skiing and snowshoeing.

SUMMARY:

Route	Distance (mi.)	Total Elevation Gain (ft.)	Time (hr.:min.)	Exertion Rating
Circuit	9.6	710	5:31	16.1

FINDING THE ACCESS POINTS: Both access points are on US 34 north of Grand Lake Village. The Kawuneeche Visitor Center is 0.3 mi. south of the Grand Lake Entrance Station; the Green Mountain Trailhead is 2.7 mi. north of the entrance station. For those driving from the park's eastern side, access points are 20.7 and 17.7 mi. southwest, respectively, from the Alpine Visitor Center on Trail Ridge Road. Both access points have **toilets,** but there is drinking **water** only at the visitor center. Remember to treat or filter any water you take from natural sources.

TRAIL DESCRIPTION (clockwise from Kawuneeche Visitor Center): The circuit can be walked in either direction from either access point. We describe it clockwise from the Kawuneeche Visitor Center because this routing lets you get the least scenic and somewhat tricky part over with first. From the Colorado River to Big Meadows, the circuit route follows the Continental Divide National Scenic Trail.

1) The beginning of this circuit can be tricky in places, so pay attention to the instructions and the map. From the center of the parking lot for the Kawuneeche Visitor Center, walk west through the trees and cross US 34 to find the trail into the woods. A few feet before you encounter the first road, the trail turns sharply right over a hill and across a small wet area before crossing this road. It is easier to leave the trail briefly, walk to the road (which is just at the point where the pavement ends), turn right onto the paved portion, and walk about 100 ft. to meet up with the trail crossing. On the other side of the road, the trail runs north of the maintenance buildings. Eventually, it leads out onto the county road, which you will have to follow north for a few minutes until the trail leaves left into the Lodgepole Pines. (The county road was formerly unpaved so met our criterion that hikers never have to walk a paved road; now it's the short exception to our rule.) Several minutes later, the trail again emerges from the woods, crosses the county road obliquely, and briefly follows along a rustic log fence. Finally, about 51 min. after leaving the visitor center, arrive at the junction with the River Trail.

2) Go straight at the trail junction and walk 1 hr., 15 min., first heading north along the North Fork of the Colorado River, then drifting northeast toward US 34, hugging the edge of the highway before crossing it and arriving at the Green Mountain Trailhead. On this scenic leg, beware of dead-end fishing trails leading down along the river's edge. Also, pass the junction where the Powerline Trail leaves the River Trail before later rejoining it. Eventually pass the remains of an old log cabin, then some modern cabins very much in use, and continue between the stables and the road. At the stables, look for mules—an increasingly rare beast in the United States. Cross a dirt road by an attractive little cabin and eventually emerge on the highway about 50 ft. south of the Green Mountain Trailhead on the other side of the road.

3) From the Green Mountain Trailhead, walk uphill (east) for 1 hr., 28 min., following a creek (expect mosquitoes) most of the way to **Big Meadows,** where you will arrive at a trail junction. When you reach higher ground near the end of this leg, keep an eye out to your right, where there are small meadows that may contain Moose. The trail junction is the high point of the circuit.

4) At the junction, go right (south) on the Tonahutu Creek Trail, following the creek downhill for 1 hr., 39 min. to a trail junction. On this pleasant leg of the circuit, the route passes just west of Big Meadows and the narrow, intermittent meadows at its southern end. *The Arapahos brought here in 1914 said that* Tonahutu *(pronounced Toe-na-HU-tu) means "big meadow."*

5) At the trail junction—the first you will come to after leaving Big Meadows—go right for 18 min. on the Tonahutu Spur Trail to return to the Kawuneeche Visitor Center.

Counterclockwise walking time is the same overall, but individual segments differ from the clockwise circuit because the elevation gains are in different places. From the Kawuneeche Visitor Center counterclockwise: **(5)** walk east 24 min. on the Tonahutu Spur Trail to the trail junction; **(4)** turn left onto the Tonahutu Creek Trail and walk a whopping 2 hr., 14 min., following Tonahutu Creek north uphill to the trail junction west of Big Meadows; **(3)** go left on the Green Mountain Trail and descend 51 min. to the Green Mountain Trailhead; **(2)** cross US 34 and walk south for 1 hr., 9 minutes, bearing right at the first fork in the trail, following along the North Fork of the Colorado River, and passing two additional trail junctions before arriving at a third; and finally **(1)** continue south and east 52 min. back to the Kawuneeche Visitor Center.

From the Green Mountain Trailhead: clockwise, segments are done in the following order—3, 4, 5, 1, and 2; counterclockwise, the order is 2, 1, 5, 4 and 3.

OUR HIKING NOTES: The formula time for this hike is 5 hr., 31 min.; we walked it easily in early August in 4 hr., 54 min.

Habitats traversed: This is among the most varied circuits hiked in well less than a full day, going as it does through Lodgepole pinewoods, by riparian habitat and along extensive marsh, up through mixed coniferous woods, and opening into high meadow. **Wildflowers noted:** A white daisy (*Erigeron*), Aspen Daisy, Cow Parsnip (past its peak), Heartleaf Arnica, Yarrow, Mountain Harebell, Red Clover, White Clover, Pinedrops, Yellow Pondlily, and Common Fireweed. **Other plants and fungi found:** Common Juniper and Shrubby Cinquefoil (shrubs), a raspberry just in berry, and mushrooms.

Birds seen or heard: Osprey, Broad-tailed Hummingbird, Northern Flicker, Gray Jay, Steller's Jay, American Crow, Cliff Swallow, Mountain Chickadee, Ruby-crowned Kinglet, Chipping Sparrow, and Dark-eyed Junco. **Mammals encountered:** Red Squirrel.

Continental Divide

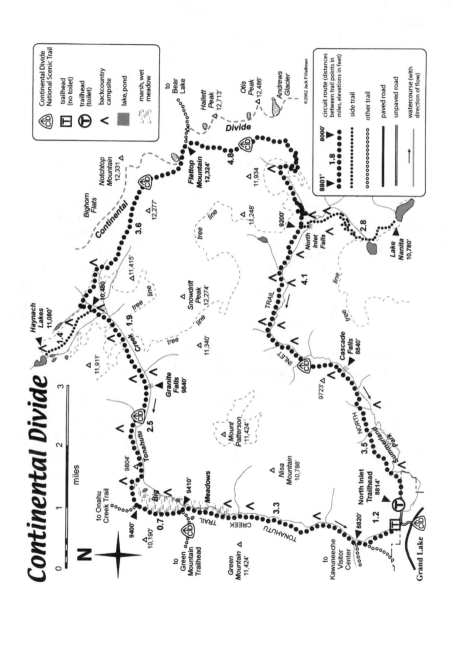

CONTINENTAL DIVIDE CIRCUIT

FORMULA TIMES: 16 hours, 19 minutes for the circuit; 22 hours, 42 minutes including both side trips.

HIKING ELEVATIONS: 8814 to 12,324 feet.

EXERTION RATINGS: 51.1 (off the scale) to 70.7 (off the scale) with both side trips. These exertion ratings would be for a continuous day hike, but as this is too long a circuit to be done in one day, the ratings have limited planning usefulness.

FEATURES: This is the only circuit in the park that follows along the Continental Divide National Scenic Trail for a substantial distance. It is also the longest circuit in the park and the one with the most mileage above tree line. On the west, the route runs the entire length of Big Meadows, the largest alpine meadow in Rocky Mountain National Park. The trail also passes both Granite Falls and Cascade Falls. From almost any perspective, this circuit is a premier backpacking adventure.

ACCESS POINT: North Inlet Trailhead near the village of Grand Lake.

SEASONS: Unless you are an experienced winter backpacker, we recommend sticking to summer trips. The elevations are extremely high, especially in the middle section of the hike; dangerous storms can threaten even in summer; and you are farther from help in an emergency than on any other circuit in this book.

SUMMARY:

Route	Distance (mi.)	Total Elevation Gain (ft.)	Time (hr.:min.)	Exertion Rating
Circuit	25.6	3520	16:19	51.1
Roundtrip to Haynach Lakes	2.8	600	2:00	6.3
Roundtrip to Lake Nanita	5.6	1580	4:23	13.3
Totals	34.0	5700	22:42	70.7

FINDING THE ACCESS POINT: From Kawuneeche Visitor Center, drive 1.4 mi. south on US 34 to Grand Lake Village. Turn left (before the Conoco Station) into Grand Lake Village and drive 0.3 mi., passing stables on the right, to a fork in the road, where you will see the Mountain Food Market on the right. Take the left fork and go 0.8 mi. on the paved road, which is West Portal Road. Turn left and head uphill on the uninviting, unpaved, Grand County Road 633 for 0.3 mi. The road turns right at the Tonahutu Trailhead (no parking here), descends to cross a river, then ascends to the lower North Inlet Trailhead parking lot, which has **toilets** on the left. There is also an upper parking lot, larger than the one by the trailhead itself. There is **no drinking water** at either trailhead. Remember to treat or filter all water you take from natural sources.

TRAIL DESCRIPTION (clockwise from North Inlet Trailhead): We recommend a clockwise circuit in order to avoid lugging full backpacks on a punishing climb (3000 ft. in elevation gain) up switchbacks along the southeastern part of the loop. The clockwise route spreads out the elevation gain more evenly, and your backpacks will be lighter when you descend the switchbacks because you will have eaten much of your food. This circuit is a minimum three-day backpacking trip, with the middle day spent crossing the tundra.

1) From the North Inlet Trailhead, walk back along the unpaved road to the Tonahutu Trailhead and take the Tonahutu Creek Trail north to the second trail junction, which you will reach in about 36 min. (At the first junction, a trail leaves left to the Grand Lake Lodge beyond the park boundary. At the second junction, a trail leaves left to the Kawuneeche Visitor Center 0.6 mi. away.)

2) At the junction, continue straight (north) for 2 hr., 14 min., slowly gaining altitude as you follow Tonahutu Creek upstream. The Lodgepole Pine woods eventually open out into **Big Meadows,** the largest montane meadow in RMNP. *Meadows of various types originate in various ways. Here, the relatively flat land allows Tonahutu Creek to create a wet area as it meanders and sometimes floods. The slow-moving water deposits fine-grained silt, and the wet soil does not support forest. Herbs and shrubs move in, providing spectacular displays of wildflowers, especially in late spring.* Reach a junction with the trail leaving left down to the Green Mountain Trailhead.

3) Walk for just 21 min. to the next trail junction, with expansive meadows off to the right. Here, our circuit joins the **Continental Divide National Scenic Trail** and remains with it for the duration of the hike. *The National Trails System Act of 1968 spurred development of national scenic trails with federal support. The Continental Divide NST is one of eight, the first and most famous being the Appalachian Trail. The Continental Divide Trail was designated a national scenic trail on November 10, 1976. When completed, it will be approximately 3260 mi. long, running through Montana, Idaho, Wyoming, Colorado, and New Mexico.* The trail leaving left goes to Onahu Creek.

4) Bear right at the trail junction. The circuit now heads east for 1 hr., 41 min., skirting the north end of Big Meadows on the way to **Granite**

Falls. Shortly after passing Big Meadows, the trail runs through a narrow stretch between the creek and a wooded hill to the north.

5) From Granite Falls, continue for another 1 hr., 35 min. to the junction with the trail leaving left for Haynach Lakes. Notice that on this stretch the forest has begun thinning out and the trees are smaller. **Note:** We recommend getting a permit for a campsite in this vicinity; that way, you can begin your tundra crossing early the following morning.

5a) The faint trail to **Haynach Lakes** takes you on a relatively easy, though often wet, two-hour roundtrip to the base of the largest lake. Taking some additional time to climb the steep slope and see the lake, perhaps snapping a great photo with Nakai Peak in the distance, is worth considering. Fly fishers note: there are supposed to be fish in these high lakes, perhaps originally stocked with hatchery fry dropped from a low-flying airplane. Yes, this is how fish made their way into many montane lakes in the western United States. *In 1914, some elderly Arapahos brought to the park were asked to remember from their childhood the names for local landscape features. They explained that their word for lakes on the tundra was "HAA-nach," meaning "snow water."*

---

6) Now begin the first part of a long hike across the tundra, ascending for 3 hr., 39 min. until you reach the trail junction at **Flattop Mountain.** Get a very early start so that you can cross the 7 or so mi. in the open before afternoon thunderstorms form. Once up on the open tundra, watch for alpine birds and mammals such as Brown-capped Rosy Finches, Water Pipits, White-tailed Ptarmigans, Bighorn Sheep, American Pikas, and Yellow-bellied Marmots. The trail leaving left goes down to Bear Lake, a bail-out possibility if you are caught in severe weather.

7) Continue 2 hr., 24 min. to a junction with the trail leaving left for Lake Nanita. Along the way, cross another long stretch of tundra before reaching tree line and descending a whopping 3000 ft. on two sets of switchbacks to arrive at the trail junction. It might be a good idea to plan on camping in one of the backcountry sites in this area.

7a) Having just descended 3000 ft. in elevation, only gluttons for punishment will now want to climb 1500 ft. to **Lake Nanita,** but many other hikers will probably want to walk the 0.3-mi. roundtrip on the side trail to visit the **North Inlet Falls.** The formula time for a roundtrip to Lake Nanita is a whopping 4 hr., 23 min. and it is not an easy hike, but it may be attractive for photographers and fly fishers. Nanita *(pronounced NA-ni-ta) is a Native American word whose language of origin remains in dispute between two possibilities.*

---

8) For the next 2 hr., 3 min., enjoy an easy downhill walk to pleasant **Cascade Falls**. It's not a very precipitous waterfall, but it makes a nice photo if you're willing to hop out on some rocks below the falls.

9) It is now just 1 hr., 45 min. to the North Inlet Trailhead. Keep an eye out to your left, watching the areas by the creek for Moose, as they seem especially numerous here. The open area of **Summerland Park** (with a nearby private cabin) is a good place to find birds. From here on, the route follows an old road, soon skirting the park boundary before reaching the trailhead.

Counterclockwise walking time is the same overall, but individual segments differ from the clockwise circuit because the elevation gains are in different places. From the North Inlet Trailhead **(9)** walk northeast 1 hr., 47 min. to Cascade Falls, then **(8)** ascend 2 hr., 25 min. to the trail junction near North Inlet Falls. Camping at one of the backcountry sites in this area will allow you to get an early start on your climb to the tundra the following morning. The next leg **(7)** involves a punishing climb gaining 3000 ft. in elevation on two sets of switchbacks before breaking out onto open tundra. The formula time to the trail junction at Flattop Mountain is a whopping 5 hr., 31 min. From the trail junction on the tundra **(6)** walk 1 hr., 48 min. to the junction with the trail going to Haynach Lakes; **(5)** descend 57 min. to Granite Falls; **(4)** continue west 1 hr., 15 min. to the next junction; **(3)** bear left and walk 22 min. to the Green Mountain Trail; **(2)** continue south 1 hr., 39 min. along the creek to the junction with the trail to the visitor center; **(1)** bear left, and left again at the next trail junction, walking a total of 36 min. back to the trailhead.

OUR HIKING NOTES: This circuit is on our list for the next backpacking trip in the park, but we have walked parts of it on three different trips in early August.

Habitats traversed: You name it, and this circuit passes through it. From humdrum Lodgepole Pine forests through riparian habitats, wet meadow, montane lakes, subalpine coniferous forest, and open tundra, this circuit showcases most of the habitats found in Rocky Mountain National Park, all on a single (if long) trip. **Wildflowers noted:** A white daisy *(Erigeron)*, Aspen Daisy, Common Dandelion, Cow Parsnip, Heartleaf Arnica, Yarrow, Mountain Harebell, Red Clover, White Clover, Pinedrops, and Common Fireweed. **Other plants found:** Common Juniper, Bush-cranberry, and Shrubby Cinquefoil (shrubs); a raspberry in fruit.

Cascade Falls is one of several waterfalls on the Continental Divide Circuit.

Birds seen or heard: Broad-tailed Hummingbird, Northern Flicker, a flycatcher, Gray Jay, Steller's Jay, American Crow, Violet-green Swallow, Mountain Chickadee, Red-breasted Nuthatch, American Robin, and a female tanager. **Mammals encountered:** A chipmunk species, Golden-mantled Ground Squirrel, Red Squirrel, Mule Deer, and Moose.

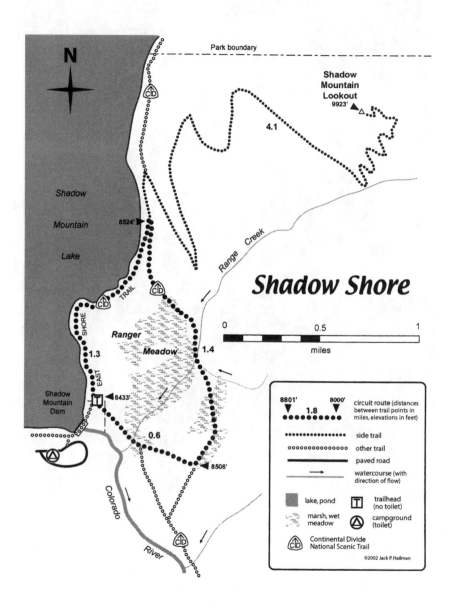

Shadow Shore

Park boundary

Shadow Mountain Lookout
9923'

4.1

Shadow

Mountain

Lake

8524'

Range Creek

TRAIL

SHORE

Ranger
Meadow

EAST

1.3

1.4

Shadow
Mountain
Dam

8433'

0.6

8506'

Colorado

River

0   0.5   1

miles

8801'   8000'
1.8
circuit route (distances
between trail points in
miles, elevations in feet)

side trail

other trail

paved road

watercourse (with
direction of flow)

lake, pond

marsh, wet
meadow

trailhead
(no toilet)

campground
(toilet)

Continental Divide
National Scenic Trail

©2002 Jack P. Hailman

SHADOW SHORE CIRCUIT

FORMULA TIMES: 1 hour, 44 minutes for the circuit; 5 hours, 56 minutes with the optional climb to Shadow Mountain Lookout.

HIKING ELEVATIONS: 8400 to 8524 feet, to 9923 feet on the side trip.

EXERTION RATINGS: 4.9 (very easy) for the circuit, to 21.1 (moderately strenuous) with the side trip.

FEATURES: This is the only trail in the park to run alongside a large body of water, in this case Shadow Mountain Lake. The inland portion passes through the extensive Ranger Meadow, and both lakeside and inland trails are alternative arms of the Continental Divide National Scenic Trail.

ACCESS POINT: East Shore Trailhead, reached through Arapaho National Recreation Area of the U.S. Forest Service (the trail itself is entirely within Rocky Mountain National Park).

SEASONS: Summer is pleasant, but fall and spring are wonderful. The views of the lake, bright fall foliage in the crisp air, copious spring wildflowers, and good wildlife viewing in Ranger Meadow make this relatively little-known circuit a special place. Even the snows do not get deep enough to hinder activity until midwinter.

SUMMARY:

Route	Distance (mi.)	Total Elevation Gain (ft.)	Time (hr.:min.)	Exertion Rating
Circuit	3.3	91	1:44	4.9
Roundtrip to Shadow Mt. Lookout	8.2	1399	4:12	16.2
Totals	11.5	1490	5:56	21.1

FINDING THE ACCESS POINT: From Grand Lake Entrance Station, drive 4.5 mi. (or from Grand Lake Village drive 2.8 mi.) south on US 34 to the entrance road for Arapaho National Recreation Area (ANRA) on the left. The road is signed on the highway as Grand County Road 66. Turn left (east) and drive 1.1 mi., passing a maintenance area and then a picnic area (both to your left) before crossing a canal and arriving at the access road that goes left to the boat launch area and fee station. If you hold the Golden Age or Golden Access passport or already have a use permit for ANRA, display the passport or permit on your dashboard and keep driving another 0.3 mi. to the campground entrance road. (Otherwise, turn left into the boat launch area and drive down to the waterfront. The fee station is to the right of the boat ramp, near the toilet building. Purchase

The Shadow Shore Circuit passes through lovely Ranger Meadow.

a permit, display it on your dashboard, return to the road, and drive 0.3 mi. farther to the campground access road.) Turn left onto the campground access road, pass the campground fee station on the right, and turn right on the first road, which leads to campsites 41 through 70.

Continue past the campsites to an open area for angler parking below the Shadow Mountain Dam; there are **outhouses** here and flush **toilets** in the campground. Drinking **water** is available at the campground. Park and lock your vehicle, then climb the path to the dike on the west side of the spillway complex. Walk right (northeast) across the spillway complex to the end of the dike, where Rocky Mountain National Park begins and the East Shore Trailhead sign is evident.

TRAIL DESCRIPTION (clockwise): This circuit could be walked in either direction. Those taking the optional side trip to Shadow Mountain Lookout may prefer clockwise in order to do the climb early in the day. The formula time, especially for the middle leg, may be a little short because it does not take into account the minor ups and downs in the Ranger Meadow area.

1) From the East Shore Trailhead, walk north for about 44 min. along the shore of **Shadow Mountain Lake.** This is the only section of trail in this book that follows the shore of a large lake. Obviously, this lake is a man-made reservoir, as is Lake Granby farther downriver on the Colorado. *Grand Lake (the smaller lake to the north), however, is naturally dammed by the terminal moraine of the huge montane glacier that scoured out the Kawuneeche Valley. Water levels in Shadow Mountain Lake are kept high enough so that water can be pumped into the Alva B. Adams Tunnel at West Portal, which runs under the park and hence under the Continental Divide to East Portal (see the Wind River Circuit). If levels are low, water is pumped back up into Shadow Mountain Lake from Lake Granby, allowing the Colorado River to continue flowing below Shadow Mountain Dam.*

2) At the trail junction, turn sharp right, effectively reversing direction, and walk for 42 min., passing through lovely **Ranger Meadow,** which is watered by Range Creek. *Why the meadow ends in "r" and the creek does not is a question we were unable to answer. The origin of these names is apparently unknown, though we might hazard a guess that the meadow was a place to range cattle.*

2a) Before taking the pleasant walk through the meadow, you may wish to climb to **Shadow Mountain Lookout** for the spectacular view. The hike gains nearly 1500 ft. in elevation and is 8.2 mi. roundtrip, with a formula time of 3 hr., 11 min.—admittedly a significant detour. The view, however, is worth the trip. Continue north along the lakeside and bear sharp right at the junction with the trail to Shadow Mountain Lookout.

---

3) At the trail junction, go right. The sign at the junction reads 8.9 mi. to Grand Lake back to the way we came, and 4.1 mi. straight ahead to Columbine Creek (the route also signed for the Continental Divide National Scenic Trail). The trail you take to the right is signed to East Shore Trail and Shadow Mountain Dam. In 18 min. return to the trailhead, passing over Range Creek on an unusual causeway: gravel built up on logs. For a slightly longer hike, instead of turning right at the junction, continue about 6 min. farther down the trail to meet the trail that runs alongside the Colorado River. Turn right and walk for 23 min. back to the trailhead. This optional extension lengthens the circuit by only 0.4 mi. (14 min. of walking time), and raises the exertion rating from 4.9 to 5.6.

Counterclockwise walking time is the same overall, but individual segments differ from the clockwise circuit because the elevation gains are in different places. From the trailhead **(3)** turn right and walk for 22 min., bearing left at the junction where the trail following alongside the river departs; **(2)** when you come to the second trail junction, turn left and walk north through Ranger Meadow for 43 min.; and finally **(1)** head south on the East Shore Trail for 39 min. The optional side trip is the same as in the main description.

OUR HIKING NOTES: The formula time for the circuit is 1 hr., 44 min.; we took 1 hr., 25 min. in early August, stopping often to identify birds and photograph flowers.

Habitats traversed: Lakeshore, as well as Lodgepole woods, a few aspen groves, a beautiful meadow, and some riparian habitat. **Wildflowers noted:** Brown and green grasses, a blue gentianlike monocot, a bunchy yellow composite, a rabbitbrush, a ragwort, Aspen Daisy, Bigelow Groundsel, Common Dandelion, Cow Parsnip, a dandelion-like flower, False Dandelion, Salsify, Wild Chamomile, Yarrow, Mountain Harebell, a lupine, Blue Flax, Pinedrops, Common Fireweed, and Western Scarlet Gilia. **Other plants found:** A horsetail or scouring rush (primitive plant related to ferns); Common Juniper, Mountain Sagebrush, and Shrubby Cinquefoil (shrubs).

Birds seen or heard: Canada Goose, Mallard, Osprey, Swainson's Hawk, Spotted Sandpiper, Broad-tailed Hummingbird, Hairy Woodpecker, Northern Flicker, Olive-sided Flycatcher, Say's Phoebe, Gray Jay, Mountain Chickadee, American Robin, a warbler, Chipping Sparrow, and Dark-eyed Junco. **Mammals encountered:** Golden-mantled Ground Squirrel and Red Squirrel.

Shadow Mountain Lake seen from the Shadow Shore Circuit.

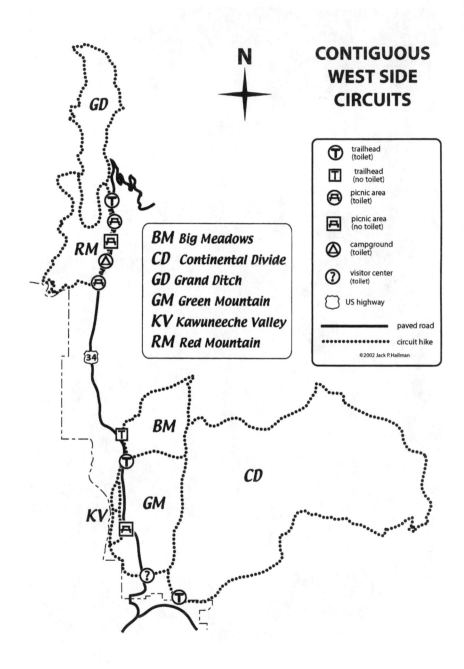

N

CONTIGUOUS
WEST SIDE
CIRCUITS

BM *Big Meadows*
CD *Continental Divide*
GD *Grand Ditch*
GM *Green Mountain*
KV *Kawuneeche Valley*
RM *Red Mountain*

GD

RM

34

BM

CD

GM

KV

trailhead
(toilet)

trailhead
(no toilet)

picnic area
(toilet)

picnic area
(no toilet)

campground
(toilet)

visitor center
(toilet)

US highway

paved road

circuit hike

©2002 Jack P. Hailman

COMBINING WEST SIDE CIRCUITS

Because there are relatively few circuits on the West Side, there are few opportunities to combine them. As the accompanying map shows, Grand Ditch and Red Mountain could be combined although the extended circuit is too long for a day hike so best done as a backpacking trip. Big Meadows and Green Mountain could be combined into a longer circuit that is feasible as a day hike. The Green Mountain Circuit already incorporates half of the Kawuneeche Valley Loops and therefore could not be combined for a longer circuit. Finally, the imposing Continental Divide Circuit shares trail segments with both the Big Meadows and Green Mountain Circuits, but it seems unlikely that you'd want to add one (or both) of these relatively short day hikes onto what is already a multiday backpacking trip.

Natural History Appendix

THE MOUNTAINS

The mountains determine everything else about natural history in Rocky Mountain National Park. They decide where creeks and rivers will flow, and where lakes will form. They decide, with a little help from man, where the roads and trails shall be placed. They decide by altitude and orientation of slopes which plants shall grow where. And they decide by altitude, topography and plant life where different species of animals shall live.

The mountains are new, the rocks that compose them ancient, and the glaciers that carved them recently deceased. That is a fair summary of the history of the Rocky Mountains in geological time. The rocks that form the core of mountains in the park are among the oldest anywhere on the continent, being of preCambrian origin some 1.5–2.5 *billion* years ago. Yet the mountains pushed up from these rocks began forming only about 65 million years ago, so consequently are among the youngest large mountains anywhere in the world. Within the last million years, the Northern Hemisphere has cycled through temperature extremes that brought repeated glaciations that carved the mountains. The human species had already immigrated to North America over the Bering land bridge and inhabited what is now Colorado when the last major episode of glaciation ended approximately 10,000 years ago.

The ancient rocks are igneous granites and metamorphic gneisses and schists—all containing embedded crystals of wonderful colors. Admire these beautiful works of nature on your hikes, but don't ask us how to tell them all apart. There are also pockets of nearly pure white **quartz** in the park, some of which can be seen on hikes in this book. The **granites** cooled to crystalline form from molten rock within the earth. The **gneisses**

and **schists** may have been laid down as sedimentary rocks, and were certainly later crystallized by metamorphism—which is to say, extremely high temperatures and pressures that transformed the rocks without actually melting them. The crystals in these rocks are large enough to see without a lens, but the crystals of quartz are so microscopic than not even a hand lens will resolve them.

The mountain-building episode that created the modern Rockies at the beginning of the Cenozoic era is called the **Laramide Orogeny**, after Laramie, Wyoming, to the northwest of Rocky Mountain National Park. There were previous mountains on this site, the so-called Ancestral Rockies that originated in the Pennsylvanian period some 300 million years ago. But they all eroded away long ago and are in no reasonable sense ancestors of today's mountains. Details of how the modern Rockies formed are still under intense study by geologists, but the general picture is clear enough. The earth's skin is composed of great "floating" plates, over which the oceans lie and on which the continents sit. About 65 million years ago the Pacific plate pushed eastward into the North American plate, diving under it at a shallow angle and creating great pressures eastward and upward. Younger rocks overlying the preCambrian granites, geneisses and schists were tilted and crumpled on the east, and you can see these dramatically up tilted, younger rocks as you drive between Estes Park and Loveland through the Big Thompson Canyon east of Rocky Mountain National Park.

Erosion and uplifts preceded glaciation in the new Rockies, as Mother Nature always begins tearing down mountains as soon as she builds them—and she had nearly 65 million years to work with before the Pleistocene glaciations. During those 65 million years, there were smaller uplifts and volcanic action to offset somewhat the erosion by water and wind that was tearing down the Rockies. Then about 1.5 million years ago the glaciations began.

Four periods of glaciation have been identified in Rocky Mountain National Park. The **earliest** involved two advances of ice from the highest and coldest land down toward lower altitudes, beginning about 1.5 million years ago. The second period, called the two **Bull Lake** glaciations, occurred about 500,000 and 80,000 years ago. Correlated with the time of the great Wisconsinan continental ice sheet, the **Pinedale** montane glaciations of the park reached maximum extent about 15,000 years ago. The last major Pleistocene glaciers disappeared by about 7500 years ago during a warm period for some 5000 years, which was finally interrupted by **neoglaciation** ("the little ice age") that began 3800 years ago. This minor glaciation event included two advances and retreats in what is now Rocky Mountain National Park.

Glacially eroded features impart dramatic scenery to the park. When an ice stream moves down a river valley, it straightens, widens and deepens the feature, resulting in a **U-shaped valley**. Unglaciated valleys are V-shaped. Tributary ice streams do not erode as quickly as those into which they flow, so can leave **hanging valleys**, in which lakes tend to form and then overflow the cliff edge as waterfalls. Ice plucks the face from peaks, creating amphitheater-shaped hollows known as **cirques**. If a lake forms in the floor of a cirque, especially if it is fed from a glacier, it is called a **tarn**. When the ice plucks both sides of a mountain, it leaves a sharp ridge known as an **arête**, and when plucking a mountain from several sides leaves a jagged peak called a **horn**.

Depositional features are also prominent results of glaciation. An ice tongue bulldozes rocks and debris—under it, along its sides and at the extending end. When the ice melts down (retreats), it thus leaves rounded hills along its sides, the **lateral moraines**. Moraine Park, near the Beaver Meadows Entrance Station, lies between two such east-west lateral moraines. The debris pile left at the end of the glacier is simply an **end moraine**, as near the Beaver Meadows Entrance Station and Aspenglen Campground.

BIOTIC ASSOCIATIONS

The broadest geographic associations among plants and consequently the animals that depend upon them are called **biomes**. The Colorado Rockies are part of the great **Coniferous Forest** biome of North America, which includes most of Canada as well as the high country of the American west. Here altitude plays a major role in determining which plants will grow where.

A pioneering ecologist of the nineteenth century, A. Hart Merriam, recognized that in the Arizona mountains plants (and the animals that depend upon them) tended to occur at specific elevations. Each species had its own altitudinal belt on the mountainside, and although these belts overlapped, there was also a distinct tendency toward typical biotic associations. He called these associations **life zones** and named them (from the Sonoran desert upward) Lower Sonoran, Upper Sonoran, Transition, Canadian, Hudsonian, and Alpine.

ALTITUDINAL LIFE ZONES

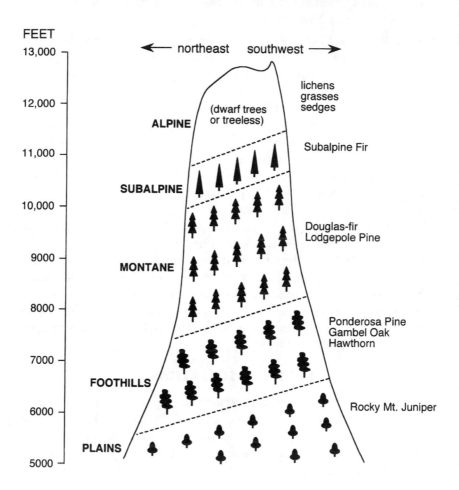

FEET

← northeast   southwest →

13,000 —

12,000 —

11,000 —

10,000 —

9000 —

8000 —

7000 —

6000 —

5000 —

ALPINE (dwarf trees or treeless)

lichens grasses sedges

Subalpine Fir

SUBALPINE

Douglas-fir Lodgepole Pine

MONTANE

Ponderosa Pine Gambel Oak Hawthorn

FOOTHILLS

Rocky Mt. Juniper

PLAINS

Similar zones occur in all mountain ranges of western North America, although the species composing the zones differ somewhat geographically. Despite the differences, the zones were found to be similar in composition. For example, the trees growing at highest elevations tended always to be spruces and firs, regardless of species. Merriam's Lower Sonoran zone does not occur in Colorado, but the others do and can be given names more evocative of their elevation: Plains, Foothills, Montane, Subalpine, and Alpine.

Elevations of the life zones differ, even on one mountain. Plants on the southwest slopes take advantage of the warming sun and grow to higher elevations than those on northeast slopes. Local conditions also help dictate what plants occur; factors such as sheltered ravines, reliable summer water, and good soil promote species that would ordinarily occur only at lower elevations. So life zones are not sharply delineated and immutable, but they are a useful first approximation to understanding ecological associations.

The traveler can see the vegetation change with loss or gain of altitude. **Plains** plants occur at low elevations, as around Loveland east of the park, where Rocky Mountain Juniper is an indicator species. **Foothill** vegetation is characterized by Ponderosa Pine, as around Estes Park and many places on the east side of Rocky Mountain National Park. Douglas-fir is an indicator species for the **Montane** zone, typical of the coniferous forest in the area of Glacier Gorge Junction and Bear Lake. Most of the hikes in this book are within the Montane zone. Above 10,000 feet, watch for Subalpine Fir as an indicator species for the **Subalpine** zone. The treeless tundra of the **Alpine** zone is most easily viewed along Trail Ridge Road.

Ecosystems and communities are terms ecologists use for smaller, habitat-specific biotic associations. Within an altitudinal life zone there may be several such associations that depend upon the topography, soil, drainage, and so on. Many ecosystems can be found in Rocky Mountain National Park.

Riparian ecosystems occur along rivers (hence the term "riparian"), creeks, and edges of lakes. Moraine Park, along the Big Thompson River, is a typical riparian area. The indicator trees are willows, birches, and Thinleaf Alder. Here the hiker may encounter Shrubby Cinquefoil, chiming-bells, Cow Parsnip, dragonflies, American Dipper, Song Sparrow, and Wilson's Warbler among many other plants and animals.

Meadows, and their associated shrub lands on drier ground, occur in moist places fed by creeks. Upper Beaver Meadows is a typical example. There are no trees, by definition, but woody indicator plants include Shrubby Cinquefoil and shrubs such as sagebrush. The hiker will see the most wildflowers in such areas, including things such as Golden Banner, Black-eyed-susan, loco, Common Dandelion, Blanketflower, and Sulphurflower. Birds are usually abundant; watch for such species as Mountain Bluebird and Savannah Sparrow. This is the habitat for Elk, and other mammals you are likely to encounter include chipmunk, Golden-mantled Ground Squirrel, and Wyoming Ground Squirrel.

Ponderosa parks occur on sunny slopes, usually south-facing. Moraine Park Campground is in such a ponderosa park. Besides Ponderosa Pine, the common trees include Douglas-fir, Limber Pine, and Rocky Mountain Juniper. Sulphurflower and Scarlet Paintbrush are two common wildflowers, and typical birds include Northern Flicker, Steller's Jay, Mountain Chickadee, White-breasted Nuthatch, and Chipping Sparrow. Mammals likely to be encountered are chipmunk, Golden-mantled Ground Squirrel, Mountain Cottontail, Mule Deer, and (if you are lucky) Abert's Squirrel, with the attractive ear-tufts. At night, listen for the yipping of Coyote packs.

Douglas-fir forests dominate the wetter, north-facing slopes. Most of the hikes in this book go through these forests on part of the circuit. Trees mixed in with the Douglas-fir usually include some Ponderosa Pine, Lodgepole Pine, Engelmann Spruce, and Subalpine Fir. Smaller woody plants include Common Juniper and Mountain Maple. Wildflowers are relatively few, and birds are widely scattered; look and listen for Steller's Jay, Mountain Chickadee, Ruby-crowned Kinglet, Brown Creeper, Hermit Thrush, and Pine Siskin. This is the habitat of the diminutive Red Squirrel, which chatters noisily at hikers.

Lodgepole stands are the hiker's most boring habitat, usually indicating an area that burned long ago. Older stands may contain scattered other conifers that are shade-tolerant, but by and large lodgepole stands are monocultures of Mother Nature. Wildflowers are scarce, and even birds are hard to find; look for Gray Jay, Mountain Chickadee, Ruby-crowned Kinglet, and Hermit Thrush. The Red Squirrel is likely to be the only mammal encountered by the hiker.

Aspen groves complete the montane associations, widely distributed along meadows and in creek valleys, or invading after fire or avalanche. Quaking Aspen is the only common deciduous tree in the park to be found away from riparian areas. Shrubs such as rose and Common Juniper occur in aspen groves, and look also for Colorado Columbine, lupine, Fremont Geranium, and Yarrow. Aspen groves are generally too thick to walk through because the plant spreads vegetatively under ground, so a whole grove may actually be a single tree. So look along the edges for such birds as Cordilleran Flycatcher, House Wren, Mountain Bluebird, Violet-green Swallow and Warbling Vireo. The mammals typical of aspen groves are small, and tend to be burrowing or nocturnal species, but

Elk hide in the groves by day and everywhere in the park you can see the black scars on aspens where Elk have chewed the inner bark for nutrients.

Spruce-fir forests of the subalpine zone are places most hikers find special. Here Engelmann Spruce and Subalpine Fir dominate, generally from about 9500 feet to tree line. Common Juniper grows this high, too, as well as several berry plants to delight the hiker beginning in late summer. There are many special flowers such as Heartleaf Arnica, Fairyslipper, Pipsissewa, and Twinflower. Many of the coniferous-loving birds from lower elevations occur here as well, but also watch for Blue Grouse, Clark's Nutcracker, Golden-crowned Kinglet, Olive-sided Flycatcher, Townsend's Solitaire, and Pine Grosbeak. Mammals include chipmunk and Red Squirrel, but watch also for the Snowshoe Rabbit (for its large feet), also called Varying Hare (white in winter, mainly brown in summer).

Limber pinelands are uncommon, but occur in rocky, exposed sites, as along Trail Ridge Road near tree line on the east side, where the trees are blown into picturesque shapes by the prevailing gales. Limber Pine is more commonly mixed in other coniferous associations at lower elevations. Most trails do not traverse pure stands of limber pine.

Tundra is a special world of local plant communities. Only three of the very longest circuits in this book lead the hiker to or past tundra. Here watch for special birds: White-tailed Ptarmigan, American Pipit, Horned Lark, Brown-capped Rosy Finch, and White-crowned Sparrow. Mule Deer, Elk and Bighorn Sheep all frequent the tundra, when it is not too hot or too cold and snowy, and it is the best habitat to find Yellow-bellied Marmot (although this huge rodent also lives at lower altitudes). The special mammal of the tundra is the American Pika, that tiny cousin of rabbits that cures its hay harvest on rocks in the sun.

MUSHROOMS

Fungi were once considered plants but the evidence is clear that these multicellular organisms had a different evolutionary origin, so rate their own kingdom beside, if not equal in numbers and importance to, plants and animals. There are many species of free-standing mushrooms in the park, along with some bracket-fungi and other relatives. The most obvious to the hiker is the Fly Amanita, with a bright red cap decorated with white granular bumps. Like the cryptically brown amanitas, it is highly poisonous. And even though a Red Squirrel can eat a given species of mushroom with impunity, that doesn't mean the mushroom can't kill you.

LOWER PLANTS

Plants that are neither gymnosperms (including all the conifers) nor angiosperms (the flowering plants) occur in the park, although many are rare, aquatic, or microscopic so not an obvious part of a hiker's experience. The common parlance term "lower plants" includes some unicellular organisms, various unrelated (unicellular and multicellular) groups called algae, lichens, stoneworts, mosses, liverworts, horsetails, clubmosses, spikemosses, and ferns. The hiker will find **lichens**, which are peculiar combinations of an alga and a fungus, encrusting boulders, especially at high altitudes. **Horsetails** have jointed stalks, in some species with a whorl of leaf-like projections at each joint; find them mainly by creeks. Various **ferns** occur in the park, like horsetails found by streams, but also in dryer places as well.

TREES AND SHRUBS

Pines are the only conifers to have their needles bundled into little groups (called fascicles). The indicator species for the Foothills zone is **Ponderosa Pine** *(Pinus ponderosa)*, which like Quaking Aspen also invades burned areas. This is the familiar pine of western United States, growing to stately heights and displaying a distinctive red bark (which, by the way, smells like vanilla when you put your nose to it). The extremely long, graceful needles readily confirm identification; they occur in twos or threes (often on the very same tree). The cones are large and globular, with a prickle at the end of each scale. Ponderosa pines form large "parks" (open woodland) in relatively flat, dry areas; this is the "park" to which the name Estes Park refers. **Limber Pine** *(Pinus flexilis)* occurs from the Foothill zone to tree line, thus being the most altitudinally widespread pine. It is easily distinguished from ponderosa by its short, stiff needles in groups of five; also, its large cones are more columnar in shape and lack prickles on the scales. Clark's Nutcracker harvests and buries the seeds, and despite the bird's uncanny memory for caching sites, it forgets about some so helps plant new Limber Pines. **Lodgepole Pine** *(Pinus contorta)* looks a bit like Limber Pine, but its short needles are in twos and its cones are small and spherical, having prickles. Lodgepole Pine is characteristic of the montane zone, but like Ponderosa moves into burned areas.

Other conifers are as readily distinguished from one another as the pines. **Rocky Mountain Juniper** *(Sabina scopulorum)* occurs from the lowest

CONIFERS

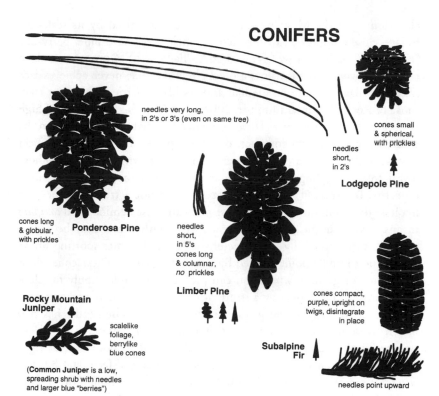

needles very long,
in 2's or 3's (even on same tree)

cones small
& spherical,
with prickles

needles
short,
in 2's

Lodgepole Pine

cones long
& globular,
with prickles

Ponderosa Pine

needles
short,
in 5's

cones long
& columnar,
no prickles

Limber Pine

cones compact,
purple, upright on
twigs, disintegrate
in place

**Rocky Mountain
Juniper**

scalelike
foliage,
berrylike
blue cones

(**Common Juniper** is a low,
spreading shrub with needles
and larger blue "berries")

**Subalpine
Fir**

needles point upward

Douglas-fir and both spruces

needles in all directions,
cones tan colored, hang down
from twigs, drop
before disintegrating

both spruces

needles stiff and
sharp, same
width to base, roll
between thumb
and finger

Douglas-fir

needles flat and soft,
attach to twig with short
stem, do not roll between
thumb and finger

"rat-tail" cones with
3-pointed brachts,
readily drop from tree

cones reluctantly but
eventually drop from tree

Blue Spruce

needles bluish, twigs not hairy,
cones long (3.5 inches)

Engelmann Spruce

needles green, twigs minutely hairy,
cones short (1.0-2.5 inches)

elevations into the Montane zone, and is characterized by its scale-like foliage closely oppressed to the stem. Female trees have blue, berry-like "cones" (extracts from which are used to flavor gin). **Common Juniper** *(Juniperus communis)* is a low-growing relative that never achieves tree size; its foliage is more needle-like and its blue "berries" are larger than those of Rocky Mountain Juniper. **Subalpine Fir** *(Abies lasiocarpa)* of high elevations is easily told at a glance by its needles that curve upward on the twigs, as well as by its compact, distinctly purple cones, which project upward on twigs. The purple cones often glisten with liquid sap. Those dwarf trees struggling for existence at the edge of the tundra are subalpine firs. **Douglas-fir** *(Pseudotsuga taxifolia)* is not a true fir, hence the hyphenated common name; *Pseudotsuga* means false hemlock and *taxifolia* means leaves like the yew. It is not a spruce, either, and may be distinguished from spruces by its characteristic "rat-tail" cones sporting bracts with a long middle point flanked by two lesser points. These cones drop readily to the ground, where you can pick up an ample supply for close inspection. Look closely at an individual needle, too: it narrows to a short stem (petiole) where it attaches to the twig. The needle has two bluish-white lines on the underside, and is flat so cannot be rolled between thumb and index finger. The needles tend to point out at right angles from the twig, and have a "soft" appearance and feel. **Blue Spruce** *(Picea pungens)*, often called Colorado Blue Spruce (although distributed over a six-state area), is one of the best known trees of the Rocky Mountains because of its unusual bluish color and beautiful symmetry. Both spruces in the park have cones that tend to persist on the tree and needles that do not narrow at the base. The needles are squarish in cross-section and can be rolled between thumb and index finger. Unlike the needles of Douglas-fir, spruce needles are stiff and sharp. The twigs are not hairy and the cones are long (3.5 inches). Find it in the Foothill and Montane zones, especially in damper areas. **Engelmann Spruce** *(Picea engelmannii)* is similar, but green like most trees; its twigs have minute hairs and its cones are noticeably smaller (1 to 2.5 inches). Engelmann Spruce overlaps Blue Spruce in the Montane zone, but ranges up into the Subalpine zone as well.

Broad-leaved trees are often easily identified by the hiker because there are relatively few common species in RMNP (compared with eastern United States, for example) and the commonest ones have distinctive leaves. **Boxelder** *(Acer negundo)*, a maple in disguise, occurs at the lowest

SOME BROAD-LEAVED TREES

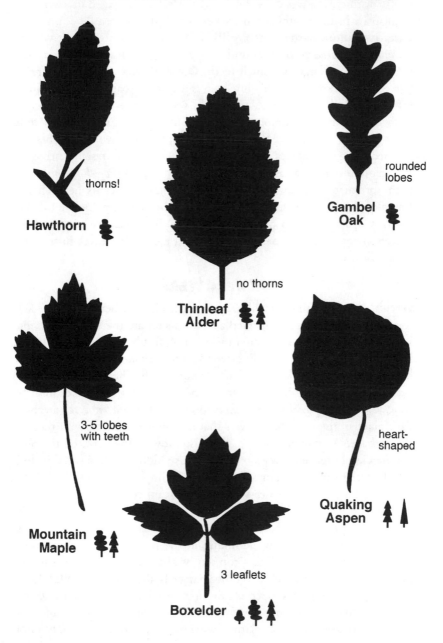

thorns!

Hawthorn

Gambel Oak

rounded lobes

no thorns

Thinleaf Alder

Quaking Aspen

heart-shaped

3-5 lobes with teeth

Mountain Maple

Boxelder

3 leaflets

185

elevations, and along creeks upward through the Montane zone. Boxelder sports distinctive leaves consisting of three leaflets arranged in a symmetric display. In the Foothills zone, where stately Ponderosa Pines predominate, two more hardwoods are likely to be encountered. **Hawthorn** *(Crataegus coloradensis)* is the only thorny tree, its leaf-edges being serrated into both large and small teeth. **Gambel Oak** *(Quercus gambelii)*, also called Rocky Mountain white oak, is the only broad-leaved tree whose leaves have rounded lobes. Along creeks watch for yet two other species, both of which are commoner in the Montane zone. **Mountain Maple** *(Acer glabrum)* leaves have the distinctive maple shape, with 3–5 lobes and toothed margins. **Thinleaf Alder** *(Alnus tenuifolia)* leaves resemble those of Hawthorn but the tree has no thorns. **Quaking Aspen** *(Populus tremuloides)* is the premier broad-leaved tree of the Montane zone. Its heart-shaped leaves quake in the slightest breeze because the leaf-stem (petiole) is flattened. Copses of aspens occur upward into the Subalpine zone and the species characteristically moves into burned areas. The leaves turn a brilliant yellow in fall.

WILDFLOWERS

Flowering plants with showy blossoms are the plants other than trees likely to grab the hiker's attention. Herbaceous species are the **wildflowers**, but some **flowering shrubs** are often included. A shrub is merely a plant that is woody, and if it is small like **Twinflower** *(Linnaea borealis)*, only the botanically minded will notice that it is not a herb. There is no distinction between herb and shrub with regard to their flowers; for example, **Shrubby Cinquefoil** *(Pentaphylloides floribunda*, formerly *Potentilla fruticosa)*, an abundant plant in the park, has flowers that are almost identical with those of the herbaceous cinquefoil species that also grow in the park. Distinctions among closely related species of herbaceous wildflowers are often technical, downright uncertain, or at least of trivial importance to the hiker. Yet genera of flowers are often easy to tell apart, and common names tend to be given to genera rather than species, reflecting these distinctions. Get out your flower books and learn first to recognize some wildflowers most likely to be encountered while hiking in the park. Along with Shrubby Cinquefoil, here is a list of the "top ten" we have noticed on our summer hikes: **Mountain Harebell** (two other harebells also occur), **Scarlet Paintbrush** (a half dozen other species can often be separated by color), **Yarrow** (no look-alike relatives but could be confused with other kinds of flowers), **Aspen Daisy** (lots of relatives with which to confuse it), **Common**

Fireweed (so named because it invades after a fire, it has one uncommon relative in the park), **chiming-bells** (two similar species), **Heartleaf Arnica** (doesn't always have heart-shaped leaves, and is similar to six other arnicas in the park), **Salsify** (a distinctive, vaguely dandelion-like flower brought to America by early colonists, subsequently spread virtually everywhere), **wallflower** (two similar species), and **rose** (three species).

INVERTEBRATES

Animals without backbones are mainly marine except for many **arthropods** or "jointed-legged" critters, including spiders, insects and their relatives, of which the hiker is likely to notice only certain kinds of **insects.** When on a religion-and-science discussion program on BBC, the distinguished biologist J.B.S. Haldane was asked by the moderator what he had learned about God through studying biology. Haldane replied that He has an inordinate fondness for **beetles.** There are more species of beetles than any other kind of animal, and this is probably true in Rocky Mountain National Park as anywhere. Nevertheless, most of us while hiking will notice only the most evident and colorful insects, such as **dragonflies** and **butterflies**, if we don't count things such as mosquitoes, gnats, flies, and no-see-ems.

VERTEBRATES

Fishes certainly rank high on the list of some outdoor enthusiasts, at least on the end of a line or on a dinner plates. Many of the lakes in the park, though, have fish that are quite "watchable" through the clear montane waters, and almost all of these are one or another species of trout, among them **Brook** *(Salvelinus fontinalis),* **Brown** *(Salmo trutta),* **Greenback Cutthroat** *(Oncorhynchus clarki),* and **Rainbow** *(O. mykiss)* **Trouts**, and **suckers** *(Catostomus,* two species).

Amphibians are basically salamanders on the one hand and frogs and toads on the other. Of the former only the **Tiger Salamander** *(Ambystoma tigrinum)* is likely to be encountered, as it is far larger than most species and ventures out in the open while other terrestrial salamanders habitually hide in leaf litter. The Tiger can be up to half a foot long, and is black with yellow markings, which range from highly conspicuous to virtually absent. Frogs and toads are likely to be heard singing from water in the spring but not much in evidence at other times of year. From marshy peripheries of lakes we have heard **Northern Chorus Frogs** *(Pseudacris triseriata),* whose song sounds like running a fingernail along the teeth of

187

a pocket comb. The **Northern Leopard Frog** *(Rana pipiens)* sings from deeper water and has a more croaking-like voice. The only species one is likely to find away from water are the uncommon **Wood Frog** *(Rana sylvatica)* and only a little commoner **Western Toad** *(Bufo boreas)*.

Reptiles are a heterogeneous lot, including turtles, snakes, and lizards— and some other creatures such as crocodilians that needn't concern us in the park. Reptiles seem uncommon in the park; at least we have never seen any. Nevertheless, we always follow our habit of stepping *up upon* a tree trunk across the trail, and then stepping down on the other side because stepping *over* a log may result in landing your foot on a snake you can't see.

Birds are by far the most numerous and diverse vertebrates encountered by hikers. Approaching 300 species have been recorded at least once from Rocky Mountain National Park, and many excellent field guides are available to aid in identifications. As with wildflowers, the best introduction is to concentrate initially in learning to recognize some of the commonly encountered species. Here is our "top ten" list of frequently encountered birds along park circuit hikes; actually, there are 11 species, but who's counting?: **Steller's Jay**, the flashy black-and-blue bird with the exaggerated crest; **Mountain Chickadee**, much like the Black-capped Chickadee (which is less common) except for an eye stripe in the black cap; **Dark-eyed Junco**, so named to distinguish it from the Yellow-eyed Junco of Mexico; **Gray Jay**, usually rather quiet in contrast with most members of the crow family; **American Robin**, the ubiquitous bird everyone knows; **Red-breasted Nuthatch**, known for its nasal "eh-eh" call; **Ruby-crowned Kinglet**, commoner than its Golden-crowned cousin; **Violet-green Swallow**, which hunts on the wing for insects over the water's surface; **Broad-tailed Hummingbird**, by far the commonest hummer in the park; **Clark's Nutcracker**, another noisy member of the crow family; and **Northern Flicker**, a woodpecker with the interesting habit of hopping around on the ground, feeding on ants.

Mammals are the favorite animals of most people, perhaps because being mammals ourselves, we unconsciously feel the familiarity of kinship. Still, we are generally aware of mainly the small number of species that are large or diurnal, or both—which means principally the large hoofed animals (ungulates) and certain rodents, mostly in the squirrel family. There are also some carnivores that the hiker might encounter, and some lagomorphs to round out the fauna.

Ungulates. The first three are in the deer family (Cervidae). Most obvious among them is the **Elk** *(Cervus elaphus)*, whose ancestors were a staple of the Lewis and Clark expedition. In September, the older males (called bulls) round up and defend "harems" of females (cows) with which to breed. Younger males bide their time living in "bachelor groups" until large enough to challenge older bulls for reproductive rights. Hundreds of cars line the park roads near meadows so the passengers can hear the evening "bugle" cry of the bulls as they guard their harems against intruders. Far slimmer and smaller, and likely to be encountered only as single individuals in the woodlands, is the **Mule Deer** *(Odocoileus hemionis)*, named for its oversized ears compared with those of its eastern cousin, the White-tailed Deer *(O. virginianus)*. The third member of the deer family in the park is the **Moose** *(Alces alces)*, originally an inhabitant but extirpated, probably by the early twentieth century. Reintroduced into the national forest to the west, Moose spread readily along the park's waterways, becoming numerous west of the Continental Divide and increasingly reported east of it. In Alaska, the Moose is considered the next most dangerous animal after the Grizzly. Never attempt to approach a Moose closely, or even an Elk for that matter. Last in the parade of hoofed mammals is the **Bighorn Sheep** *(Ovis canadensis)*, or just Bighorn, which is in the family with goats and bison (Bovidae). The male is called a ram and the female a ewe (not said, as the park story goes, "ee-wee" but rather more like the conifer "yew"). Unlike the first three ungulates, Bighorn are not commonly seen by hikers, but watch for them on the circuits that go up to the tundra along the Continental Divide.

Squirrels and another rodent. The family of rodents called Sciuridae includes a lot more critters than just those with "squirrel" in the common name. The lumbering **Yellow-bellied Marmot** *(Marmota flaviventris)* beseeches hikers at high altitudes. It's a close relative of the widespread Woodchuck *(M. monax)* but far more brazen. The **Wyoming Ground Squirrel** *(Spermophilus elegans)* is the only all gray member of the family in the park, making its colonies in the ground in open grassy areas on morainal soil at relatively low elevations. A close relative is the **Golden-mantled Ground Squirrel** *(S. lateralis)*, often mistaken for a chipmunk because of stripes on its side; but unlike a chipmunk, this squirrel has no stripes on the head and back, and is noticeably larger than its diminutive cousins. Two or possibly three species of chipmunks occur in the park and they are so similar than only an aficionado cares about the distinction. The **Least Chipmunk** *(Tamias minimus)* is by far the commonest

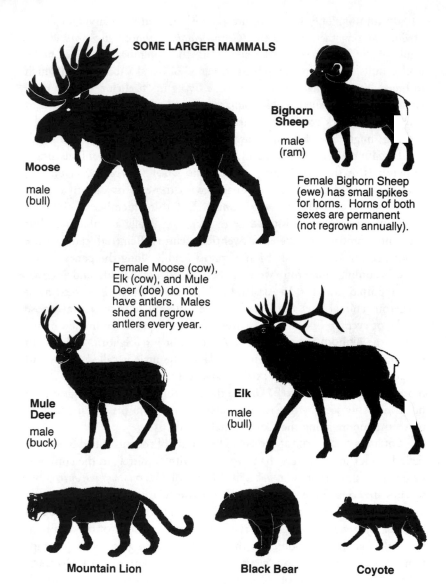

SOME LARGER MAMMALS

Moose

male
(bull)

**Bighorn
Sheep**

male
(ram)

Female Bighorn Sheep
(ewe) has small spikes
for horns. Horns of both
sexes are permanent
(not regrown annually).

Female Moose (cow),
Elk (cow), and Mule
Deer (doe) do not
have antlers. Males
shed and regrow
antlers every year.

**Mule
Deer**

male
(buck)

Elk

male
(bull)

Mountain Lion

Black Bear

Coyote

species and ranges furthest with respect to both elevation and habitats, so most of the time you'll be right calling a chipmunk a Least. From inspecting and photographing the few skins of the park collection, Jack concludes that a hiker probably cannot distinguish chipmunk species unless studying the animals with binoculars. The diminutive **Red Squirrel** *(Tamiasciurus hudsonicus)* is as often heard as seen, its trilled call greeting the hiker in Lodgepole Pine stands and any other coniferous habitat. Finally, the **Abert's** (or Tassel-eared) **Squirrel** *(Sciurus aberti)* is something quite special, and occurs only in Ponderosa Pine parks below about 8500 feet; if the park has recently burned, apparently so much the better for this beautiful, large, and usually quiet squirrel with tufts of hair on its ears. Most rodents are nocturnal or burrow into the ground, so you are not likely to come across pocket gophers, kangaroo mice, native rats, mice and voles, jumping mice, and so on. But that large aquatic rodent, the **American Beaver** *(Castor canadensis)* is common in appropriate habitats such as the streams in Glacier Basin near Sprague Lake. These water-loving rodents have their own family, the Castoridae.

Carnivores. The flesh-eating mammals constitute an order represented by members of at least four families that the hiker could encounter. Of the bears (family Ursidae) only the **Black Bear** *(Ursus americanus)* inhabits the park, although it is fairly certain that the Grizzly Bear *(U. horribilis)* was here in historical times. Despite the name, Black Bears may be brown or even blond in coloration. Whereas Black Bears in eastern United States commonly weigh up to 400 or more pounds, those in the park are far smaller, weighing in at about 150 pounds on the average. Black Bears are usually not dangerous; just give them wide berth, and stand your ground, looking as large as possible, if they try a sham attack at you. The hiker is quite unlikely to be attacked by a Black Bear, except if getting between a mother and her cub, but if that rare exception occurs, *fight back!* Hit the bear with anything you can—fists if nothing else is available. The commonest member of the weasel and skunk family (Mustelidae) seen by the hiker is the **Long-tailed Weasel** *(Mustela frenata)*, a small but beautiful, long, slinky animal that is brown above and light below, with *brown paws*. Why we never see the similar **Short-tailed Weasel** *(M. erminea)* is unclear, but if the weasel you see has *white paws*, it is of this species. Only once on a hike did we see a **American Marten** *(Martes americana)*, which is somewhat similar to weasels but is larger and has brownish underparts. The third family of carnivores in the park are dog relatives (Canidae). Probably sneaky foxes occur, but the only canid we see is the **Coyote**

SOME SMALLER MAMMALS

Wyoming Ground Squirrel

Golden-mantled Ground Squirrel

Yellow-bellied Marmot

Abert's Squirrel

Least Chipmunk

American Marten
female smaller

Red Squirrel

Muskrat

Long-tailed Weasel
female smaller

Snowshoe Hare
brown in summer, white in winter

American Pika

American Beaver

Mountain Cottontail

(Canis latrans), which seems to be commonest in the parks at relatively low altitudes. Coyotes yip, by the way, rarely howling like wolves and dogs. Finally, there are the cats (Felidae), which take stealth to its logical extreme. We've never seen a **Bobcat** *(Lynx rufus)* in the park—we frequently see them in Florida—but they are here. Similarly, we'd be joyed to see a **Mountain Lion** *(Felis concolor)*, but it is the runners, not hikers, on park trails that stimulate these magnificent cats to give chase. As with a Black Bear, if attacked by a Mountain Lion, *fight back*: convince the cat to look for easier prey.

Lagomorphs. There are two members of the hare and rabbit family (Leporidae) we run across while hiking: the **Mountain Cottontail** *(Sylvilagus nuttalli)*, with its gray-brown fur and white powder-puff tail, and the **Snowshoe Hare** or **Varying Hare** *(Lepus americanus)*, whose coloration changes during the year. In winter it is all white, blending into the snow, and in summer all brown. (Well, it does have black tips to the ears at all times.) When they are molting into the alternative coat, they become a mixture of colors, often brown with white feet. And the hind feet, by the way, are huge, probably because they do indeed act like snowshoes. In a different family (Ochotonidae) of the same order is the tiny **American Pika** *(Ochotona princeps)*, looking perhaps more like a rodent than a rabbit relative because of its short ears. They scurry around rocky areas on the tundra, harvesting grasses and drying them in the sun. Beavers are industrious, but the time-honored expression could just as readily be "busy as a Pika."

Other mammals occur in the park. We have selected those most likely to be seen by the hiker, and that's a pretty exciting collection.

OTHER SOURCES OF NATURAL HISTORY INFORMATION

To learn more about the natural history of Rocky Mountain National Park several avenues are open. One is to study the publications listed in the bibliography near the end of this book. For the computer minded another is to view the CD-ROM "Magnificent Rocky," which runs on both Macintosh and Windows machines. In the book nooks at visitor centers you can find other CD-ROMs and also video tapes relating to the park's natural history. A third way is to look at the displays in the park's visitor centers, and especially the museum in Moraine Park. Still another source of information is the (free) evening programs by rangers, given during summer months at all the campgrounds and at the park headquarters.

Last, but (as the saying goes) no way least, is to take (again, free) walks with rangers, most of which are devoted mainly to natural history. These campfire programs and ranger-led walks are listed in the park newspaper given out at all entrance stations.

Fee Schedules

Specific fee amounts are given here (nowhere else in the book) so that as they change the new values can be penciled in by the reader in one place. The two relevant places charging fees are the park and (for access to one park trail) the Arapaho National Recreation Area. The values given below were those current in the summer of 2002.

PASSPORTS COVERING BOTH ROCKY MOUNTAIN NATIONAL PARK AND ARAPAHO NATIONAL RECREATION AREA

Golden Age Passport: Available to U.S. residents age 62 or older. A one-time $10 fee provides free lifetime entrance to most federal fee areas, including Rocky Mountain National Park and Arapaho National Recreation Area. The Golden Age Passport also provides a 50 percent discount on camping fees. Note that this discount does *not* apply to the "administrative fee" for backcountry camping in Rocky Mountain National Park.

Golden Access Passport: Available to disabled U.S. residents, this passport is free and provides the same benefits as the Golden Age Passport.

Golden Eagle Passport: $65 per year per family. The passport provides free entrance to most federal fee areas, including Rocky Mountain National Park and Arapaho National Recreation Area.

ANRA/RMNP Passport: $50 per year per family. The passport provides free entrance to Rocky Mountain National Park and the Arapaho National Recreation Area (but no other federal areas).

FEES FOR ROCKY MOUNTAIN NATIONAL PARK (RMNP)

National Parks Pass: $50 per year. The pass covers entrance to all national parks, including RMNP.

Annual Pass: $30 per year. The pass covers entrance to RMNP only.

Vehicle Entrance Fee: for RMNP is $15 per week for noncommercial vehicles.

Individual Entrance Fee: for RMNP is $5 per week for one person on foot, horseback, motorcycle, or bicycle.

Campground Fees: $18 a night per campsite at all family campgrounds in RMNP, with 50 percent discounts to holders of Golden Age and Golden Access Passports. (Special fees apply to group camping facilities. There is also a campsite reservation fee for those campgrounds accepting reservations.)

Backcountry Camping Permits: $15, and discounts do not apply.

Shuttle Bus Services: No charge.

FEES FOR ARAPAHO NATIONAL RECREATION AREA (ANRA)

Annual Pass: for ANRA is $30 per family.

7-day Pass: for ANRA is $15 per vehicle.

3-day Pass: for ANRA is $10 per vehicle.

1-day Fee: for ANRA is $5 per vehicle.

7-day Nonmotorized Pass: for ANRA is $10 per person.

3-day Nonmotorized Pass: for ANRA is $5 per person.

1-day Nonmotorized Pass: for ANRA is $2 per person.

Local Hiking Equipment Stores

The following retailers near Rocky Mountain National Park carry a complete line of hiking supplies and equipment: day packs, hiking boots and boot socks, hats, jackets, rainwear, walking sticks, water bottles, trail snacks, first-aid kits, compasses, topographic maps, guidebooks, and more. In addition, those stores marked with an asterisk (*) also carry a complete line of backpacking supplies and equipment: backpacks, sleeping bags and pads, tents, water filters and purifiers, backpacking stoves, cookware, utensils, freeze-dried food, and more. All items were in stock when field checked by us in summer 2002.

ESTES PARK

Moraine Avenue (road to Beaver Meadows Entrance Station)

*Scot's Sporting Goods, 870 Moraine Ave., Estes Park, CO 80517; phone 970/586-2877.

*The Warming House, 790 Moraine Ave., P.O. Box 3368, Estes Park, CO 80517; phone 970/586-2995; www.warminghouse.com.

Elkhorn Avenue (principal downtown street)

The Hiking Hut, 110 East Elkhorn Ave., P.O. Box 1318, Estes Park, CO 80517; phone 970/586-0708.

*Outdoor World, 156 East Elkhorn Ave., P.O. Box 2800, Estes Park, CO 80517; phone 970/586-2114; fax 970/577-1835; www.RMConnection.com; orders@RMConnection.com.

*Estes Park Mountain Shop, 358 East Elkhorn Ave., Estes Park, CO 80517; phone 970/586-6548; toll-free 800/504–6642; www.estesparkmountainshop.com.

Grand Lake (west side of Park)

*Never Summer Mountain Products, 919 Grand Ave., P.O. Box 929, Grand Lake, CO 80447; phone 970/627-3642; fax 970/627-3868.

Organizations You Can Join

We are a gregarious species and often seek out people with similar interests. There are many organizations that hiking enthusiasts can join. These associations, societies, and clubs offer a variety of activities aimed at enhancing our national parks, developing hiking trails, encouraging "silent" sports, and working for conservation in general. Get involved; you'll be glad you did.

Rocky Mountain Nature Association, P.O. Box 3100, Estes Park, CO 80517; phone 800/816-7662; www.rmna.org.

American Hiking Society, P.O. Box 20160, Washington, DC 20041-2160; phone 301/565-6704; www.americanhiking.org.

Continental Divide Trail Alliance, P.O. Box 628, Pine, CO 80470; phone 303/838-3760 or 888/909-CDTA (2382); www.CDTrail.org.

Sierra Club, 85 Second St., San Francisco, CA 94105; phone 415/977-5500 or 800/477-2627; www.sierraclub.org.

Suggested Reading and Reference

Most of the guidebooks listed are currently available, but we also include (mainly for historical interest) older standards that are probably out of print, accessible only in libraries or used-book stores. We have omitted books and videos that are narrowly specialized (focusing, for example, on a single animal species), as well as titles that are essentially photo essays. Guides on certain topics, such as wildflowers and birds, are so abundant that we list only a sampling of those available.

Items that were stocked by the Rocky Mountain Nature Association at one or more RMNP visitor centers in the summer of 2002 are marked with an asterisk (*). Some items are also available from Association's website (www.rmna.org) or by phone (800/816-7662). Space is limited, so not all items are available at all visitor centers; the most complete inventory is usually at Beaver Meadows. Many of the books, maps, and CD-ROM maps listed are also available at retail stores in Estes Park and Grand Lake.

OUR CHOICE

*Dannen, Kent, and Donna Dannen. *Hiking Rocky Mountain National Park Including Indian Peaks.* 8th ed. Guilford, CT: Globe Pequot, 1994. [Buy this guide first. It covers nearly every trail in the park—albeit in less detail than the more focused books—and is written by an extraordinarily qualified husband-and-wife team.]

OTHER RMNP TRAIL GUIDES

*Dannen, Kent, and Donna Dannen. *Short Hikes in Rocky Mountain National Park.* Allenspark, CO: Tundra, 1986.

———. *Best Easy Day Hikes in Rocky Mountain National Park.* Guilford, CT: Globe Pequot, 2002.

*Donahue, Mike. *The Longs Peak Experience and Trail Guide.* Loveland, CO: Indiana Camp Supply, 1992.

*Evans, Lisa Gollin. *An Outdoor Family Guide to Rocky Mountain National Park.* 2nd ed. Seattle: Mountaineers, 1998.

*Heasley, John E. *Leaving the Crowds Behind: A Guide to Backcountry Camping in Rocky Mountain National Park.* Fort Collins, CO: RAS, 2002.

*Malitz, Jerome. *Rocky Mountain National Park Dayhiker's Guide.* Boulder, CO: Johnson Books, 1993.

*Mendon, Laurie. *Rocky Mountain National Park Trail Guide and Journal.* 2nd ed. Estes Park, CO: Pinnacle Ventures, 1994.

Nesbit, Paul W. *Longs Peak: Its Story and a Climbing Guide.* 7th ed. Colorado Springs, CO: Paul W. Nesbit, 1969.

*Rusk, Dave. *Rocky Mountain Day Hikes.* Estes Park, CO: Barefoot Publications, 1998.

*Salcedo, Tracy. *12 Short Hikes: Rocky Mountain National Park: Estes Park.* Guilford, CT: Globe Pequot, 1995.

*————. *12 Short Hikes: Rocky Mountain National Park: Grand Lake.* Conifer, CO: Chockstone, 1997.

Soran, Patrick. *Rocky Mountain National Park Walks & Easy Hikes.* Canmore, Alberta: Altitude, 2002.

TRAIL GUIDES THAT INCLUDE SELECTED RMNP TRAILS

Boddie, Caryn, and Peter Boddie. *Hiking Colorado.* Helena, MT: Falcon, 1991.

————. *Hiking Colorado II.* Guilford, CT: Globe Pequot, 1999.

Brown, Robert L. *Colorado on Foot.* Caldwell, ID: Caxton, 1994.

*Dawson, Louis W., II. *Dawson's Guide to Colorado's Fourteeners.* Vol. 1, *The Northern Peaks.* Colorado Springs, CO: Blue Clover, 1999.

Gaug, Maryann. *Hiking Colorado III.* Guilford, CT: Globe Pequot, 2002.

Hagen, Mary. *Hiking Trails in Northern Colorado.* Boulder, CO: Pruett, 1979.

*Irwin, Pamela. *Colorado's Best Wildflower Hikes.* Vol. 1, *The Front Range.* Englewood, CO: Westcliffe, 1998.

Jacobs, Randy. *The Colorado Trail: The Official Guidebook.* 4th ed. Englewood, CO: Westcliffe, 1994.

*Keilty, Maureen. *Best Hikes With Children in Colorado.* Seattle: Mountaineers, 1998.

Lowe, Don, and Roberta Lowe. *80 Northern Colorado Hiking Trails.* Beaverton, OR: Touchstone, 1973.

Martin, Bob. *Hiking the Highest Passes of Colorado.* 2nd ed. Boulder, CO: Pruett, 1998.

Ormes, Robert, and the Colorado Mountain Club. *Guide to the Colorado Mountains.* 6th ed. Chicago: Swallow, 1970.

*Schneck, Stuart A., and Ida I. Nakashima. *The Geezers' Guide to Colorado Hikes.* Boulder, CO: University Press of Colorado, 2002. [An unusual trail guide by two physicians—a husband-and-wife team of self-proclaimed "geezers," who identify and address the concerns of older hikers.]

*Warren, Scott S. *100 Classic Hikes in Colorado.* 2nd ed. Seattle: Mountaineers, 2001.
*Williams, Christina. *The Best Hikes of Colorado.* Denver: Altitude, 1999.

RMNP MAPS

National Geographic Rocky Mountain National Park Topographic Map. Trails Illustrated. Scale approx. 1:59,000, contour interval 80 feet. Printed on plastic. [Shows all trails in this book. The best map for hikers currently available.]

Rocky Mountain National Park, Colorado. U.S. Geological Survey. Scale 1:50,000, contour interval 80 feet. Printed on plastic. [The map of largest scale that covers the entire park; its usefulness is somewhat offset by woefully outdated trail data.]

Rocky Mountain National Park/Indian Peaks Wilderness Trails. Skyterrain. Scale 1:40,000, contour interval 80 feet, shaded relief. [Covers only the southeastern part of the park.]

Rocky Mountain National Park Panoramic Hiking Map. Fern/Horn Endeavors (www.trailtracks.com). Perspective graphics—not topographic. Paper. [A fun map to put up on your wall, but don't use it for hiking. Does not show all the trails in this book.]

Rocky Mountain National Park Recreation Map. Trails Illustrated Topo Maps. Approx. 1:59,000, contour interval 80 feet. Paper. [Text in English, Deutsch, Español, Français, and Nihon Go. Does not show all the trails in this book. Although it is subject to water damage, you can buy about five of these for the same price as a similar map printed on plastic.]

CD-ROM MAPS

Colorado Front Range Cities and Recreation Areas. San Francisco: Wildflower Productions, 1998. [For Windows 3.1, 95, 98, and NT.]

National Park Maps. San Francisco: Wildflower Productions, 1999. [For Windows 95, 98, and NT.]

Rocky Mountain National Park. Washington, DC: National Geographic Maps, 2000. [For Macintosh and most(?) versions of Windows.]

BACKPACKING AND WILDERNESS SKILLS

*Curtis, Rick. *The Backpacker's Field Manual: A Comprehensive Guide to Mastering Backcountry Skills.* New York: Three Rivers Press, 1998.

Hailman, Jack P., and Elizabeth D. Hailman. *Backpacking Wisconsin.* Madison, WI: University of Wisconsin Press, 2000. [Included here for readers interested in our views on backpacking equipment and procedures.]

*Kavanagh, J., and R. Leung. "Wilderness Survival: How to Stay Alive in the Wilderness." Blaine, WA: Waterford, 2001. [A fold-out guide printed on plastic.]

*McGivney, Annett. *Leave No Trace: A Guide to the New Wilderness Etiquette.* Seattle: Mountaineers, 1998.

*Smith, Lucy. *Improve Your Survival Skills.* Tulsa, OK: EDC, 1987.

*Wood, Robert S. *The 2 oz. Backpacker: A Problem Solving Manual for Use in the Wilds.* Berkeley, CA: Ten Speed, 1982.

FIRST AID, HEALTH, AND SAFETY

*Bezruchke, Stephen. *Altitude Illness Prevention & Treatment.* Seattle: Mountaineers, 1994. [An authoritative volume written by a physician.]

*Johnson, J. Leslie. *An Altitude Superguide: Basic Mountain Safety from A to Z.* Canmore, Alberta: Altitude, 2001.

*Kavanagh, J. "Emergency First Aid: Recognition and Treatment of Medical Emergencies." Blaine, WA: Waterford, 2001. [A fold-out guide printed on plastic.]

*Preston, Gilbert. *Wilderness First Aid: When You Can't Call 911.* Helena, MT: Falcon, 1997. [An authoritative volume written by a physician.]

ECOLOGY AND NATURAL HISTORY (GENERAL)

*Alden, Peter, and John Grassy. *National Audubon Society Field Guide to the Rocky Mountain States.* New York: Alfred A. Knopf, 1998.

*Bezener, Andy, and Linda Kenshaw. *Rocky Mountain Nature Guide.* Edmonton, Alberta: Lone Pine, 1999.

*Emerock, John C. *Rocky Mountain National Park Natural History Handbook.* Niwot, CO: Roberts Rinehart, 1995.

Ferguson, Gary, John Clayton, and Maureen B. Keilty. *Guide to America's Outdoors: Southern Rockies.* Washington, DC: National Geographic, 2001.

*Gunn, John, ed. *Bear Lake Nature Trail.* Rocky Mountain Nature Association, n.p., n.d.

Whitney, Stephen. *Western Forests.* New York: Alfred A. Knopf, 1985. [This work covers forest ecosystems, including animals, trees, and all kinds of plants.]

*Wuerthner, George. *Rocky Mountain: A Visitor's Companion.* Mechanicsburg, PA: Stackpole, 2001.

Zim, Herbert S. *The Rocky Mountains: A Golden Regional Guide.* New York: Golden Press, 1964.

GEOLOGY

*Chronic, Halka. *Roadside Geology of Colorado.* Missoula, MT: Mountain Press, 1980.

Harris, Ann G., and Esther Tuttle. *Geology of National Parks.* 4th ed. Dubuque, IA: Kendall/Hunt, 1990.

Pearl, Richard M. *Colorado Gem Trails and Mineral Guide.* Denver: Sage Books, 1958.

FLORA (GENERAL)

*Beidleman, Linda H., Richard G. Beidleman, and Beatrice E. Williard. *Plants of Rocky Mountain National Park.* Helena, MT: Rocky Mountain Nature Association and Falcon, 2000.

*Kavanagh, J., and R. Leung. "Rockies Trees and Wildflowers: An Introduction to Familiar Species." Blaine, WA: Waterford, 2000. [A fold-out guide printed on plastic.]

*Kershaw, Linda, Andy MacKinnon, and Jim Pojar. *Plants of the Rocky Mountains.* Edmonton, Alberta: Lone Pine, 1998.

Nelson, Ruth Ashton. *Plants of Rocky Mountain National Park.* Rocky Mountain Nature Association, n.p., 1970.

*———. *Handbook of Rocky Mountain Plants.* Rev. ed., Roger L. Williams. Niwot, CO: Roberts Rinehart, 1992.

TREES

*Feucht, James R. *Illustrated Guide to Trees and Shrubs of Rocky Mountain National Park.* Granby, CO: Kopycat, 1999.

*Watts, Tom. *Rocky Mountain Tree Finder.* Berkeley, CA: Nature Study Guild, 1972. [We are fond of this small book, which fits into a shirt pocket and is remarkably good at identifying tree species quickly.]

WILDFLOWERS

*Dahns, David. *Rocky Mountain Wildflowers Pocket Guide.* Windsor, CO: Paragon, 1999.

*Dannen, Kent, and Donna Dannen. *Rocky Mountain Wildflowers.* Allenspark, CO: Tundra, 1981.

*Guennel, G. K. *Guide to Colorado Wildflowers.* Vol. 2, *Mountains.* Englewood, CO: Westcliffe, 1995.

*Miller, Millie. *Mountain Blooms: Wildflowers of the Rockies.* Boulder, CO: Johnson Books, 2000.

Roberts, Rhoda N., and Ruth Ashton Nelson. *Mountain Wild Flowers of Colorado and Adjacent Areas.* Denver: Denver Museum of Natural History, 1967.

*Robertson, Leigh. *Southern Rocky Mountain Wildflowers: A Field Guide to Wildflowers in the Southern Rocky Mountains, Including Rocky Mountain National Park.* Helena, MT: Falcon, 1999.

*Wingate, Janet L. *Rocky Mountain Flower Finder: A Guide to Wildflowers Found Below Treeline in the Rocky Mountains.* Rochester, NY: Nature Study Guild Publications, 1990.

MUSHROOMS

*Evenson, Vera Stucky. *Mushrooms of Colorado and the Southern Rocky Mountains.* Englewood, CO: Denver Botanic Gardens, Denver Museum of Natural History, and Westcliffe, 1997.

*Lincoff, Gary H. *National Audubon Society Field Guide to North American Mushrooms.* New York: Alfred A. Knopf, 1981.

McKnighty, Kent H., and Vera B. McKnighty. *A Field Guide to Mushrooms of North America.* Boston: Houghton Mifflin, 1987.

FAUNA (GENERAL)

*Kavanagh, J. "Rocky Mountain Wildlife: An Introduction to Familiar Species." Blaine, WA: Waterford, 2000. [A fold-out guide printed on plastic.]

MAMMALS

*Halfpenny, James C. *Scats and Tracks of the Rocky Mountains.* 2nd ed. Guilford, CT: Globe Pequot, 2001.

*Kavanagh, J. "Animal Tracks: An Introduction to the Tracks and Signs of the Familiar North American Species." Blaine, WA: Waterford, 2000. [A fold-out guide printed on plastic.]

Rodeck, Hugo G. *Guide to the Mammals of Colorado.* Boulder, CO: University of Colorado Museum, 1969.

*Russo, Ron. *Mountain State Mammals: A Guide to Mammals of the Rocky Mountain Region.* Rochester, NY: Nature Study Guild, 1991.

*Sheldon, Ian. *Animal Tracks of the Rockies.* Edmonton, Alberta: Lone Pine, 1997.

Whitaker, John O., Jr. *National Audubon Society Field Guide to North American Mammals.* Rev. ed. New York: Alfred A. Knopf, 1996.

BIRDS

**Field Guide to the Birds of North America.* 3rd ed. Washington, DC: National Geographic Society, 1999.

Gray, Mary Taylor. *Watchable Birds of the Rocky Mountains.* Missoula, MT: Mountain Press, 1992.

*——. *The Guide to Colorado Birds.* Englewood, CO: Westcliffe, 1998.

Holl, Harold R., and James A. Lane. *A Birder's Guide to Colorado.* 2nd ed. Colorado Springs, CO: American Birding Association, 1988.

*Kaufman, Kenn. *Birds of North America.* Boston: Houghton Mifflin, 2000.

*Kavanagh, J., and R. Leung. "Rocky Mountain Birds: An Introduction to Familiar Species." Blaine, WA: Waterford, 2001. [A fold-out guide printed on plastic.]

Peterson, Roger Tory. *A Field Guide to Western Birds.* 3rd ed. Boston: Houghton Mifflin, 1990.

*Roederer, Scott. *Birding Rocky Mountain National Park.* Boulder, CO: Johnson Books, 2002.

*Seacrest, Betty R., and Delbert A. McNew. *Rocky Mountain Birds: Easy Identification.* Boulder, CO: Avery, 1993.

*Sibley, David Allen. *The Sibley Guide to Birds.* New York: Alfred A. Knopf, 2000.

*Tekiela, Stan. *Birds of Colorado Field Guide.* Cambridge, MN: Adventure, 2001.

REPTILES AND AMPHIBIANS

Stebbins, Robert C. *A Field Guide to Western Reptiles and Amphibians.* Boston: Houghton Mifflin, 1966.

BUTTERFLIES

*Mitchell, Robert T., and Herbert S. Zim. *Butterflies and Moths: A Guide to the More Common American Species.* New York: St. Martin, 1987.

Opler, Paul A., and Amy Bartlett Wright. *Western Butterflies.* Boston and New York: Houghton Mifflin, 1999.

PERIODICALS

Backpacker. 33 E. Minor St., Emmaus, PA 18098; phone 800/666-3434; www.bpbasecamp.com.

Index

Names of circuits and page numbers of their accounts are in **boldface**.
Page numbers of entries shown in maps and figures are in *italics*.

Access points, xii (map), 18; definition of, 6–7; types of, *xii*
Acclimation. *See* Altitude
Accounts, circuit, 17–21; maps, 20–21; text, 17–20. *See also* individual accounts by name
Admiral, Weidemeyer's (butterfly), 55
Alaska, 189
Alberta Falls, 101, *104*, 105, 108, *110*, 111, 114, 115, *126*, 127, 131
Alder, 49, 145; identification of, *185;* Thinleaf, 77, 88, 89, 145, 151, 179
Algae, 182
Allenspark, 66, 67
Alpine Brook, *56*, 58
Alpine Lakes Circuit, 3, 71, 101, 110 (map), **111–115**, 131, *132*
Alpine Life Zone, 177, *178*, 178, 179
Alpine Visitor Center, 137, 141, 147, 153, 157
Altitude, 4; acclimation to, 5; acute mountain sickness (AMS), 9; air pressure, 6; effect on exertion rating, 5–6; high-altitude pulmonary edema (HAPE), 10; sickness, 9–10. *See also* Elevation
Alumroot, Bracted, 63
Alva B. Adams Tunnel, 169
Amanita, Fly (mushroom), 83, 114, 125, 181
Amphibian. *See* Frog; Salamander, Tiger
AMS (acute mountain sickness). *See* Altitude
Andrews, Edwin B., 130
Andrews Creek, *126*, 130
Andrews Glacier, 113, *126*, 127, 128, 129, 130, 131, *160*
Andrews Tarn, 113, *126*, 127, 128, 130

Animal: feeding of prohibited, 11, 15; names of, 19–20. *See also* Bird; Butterfly; Frog; Mammal; Salamander, Tiger
Annual Pass. *See* Pass/Passport
Ant, 188
Antacid, 9
Appalachian Trail, 148, 162
Arapaho National Recreation Area, 167, 195, 195
Arapahos, 148, 153, 163
Arch Rocks (the Arches), *78*, 80, *120*
Arete, 177
Arnica, Heartleaf, 49, 83, 89, 115, 151, 159, 164, 181, 187
Arthropod, 187
Aspen, 2, 29, 77, 79; Elk-chewed, 46; groves, 180; identification of, *185*, 186; Quaking, 37, 39, 43, 49, 55, 83, 89, 114, 115, 145, 148, 151, 180, 182
Aspen Brook, *50*, 51, 53, 55
Aspenglen Campground, *30*, 32, 33, 34, 177
Aster, 145; Golden (*see* Golden Aster); Hairy Golden (*see* Golden Aster, Hairy); purple, 37, 49, 63, 151

Backcountry campsite. *See* Campsite, backcountry
Backcountry office, 58
Backpack, 4
Backpacking, 11, 13; books, 203–204; circuits, 3, 23, 57, 58, 125, 133, 139, 161, 162, 164, 173
Bacteria, 7; tetanus, 7
Balanced Rock, *24*, 25, 27, 29

Bandana, 13
Banner. *See* Golden Banner
Battle Mountain, *56*
Bear: Black, *190,* 191, 193; Grizzly, 1, 10,
    122, 191, 193
Bear Lake, 3, *56,* 70 (photo), *98,* 101, *110,*
    114, *116,* 117, 119 (photo), *120,* 124,
    125, *126,* 128, 129, 163, 179; how
    named, 80; origin of, 118, 121
Bear Lake Circuit, 3, 20, 71, 116 (map),
    117–118, 132 (map)
Bear Lake Road, *xii,* 23, *30, 56,* 57, 62, 69,
    71, *72,* 75, 77, *84, 90, 94, 96, 98,* 100,
    101, *104, 110,* 112, *116,* 117, *120,*
    121, *126, 132,* 133
Bear Lake Road circuits, 71–133; access
    points for, *xii,* 3; combining, 133;
    introduction to, 71
Bear Lake Trailhead, 3, 71, 99, 100, 105,
    106, 111, 112, 117, 121, 122, 127,
    128, 131, 133
Beaver, 193; American, 55, 92, 96, 191,
    192; dam, 28, 47, *38,* 47, 92 (photo),
    96; pond, 29, 83, *90, 94,* 95, 149
Beaver Brook, *30, 38,* 39, 43
Beaver Brook Circuit, 38 (map), **39–43,** *68,*
    69
Beaver Meadows Entrance Station, *30,* 58,
    71, *72,* 177
Beaver Meadows Trailhead, 69
Beaver Meadows Visitor Center, 31, 201. *See
    also* Park Headquarters
Beaver Mountain, *38,* 41, 43
Beetle, 187
Bekoff, Marc, 144
Berries, picking of allowed, 15
Bicycles, 15
Bierstadt, Albert, 100
Bierstadt Lake, *98,* 99, 101, 103, 122, 125,
    129
Bierstadt Lake Trailhead, 46, *56,* 57, 58, 60,
    62, *98,* 99, 100, 101, 103, *104,* 106
Bierstadt Moraine, 96, *98,* 99, 103
Bierstadt Moraine Loops, 71, 98 (map),
    99–103; East Loop, 99, 103, *132;* West
    Loop, 99, 100, 101, 103, *132*
Big Dutch Creek, *136*
Bighorn Flats, *160*

Bighorn Sheep. *See* Sheep, Bighorn
Big Meadows, *146,* 147, 149, 150 (photo),
    151, *156,* 157, 158, 159, *160,* 161,
    162, 163; origins of, 162
Big Meadows Circuit, 135, 146 (map),
    147–151, *172,* 173
Big Thompson Canyon, 176
Big Thompson River, *72,* 73, 74, 75, 77,
    78, 80, 81, 83, *120,* 121, 122, 123,
    124, 170
Binoculars, 12, 13
Biome, 177
Biotic associations, 177–181
Bird, 10, 179, 188; fledged young, 43;
    names of, 19; nest, 43; top ten, 188;
    where to see, 25, 26, 28, 46, 73, 81,
    164. *See also* individual species by name
Blackbird, Red-winged, 92, 145
Black Canyon Creek, *24,* 28
Black-eyed-susan, 29, 55, 179
Black Lake, 3, 114
Blanketflower, 43, 55, 77, 89, 179
Blisters, 11, 12
Bluebird, Mountain, 26, 29, 43, 77, 115,
    155, 179, 180
Bobcat, 193
Bolete, King, 89, 125
Books. *See* Guide
Boots, hiking. *See* Footwear
Boulder, house-sized, 59
Boulder Brook, *56,* 60, 61, *90,* 95, 96, 99,
    104, 106, 108, 133
Boulder Brook Circuit, 71, 104 (map),
    105–108, *132*
Boulder Field, *56,* 57, 59, 61
Box-elder, 184–186; identification of, *185*
Bracket-fungus, 181
Breathing rate, 9
Bridal Veil Falls, 3, *24,* 25, 28, 29
Buckwheat, 37, 55
Bull Lake Glaciation, 176
Bus, shuttle. *See* Shuttle bus
Bush-cranberry, 49, 164
Butter-and-eggs, 29
Buttercup, 108
Butterfly, 55, 89, 187; orange, 49. *See also*
    Admiral, Weidemeyer's; Checkerspot,
    Arnica; Swallowtail, Western Tiger

Cables on Long's Peak, 59
Cactus. See Pricklypear, Plains
Cairn, 60, 129
Calypso bulbosa, 66
Calypso Cascades, *64,* 65, 66, 67
Camera, 12, 13
Campground, 193; fees, 14, 195; hiking
    from, 23, 46, 49, 58, 71, 73, 79, 95,
    96, 97, 135, 141, 142, 143, 144. See
    also specific campgrounds by name
Campsite, backcountry, 3, 69, 163, 164;
    fees, 14–15, 195; in maps, 20
Canadian Life Zone, 177
Carnivore, 188, 191, 193
Cascade Falls, *160,* 161, 164, 165 (photo)
Castle Rock, *120*
Cat family, 193. See also Bobcat; Mountain
    Lion
CD-ROM: "Magnificent Rocky," 193; maps
    (*see* Map)
Cell phone, 13–14
Cenozoic Era, 176
Chamomile, Wild, 170
Chaos Creek, *110, 126*
Chaos Glacier, *126,* 127, 129
Chasm Falls, 114, 131
Chasm Lake, *56,* 58, 59
Checkerspot, Arnica, 77, 89
Chickadee: Black-capped, 188; Mountain,
    29, 37, 43, 49, 63, 67, 77, 83, 92, 103,
    108, 115, 118, 125, 155, 159, 165,
    170, 180, 188
Chickweed, 43
Children, hiking with, 37
Chiming-bells, 63, 89, 108, 125, 151,
    179, 187; Tall, 115, 118, 145
Chipmunk, 11, 67, 118 (photo), 151, 165,
    180, 189; Least, 29, 43, 55, 63, 77,
    103, 108, 112, 115, 118, 125, 128,
    131, 145, 155, 189, 191, *192;* Uinta,
    29
Chorus Frog, Northern, 115, 187–188
Christian, Barb, xi
Cinquefoil, 108; herbaceous, 43, 155;
    Shrubby, 43, 55, 63, 77, 83, 89, 108,
    125, 145, 151, 155, 159, 164, 170,
    179, 186
Circuit: clockwise versus counterclockwise,

18; definition of, 2; table of, xiii. *See also*
    individual circuits by name
Cirque, 177
Climbing, rock/mountain/technical, 26
Clothing, 12, 13
Clover: Red, 159, 164; White, 89, 125,
    155, 159, 164
Clubmoss, 182
Colorado, 148, 163, 175
Colorado River, *166, 169,* 170. *See also*
    North Fork Colorado River
Colorado River Trail, *136,* 139, 143
Colorado River Trailhead, 135, *136,* 137,
    139, *140,* 141, 142, 144
Columbine, Colorado (wildflower), 83, 125,
    151, 180
Columbine Creek, 170
Columbine Falls, *56,* 57, 58, 59, 62
Comfort, hiking in, 7–10
Compass, 13
Composite, 55; yellow, 29, 49, 63, 145,
    170. *See also* individual species by name
Condition, physical, 4
Coneflower, 49
Conifer, 29, 63, 66, 177, 182–184, 183
    (figure). *See also* individual species by
    name
Continental Divide, 123, 129, *136, 160,*
    169, 189
Continental Divide Circuit, 127, 135, 160
    (map), **161–165,** *172,* 173
Continental Divide National Scenic Trail,
    148, *152,* 155, 157, *160,* 161, 162,
    166, 167, 170
Continental Divide Trail, 148, 162
Contour line. *See* Map
Cony, 66
Cony Creek, *64,* 66
Cooper, William, 66
Copeland, John B., 67
Copeland Falls, *64,* 65, 67
Coralroot, 37; Spotted, 125
Cottontail, Mountain, 43, 180, *192,* 193
Cottonwood, 79
Cow Creek, *24,* 26, 27, 28, 29
Cow Creek Trail, 28
Cow Creek Trailhead, *24,* 25, 28
Cow Parsnip, 145, 151, 159, 164, 170, 179

Coyote, 63, 108, 144, 153, 180, *190,* 191, 193

Cranberry. *See* Bush-cranberry

Creeper, Brown, 29, 43, 49, 67, 92, 115, 125, 180

Crossbill, Red, 29, 43, 77, 115, 125

Crow, American, 77, 83, 92, 115, 145, 155, 159, 165

Cub Lake, 75, *78,* 80, 83, *84,* 85, 86, 89, *120,* 122, 124; how named, 80; origin of, 80

Cub Lake Circuit, 71, 78 (map), **79–83,** 85, 122, *132*

Cub Lake Trail, 83, 86, 89, 122, 124

Cub Lake Trailhead, 71, *72,* 73, 75, 77, *78,* 79, 80, 83, 86, 133

Currant, 55

Daisy: Aspen, 63, 103, 108, 145, 159, 164, 170, 186; Cutleaf, 55; white (Erigeron), 49, 55, 103, 159, 164

Damselfly, 83

Dandelion: Common, 145, 155, 164, 170, 179; False, 170

Day pack, 4; contents, 13

Deer, 189; Mule, 29, 31, 43, 55, 77, 88, 115, 151, 165, 180, 181, 189, *190;* White-tailed, 189

Deer Mountain, *30,* 31, 32, 33 (photo), 33, 34, 35, 36 (photo), 37, 129; summit, 34, 35, 37

Deer Mountain Loops, 30 (map), **31–37,** 69; North Loop, *30,* 31, 34–35, *68;* outer circuit, 32; South Loop, *30,* 31, 35–37, *68,* 69

Deer Ridge Junction, *30,* 31, 32, 33, 34, 35, 37

Dehydration, 7–8

Denver, Colorado, 100

Devils Gulch Road, *24,* 25

Dicot, 19

Dipper, American, 66, 67, 83, 114, 115, 122, 125, 179

Distance: hiking, 18; in maps, 20; sources of, 20

Ditch Camp site, *136,* 137, 138

Ditch Camp Trail, 138

Dock (wildflower), 145

Dog, 144, 193. *See also* Pet

Domes of Yosemite. *See* Yosemite National Park

Douglas-fir, 26–27, 37, 43, 46, 49, 55, 75, 77, 83, 89, 115, 151, 180; as indicator species, *178,* 179; forests, 180; identification of, *183,* 184

Dragonfly, 83, 89, 179, 187

Dream Lake, *110,* 111, 112, 113, 114, 118, *126;* origin of, 112–113

Drummond, Alexander, xi

Duck, 51, 86; Ring-necked, 55, 83, 103. *See also* Mallard

Duct tape, 11–12

Eagle, Golden, 37

East Longs Peak Trail, 58

East Portal, *44,* 45–46, 47 (photo), 49, *56,* 60, 62, 169

East Portal Trailhead, 45

East Shore Trail, *166,* 170

East Shore Trailhead, *166,* 167, 169

East Side circuits, 23–69; access points, *xii,* 3; combining, 68 (map), 69; introduction to, 23

Ecosystems and communities, 179–181

Elevation: gain, 18; hiking, 27; in maps, 20; sources of, 20. *See also* Altitude

Elk, 10, 37, 39, 40 (photos), 83, 144, 145, 154, 179, 180, 181, 189, *190*

Emerald Lake, *110,* 111, 112, 113, *126*

Equestrians, 49, 87 (photo)

Equipment, 11–14; local stores selling, 197–198

Erosion, 176; features (*see* Arete; Cirque; Horn; Tarn; Valley)

Estes, Joel, 60

Estes Cone, 46, 52–53, 54 (photo), *56,* 60, 62

Estes Park, *xii,* 8, 25, 32, 34, 45, 57, 60, 65, 71, 91, 135, 176, 179, 182

Eugenia Mine site, *56,* 57, 60, 61, 62 (photo)

Evening-primrose, Common, 29

Exertion ratings, table of. *See* Ratings, trail

Eyeglasses, 13

Fairybells, 125

Fairyslipper, 66, 151, 181

Fall hiking, xi, 2, 8, 25, 31, 39, 45, 57, 65, 73, 79, 85, 91, 95, 99, 105, 111, 117, 121, 137, 141, 147, 153, 157, 167
Fauna. *See* Animal; Guide
Features, 18. *See also* individual features by name
Fee, 14–15; ANRA, 196; backcountry campsite, 196; campground, 196; entrance, 196; schedules, 195–196. *See also* Pass/Passport
Fern, 49, 83, 89, 182
Fern Creek, *120*, 123, 124
Fern Falls, *78*, 79, 80, 81, 83, *120*, 123, 124
Fern Lake, 101, *120*, 123, 124, 129
Fern Lake Trail, *78*, 80
Fern Lake Trailhead, *78*, 79, 81, 83, 121
Filters, water, 7, 197
Finch Lake, 66, 67
Finch Lake Trailhead, *64*, 65, 66, 67, 80
Fir: as indicator species, *178*, 179; identification of, *183*, 184; Subalpine, 108, 115, *178*, 180, 181
Fire, forest, 106
Fireweed, Common, 49, 55, 63, 103, 108, 145, 159, 164, 170, 186–187
First aid kit, 12, 13. *See also* Guide
Fish, 187; stocking of, 163. *See also* Sucker; Trout
Fish Creek, *50*, 148
Flashlight, 13
Flattop Mountain, 101, 112, 124, *126*, 129, 131, *160*, 163, 164
Flax, Blue, 77, 89, 170
Fleabane, 37, 83, 89, 155
Flicker, Northern, 29, 55, 63, 77, 108, 145, 155, 159, 164, 170, 180, 188
Flora. *See* Guide; individual plants by name
Fly, 187
Flycatcher, 164; Cordilleran, 83, 180; Empidonax, 29, 155; Olive-sided, 29, 43, 49, 170, 181
Food, 7, 13
Foothills Life Zone, *178*, 178, 179, 186
Footwear: athletic shoes, 11; hiking boots, 4, 11
Formula, hiking times. *See* Times, hiking/ walking

Fox, 191
Frog: Northern Leopard, 188; Wood, 188. *See also* Chorus Frog, Northern
Frostbite, 8
Fungus, 181, 182. *See also* Mushroom

Gem Lake, *24*, 25, 26, 29; origin of, 27
Gem Lake Trailhead, *24*, 25, 26, 27, 29
Gentian, 63, 108, 145, 155
Geology, 25
Geranium: Fremont, 43, 49, 55, 77, 89, 151, 180; Richardson's, 49
Giardia, 7, 128
Gilia, Western Scarlet, 170
Glaciation. *See* Glacier; individual glaciations by name
Glacier, 113; continental, 130, 175; definition of, 130; montane, 96, 123, 130, 169. *See also* individual glaciers by name
Glacier Basin, 93 (photo), 96, 103, 133, 191
Glacier Basin Campground, 23, 46, 49, *56*, 58, 60, 71, *94*, 95, 96–97
Glacier Basin Loops, 69, 71, 94 (map), 95–97, 133; North Loop, *94*, 95, 96, *132*; South Loop, *94*, 95, *132*
Glacier Creek, *90*, *94*, 95, 96, *98*, 99, 100, 101, 103, *104*, 106, 108, 109 (photo), *110*, 114, 131
Glacier Falls, *110*
Glacier Gorge, 114
Glacier Gorge Junction, 59, 60, 61, *98*, 99, 101, 103, *104*, 105, 106, 108, 111, 112, *126*, 127, 128, 131, 179
Glacier Gorge Junction Trailhead, 71, 100, 105, 108, *110*, 111, 114, 127
Glacier Knobs, 113, 131
Glacier National Park, 1
Global Positioning System (GPS), 14, 20, 32
Globeflower, 83, 89, 125
Gnat, 187
Gneiss, 175
Golden Access Passport. *See* Pass/Passport
Golden Age Passport. *See* Pass/Passport
Golden Aster, 63, 108; Hairy, 55
Golden Banner, 43, 77, 82 (photo), 83, 89, 125, 179

Golden Eagle Passport. *See* Pass/Passport
Goldenrod, 37, 55, 155
Goldfinch, 59
Goose, Canada, 170
Gopher, Pocket, 191
GPS. *See* Global Positioning System
Grand County Road No. 66, 167
Grand Ditch, *136*, 137, 138, 139, 141,
  142, 143 (photo), 145; construction,
  138, 142
Grand Ditch Circuit, 135, 136 (map),
  137–139, 144, *172*, 173
Grand Lake, *xii*, 8
Grand Lake Entrance Station, *152, 156*
Grand Lake Lodge, 162
Grand Lake Village, *160*, 161, 170
Granite Falls, 147, 148, *160*, 161, 162–
  163, 164
Granite formations, 28
Granite Pass, *56*, 57, 58, 59, 60, 61
Grass, 170
Grasshopper, 55
Great Plains, 66
Green Mountain, *156*, *160*
Green Mountain Circuit, 135, 156 (map),
  157–159, *172*, 173
Green Mountain Trail, *146*, 149, 151, *156*,
  159, 164
Green Mountain Trailhead, 135, *146*, 147,
  148, 149, 151, *156*, 157, 158, 159, 162
Groundsel, Bigelow, 170
Ground Squirrel, 11; Golden-mantled, 29,
  37, 43, 49, 55, 63, 67, 76 (photo), 77,
  83, 92, 103, 108, 112, 115, 118, 125,
  128, 131, 144, 145, 155, 165, 170,
  180, 189, *192;* Wyoming, 43, 75, 77,
  80, 83, 180, 189, *192*
Grosbeak, Pine, 181
Grouse, Blue, 181
Guide: birds, 206; butterflies, 207; ecology
  and natural history, general, 204; fauna,
  general, 206; first aid, health and safety,
  204; flora, general, 204–205; geology,
  204; mushrooms, 205; natural history,
  13; reptiles and amphibians, 206; trail/
  hiking, ix, 13, 201–203; trees, 205;
  wildflowers, 205

Hail, 8–9, 161
Haldane, J.B.S., 187
Hallett, William L., 130
Hallett Peak, 112, 119 (photo), 129, 130,
  160
HAPE (high-altitude pulmonary edema). *See*
  Altitude
Harbison Picnic Area, *152*, 153, 154
Hare, Snowshoe (Varying), 63, 92, 108,
  145, 181, *192*, 193
Harebell, Mountain, 37, 43, 49, 55, 63, 77,
  83, 89, 108, 145, 155, 159, 164, 170,
  186
Hat, 9, 12
Hawk: Red-tailed, 29; Sharp-shinned, 145;
  Swainson's, 170
Hawthorn, identification of, *185*, 186
Haynach Lakes, *160*, 163, 164
Health, 7–10
Heart rate, 9
Heat exhaustion, 9
Helicopter pad, 32, 35, *38*
Hell's Hip Pocket, *140*
Hike: day, 3; out and back, 1; types of, 3
Hike, circuit (loop), ix, 1; criteria for
  inclusion, 2–3; definition of, 1
Hiker, 102 (photo)
Hiking times. *See* Times, hiking/walking
Hollowell, George C., 86
Hollowell Park, 75, *84*, 85, 86, 87, 89,
  122, 124–125
Horn, 177
Horse. *See* Equestrians
Horsemint, 29
Horseshoe Park, 32
Horsetail, 151, 170, 182
Howard Mountain, *136*
Hudsonian Life Zone, 177
Hummingbird: Broad-tailed, 29, 43, 49,
  63, 77, 83, 115, 145, 159, 164, 170,
  188; Rufous, 77
Hunters Creek, *64*
Hypothermia, 8, 161

Icy Brook, *110*, 113
Idaho, 148, 162
Information in accounts, ancillary, 18
Inn Brook, *56*, 60, 61

Insect, 187
Invertebrates, 187
Iris, Mountain, 89, 125

Jacket, fleece, 12
Jay: Blue, 19; Gray, 67, 83, 92, 103, 108,
    112, 115, 118, 125, 128, 131, 145,
    151, 155, 159, 165, 170, 180, 188;
    Steller's, 19, 29, 37, 43, 55, 63, 67, 83,
    92, 103, 108, 112, 115, 118, 125, 128,
    131, 145, 155, 159, 165, 180, 188
Jeans, 12
Jewel Lake, 3, *110,* 114
Joe Mills Mountain, *120*
Jogger, 49
Junco: Dark-eyed, 29, 37, 43, 55, 67, 77,
    92, 103, 108, 115, 118, 125, 145, 151,
    155, 159, 170, 188; Yellow-eyed, 188
Juniper, 77; as indicator species, *178,* 179;
    Common, 37, 43, 46, 49, 55, 63, 77,
    83, 89, 103, 108, 115, 118, 125, 145,
    155, 159, 164, 170, 180, 181;
    identification of, 182–184, *183;* Rocky
    Mountain, 83, 89, 180, 184

Kawuneeche Valley, 169
Kawuneeche Valley Loops, 135, 152 (map),
    153–155, *172, 173;* North Loop, *152,*
    153, 154; South Loop, *152,* 153, 154
Kawuneeche Visitor Center, 145, *156,* 157,
    158, 159, 161, 162
Kettle hole, 113, 118
Keyhole, The, 59
Kingfisher, Belted, 155
Kinglet: Golden-crowned, 63, 67, 125, 181,
    188; Ruby-crowned, 29, 43, 63, 67, 108,
    115, 125, 151, 155, 159, 180, 188
Knapweed, Diffuse, 29, 145
Knife, pocket, 13
"Knobs Junction," *110,* 113, 114, *126,* 131

Lake: kettle-hole, 113, 118; rock-basin, 27,
    80, 123. *See also* Tarn
Lake Granby, 169
Lake Haiyaha, *110,* 111, 113, *126*
Lake Helene, *120,* 121, 124
Lake Nanita, *160,* 163
Lake of Glass, 113

Lake of the Clouds, *136,* 137, 138, 139
Laramide Orogeny, 176
Laramie, Wyoming, 176
Lark, Horned, 181
Larkspur, 77, 89, 195
Larkspur Creek, *56*
Lawn Lake, 28, 29
Lead Mountain, *136*
Lewis and Clark Expedition, 189
Lichen, 123, 182
Life zone: altitudinal, 177–179, *178* (figure)
    (*see also* individual life zones by name);
    elevations of, *178,* 179
Lightning, 8, 161
Lily, 83, 89
Lily Lake, *50,* 52, 54 (photo), 55
Lily Lake Loops, 50 (map); **51–55;** Inner
    Loop, 20
Lily Lake Trailhead, 51, 52, 53
Lily Lake Visitor Center, *50,* 51
Lily Mountain, *50,* 55
Line, nylon, 13
Little Dutch Creek, *136*
Little Matterhorn, 123
Liverwort, 182
Lizard, 188
Loch, The, *110,* 111, 113, *126,* 127, 130,
    131
Locke, Mr., 113, 130
Lock Vale, 113
Loco, 77, 89, 179
Lodgepole stands, 180
Longs Flank Circuit, 23, 56 (map), **56–63,**
    68, 69, 132, 133
Longs Peak, 42 (photo), 46, 52, 54 (photo),
    56, 59, 61, 63, 96, 100, 101, 103, 106,
    108, 114, 129, 131; view of, 31, 34, 41,
    66
Longs Peak Campground, 23, 58
Longs Peak Inn, 61
Longs Peak Ranger Station, 23, 58
Longs Peak Road, 57–58
Longs Peak Trailhead, *56,* 57, 58, 60, 61, 62
Loop: definition of, 2; in account names, 2
Lost Creek, *136*
Loveland, 138, 142, 176
Lower plants, 182. *See also* Fern; Horsetail;
    Lichen; Moss

Lulu City: history and naming of, 138–139; site, *136*, 137, 139
Lulu Creek, *136*, 138
Lumpy Ridge, *24*, 25, 26, 28
Lumpy Ridge Circuit, 3, 24 (map), **25–29**
Lupine, 55, 63, 155, 170, 180

Magpie, Black-billed, 43, 77, 83, 115
Mallard, 55, 81 (photo), 83, 92, 101, 103, 118, 128, 170
Mammal, 19, 188–193; larger, 190 (figure); names of, 19–20; smaller, 192 (figure); where to see, 73
Many Parks Curve, 41
Map: CD-ROM, 203; contour line, 20; topographic, 7, 13, 20, 21, 41; trail, 3, 20–21, 203; USGS topographic, 106; wheel, 20
Maple, Mountain, 37, 83, 118, 145, 180; identification of, *185*, 186
Marmot, Yellow-bellied, 59, 61 (photo), 115, 123–124, 125, 129, 131, 163, 181, 189, *192*
Marsh-marigold, 125
Marten, American (Pine), 145, 191, *192*
Matches, 13
McGregor Avenue, *24*, 25
McGregor Ranch, 25–26
Meadows, 43, 47, 63, 179. *See also* Big Meadows
Medications, 13
Merriam, A. Hart, 177
Mica, 46
Mill Creek, *84*, 85, 86, *120*, 122, 125
Mill Creek Basin, 80, *84*, 85, 86, 89, 101, *120*, 122, 125
Mill Creek Basin Trailhead, 85
Mills, Enos Abijah, 61, 86, 91, 114
Mills Lake, 3, 91, *110*, 111, 114, 131
Mills Moraine, *56*
Miners-candle, 43, 77, 89, 125
Mine site, *136*, 137, 139
Mirror, 13
Moleskin, 12
Monocot, 19
Montana, 148, 162
Montane Life Zone, *178*, 178, 179, 186
Monument-plant, 29, 37, 63, 108

Moore Park, *56*, 60, 61, 75, 80, 86
Moose, 10, 149 (photo), 149, 151, 158, 165, 189, *190*
Moraine: lateral, 74 (photo), 74, 177 (*see also* South Lateral Moraine); terminal (end), 130, 177
Moraine Park, 39, 41, 71, *72*, 73–74, 77, 83, 85, 89, 91, 100, 177, 179, 180; upper, 74 (photo)
Moraine Park Campground, *58*, 71, *72*, 73, 75, 79
Moraine Park Circuit, 71, 72 (map), **73–77, 85,** *132*
Moraine Park Museum, *72*, 100, 193
Mosquito, 151, 187
Mosquito Creek, *136*, *140*
Moss, 63, 182
Mountain, 175–177
Mountain-building, 176
Mountain Lion, 10, 19, 49, *190*, 193
Mount Cirrus, *136*
Mount Elbert, 63
Mount Lady Washington, *56*
Mount Meeker, 66, 106
Mount Patterson, *160*
Mount Rainier National Park, 1
Mount Wuh, *120*, 122
Mount Wuh Circuit, 71, 85, 86, 89, 120 (map), **121–125,** *132*
Mouse: jumping, 191; kangaroo, 191; native, 191
Mule, 158
Mushroom, 89, 151, 155, 159, 181; names of, 19. *See also* Bolete, King
Muskrat, 55, *192*

Nakai Peak, 163
Narrows, The, 59
National Parks Pass. *See* Pass/Passport
National Scenic Trails, 162; history of, 148
National Trails System Act of 1968, 148, 162
Natural history: appendix, 175–194; in accounts, 18; sources of, 193–194; where to study, 73, 75, 81, 85, 86, 91, 117
Nausea, 9
Needles, The, *24*
Neoglaciation, 176

Never Summer Mountains, *136,* 137, 139
Never Summer Ranch, *140,* 141, 142, 143, 144, 145
New Mexico, 148, 162
Nisa Mountain, *160*
North America, 175
North American Plate, 176
North Deer Mountain Trail, *30,* 32, 34
North Fork Colorado River, *136,* 137, 138, 139, *140,* 141, 142, 143, 144, *152,* 153, 154, 155 (photo), 155, *156,* 157, 158, 159
North Inlet, 129
North Inlet Falls, *160,* 163, 164
North Inlet Trail, *160*
North Inlet Trailhead, *160,* 161, 162, 164
North Longs Peak Trail, *56, 104,* 106, 108
North Saint Vrain Creek, *64,* 66, 67
No-see-ums, 187
Notchtop Mountain, 123, *160*
Notes, our hiking, 19
Nuphar, 112
Nutcracker, Clark's, 29, 37, 49, 103, 108, 112, 115 (photo), 115, 118, 125, 128, 131, 145, 181, 182, 188
Nuthatch: Pygmy, 29, 37, 43, 77; Red-breasted, 29, 49, 63, 67, 77, 83, 103, 108, 115, 125, 165, 188; White-breasted, 29, 43, 92, 180
Nymphaea, 112
Nymphaeaceae, 112
Nymph Lake, 3, 101, *110,* 111, 112, 114, *126,* 128

Oak, Gambel, identification of, *185,* 186
Odessa Lake, *120,* 121, 123, 124, 125, 129
Old Fall River Road, *xii,* 114, 131
Onahu Creek, *146,* 148, 151, *152,* 154, 155, 162
Onahu Creek Trail, *146*
Onahu Creek Trailhead, *146,* 147, 148, 151
Onion, Nodding, 63, 103, 108
Opposition Creek, 138, *140*
Orchid. *See* Fairyslipper
Organizations, 199
Osprey, 159, 170
Otis, Edward Osgood, 130
Otis Peak, *126,* 129, 130, *160*

Ouzel, 66
Ouzel Creek, *64*
Ouzel Falls, 22 (photo), *64,* 65, 66, 67
Ouzel Lake, 67

Pacific plate, 176
Pack, day. *See* Day pack
Paintbrush, 83, 125, 145, 186; Narrowleaf, 125; Rosy, 125; Scarlet, 37, 43, 46, 49, 55, 63, 77, 108, 115, 180, 186
Pants, zip-off, 12
Park Headquarters, *30,* 33 (photo), 33, 58, 193. *See also* Beaver Meadows Visitor Center
Parsley, white, 49, 55
Pass/Passport: ANRA, 196; ANRA/RMNP, 195; Golden Access, 14, 195; Golden Age, 14, 15, 195; Golden Eagle, 14; National Parks Pass, 14, 195; RMNP annual, 196. *See also* Permit
Peacock Pool, *56,* 59
Pearly-everlasting, 49, 103, 115, 145
Peneplain, 129
Penstemon, 43, 77; blue, 83, 89, 125
Periodicals, 207
Permit, 3, 14–15, 167. *See also* Pass/Passport
Pet, prohibited on trails, 15
Pewee. *See* Wood Pewee, Western
Phoebe, Say's, 49, 55, 170
Photographs, 4, 10
Pictures. *See* Photographs
Pika, American, 63, 66, 129, 131, 163, 181, *192,* 193
Pine, 182; as indicator species, *178,* 179; as lightning rod, 8; identification of, 182, *183;* Limber, 60, 114, 145, 180, 181; Lodgepole, 41, 43, 46, 49, 53, 55, 57, 63, 77, 83, 86, 89, 95, 114, 118, 122, 148, 151, 155, 158, 159, 162, 164, 170, 180, 191; Ponderosa, 26, 27, 28, 29, 35, 37, 39, 40, 41, 43, 49, 55, 75, 77, 83, 86, 87, 88 (photo), 89, 96, 97, 103, 122, 155, 180, 186, 191
Pinedale Glaciation, 74, 80, 176
Pinedrops, 151, 159, 164, 170
Pine Ridge, 56
Pipit, 115; American, 63, 181; Water, 129, 131, 163

Pipssissewa, 181
Plague, bubonic, 11
Plains Life Zone, *178*, 178, 179
Plant names, 19–20. *See also* individual
　plants by name
Platte River, 67
Play, animal, 144–145
Pleistocene Epoch, 130, 176
Poncho. *See* Raingear
Pondlily, Yellow, 80, 83, 86, 89, 112, 115,
　151, 159
Pool, The, *78*, 79, 80, 81, 83, *120*, 121,
　122, 123, 124
Powerline Trail, *152*, 154, 158
Precambrian Age, 175
Pressure: air (*see* Altitude); middle ear, 10
Pricklpear, Plains, 37, 77, 83, 89
Prospect Canyon, 60, *98*, 99, 101, *104*,
　108
Ptarmigan, White-tailed, 63, 129, 163, 181
Pulse. *See* Heart rate
Pussytoes, 103, 108, 145, 155
Putney, Dick, xi, 18
Pyrola, Star, 145

Quartz, 41, 60, 175, 176

Rabbit, 66, 181; Snowshoe (*see* Hare,
　Snowshoe)
Rabbitbrush, 37, 170; Yellow, 49
Rabies, 11
Ragwort (Senecio), 49, 55, 63, 103, 108, 170
Rain, 8
Raingear, 8, 12, 13
Range Creek, *166*, 169, 170
Ranger, park, xi
Ranger Meadow, *166*, 167, 168 (photo),
　169, 170
Raspberry, 145, 151, 159, 164
Ratings, trail: exertion categories, 6; exertion
　points, 5–6, 17, 18; hiking times, 4 (*see
　also* Times, hiking/walking); route
　classification, 5; types of, 4–6
Rats, native, 191
Raven, Common, 29, 37, 55, 63, 77, 108,
　115, 118, 131
Red Gulch, *140*, 142, 143
Red Mountain, *136*, *140*

Red Mountain Circuit, 135, 140 (map),
　141–145, *172*, 173
Red Mountain Trail, *136*, 138, 139, *140*,
　142, 143
Regulations, 15
Reptile, 188
Reservations, 3
Ribbon Falls, 114
Riparian ecosystem, 179
River Trail, *152*, 154, *156*, 158
Road, old toll, 53
Roaring Fork, 59
Robin, American, 29, 37, 43, 55, 63, 77,
　92, 108, 115, 125, 145, 151, 165, 170,
　188
Rock: age of, 175; formations, 48 (photo),
　130; outcrops, 55, 107 (photo); red, 47;
　types of, 175–176
Rocky Mountain National Park (RMNP), 1,
　86, 114, 167; fees, 195–196; publica-
　tions of, 20
Rocky Mountain Nature Association
　(RMNA), xi, 199, 201
Rocky Mountains, 117, 175; ancestral, 176;
　northern front range, 135; origin of, 129,
　175, 176
Rodent, 188, 189, 193
Rope. *See* Line, nylon
Rose, 43, 83, 89, 125, 187
Rosehips, 55
Rosy-Finch, Brown-capped, 63, 129, 163,
　181
Roughhousing, 144–145
Ruins, 53; cabin, 52 (photo), 61, 158;
　machinery, 61

Safety, 8–10
Sagebrush, 41, 179; Mountain, 43, 170
Saint Vrain brothers, 67
Saint Vrain Creek, 67
Salamander, Tiger, 55, 187
Salsify, 29, 37, 43, 77, 89, 155, 170, 187
Sandbeach Creek, *64*, 67
Sandpiper, Spotted, 92, 170
Sapsucker, 37; Red-breasted, 43, 145;
　Williamson's, 43, 83, 92
Sawmill Creek, *136*, 138
Say's Phoebe. *See* Phoebe, Say's

Scouring Rush. *See* Horsetail
Seasons, hiking, ix, 1–2, 18, 51
Shadow Mountain Dam, *166,* 169, 170
Shadow Mountain Lake, *166,* 167, 169, 171
    (photo)
Shadow Mountain Lookout, *166,* 167, 169
Shadow Shore Circuit, 135, 166 (map),
    167–170
Sharkstooth (rock spire), 130
Sheep, Bighorn, 115, 129, 163, 181, 189,
    190
Shipler, Joseph L., 139
Shipler cabin site, 137, 139
Shipler Park, *136,* 139
Shirt: tee, 12; vented nylon, 12
Shooting-star, 151
Shorts, 12
Shrub, 186; flowering, 186; identification of,
    186
Shuttle bus, 3, 14, 58, 91, 95, 122, 127,
    128, 133; Bear Lake, 71, 105, 112, 121,
    128, 133; Bear Lake Schedule 2003–
    2004, 133; Moraine Park, 71, 73, 79,
    85, 133; parking lot, 91, *94,* 96, *98,*
    100, 101, 105, 112, 117, 121, 128,
    132, 133; routes, 132 (map); used to
    complete a circuit, 133
Side trip, 2, 3, 17, 18
Siskin, Pine, 43, 49, 77, 125, 145, 180
Skiing, cross-country, 2, 45, 51, 95, 99,
    111, 137, 141, 147, 157
Skunk, 191
Sky Pond, 113, 130
Smoking, 4
Snake, 188; venomous, 10
Snipe, Wilson's, 145
Snowdrift Peak, *160*
Snowfield, 130
Snowshoeing, 2, 45, 51, 95, 99, 111, 137,
    141, 147, 157
Socks, 11, 13
Solitaire, Townsend's, 29, 37, 43, 181
Sonoran Desert, 177
Sonoran Lower Life Zone, 177
Sonoran Upper Life Zone, 177
Sortland, Herbert, 59
South Lateral Moraine, *72,* 75, *84,* 85, 86,
    87, 89

Space blanket, 13
Sparrow: Chipping, 43, 49, 55, 63, 108,
    145, 155, 159, 170, 180; Savannah, 55,
    151, 179; Song, 77, 145, 179; White-
    crowned, 115, 155, 181
Spider, 187
Spikemoss, 182
Sprague, Abner E., 80, 91, 108, 113, 114,
    130, 131
Sprague, Mary Alberta, 108, 114, 131
Sprague Lake, 46, *56, 90,* 91, 93 (photo),
    95, 96, 97, 191
Sprague Lake Circuit, 20, 71, 90 (map),
    91–92, *94,* 95, 96, 97
Sprague Lake Picnic Grounds, 71, 91, 95,
    96
Sprague Lake Trailhead, 95, 97
Spring hiking, 2, 39, 45, 65, 85, 91, 117,
    147, 153, 157, 167
Spruce, 178; Blue, 55, 77, 83, 89, 115,
    145; Engelmann, 19, 43, 115, 151, 180,
    181; identification of, *183,* 184
Spruce Creek, *120,* 123, 124
Spruce-fir forest, 181
Spruce Lake, *120,* 123, 124, 125
Spurge, 151
Squawbush, 103
Squirrel: Abert's (tassel-eared), 26, 29, 180,
    191, *192;* Red, 37, 43, 49, 55, 63, 67,
    77, 83, 92, 103, 108, 115, 118, 125,
    131, 145, 151, 155, 159, 165, 170,
    180, 191, *192. See also* Ground Squirrel
Stanley Hotel, 25
Steep Mountain, *84,* 85, 86, 89
Steep Mountain Circuit, 84 (map), **85–89,**
    132
Stonecrop, Yellow, 43, 77, 83, 89, 155
Stonewort, 182
Stores, hiking equipment, 197–198
Storm Pass, *56,* 58, 60, 61, 63, 97, 106,
    108
Storm Pass Trail, *44, 46,* 49, *94,* 96
Storm Pass Trailhead, 99, 106
Storm Peak, *56*
Subalpine Life Zone, *178,* 178, 179, 186
Sucker (fish), 187
Sulphurflower, 77, 89, 155, 179, 180
Sumac, Threeleaf, 37

Summerland Park, *160,* 164
Sunburn, 9
Sunglasses, 13
Sunscreen, 9, 13
Sunstroke, 9
Swallow: Barn, 115; Cliff, 159; Rough-winged, 115; Violet-green, 43, 49, 55, 77, 92, 103, 115, 145, 165, 180, 188
Swallowtail, Western Tiger, 77
Sweater, wool, 12
Swift, White-throated, 26
Swiss Alps, 100
Switchback, shortcutting, 15

Tanager, 165; Western, 43, 77
Tape recorder, 12
Tarn, 113, 177
Tetanus. *See* Bacteria
Thistle, 55; Canada, 29
Thompson Glacier, 74, 80
Three Chimneys Formation, 47
Thrush, Hermit, 103, 115, 125, 145, 151, 180
Thunder Lake, 67
Thunder Pass, 138, 143
Thunderstorm, 8, 161, 163
Tick, 34
Timber Creek Campground, 135, *140,* 141, 142, 143, 144
Timberline. *See* Tree line
Timberline Falls, 113
Timberline Pass, 39, 43
Times, hiking/walking: effect of altitude on, 6; formula, 4, 17, 18; table of, xiii
Toad, Western, 188
Toilet paper, 13
Tonahutu Creek, 134 (photo), *146,* 148, 151, *156, 159, 160,* 162
Tonahutu Creek Trail, *146,* 148, 151, *156,* 158, 159, *160,* 162
Tonahutu Spur Trail, *156,* 158, 159
Tonahutu Trailhead, 161, 162
Towhee: Green-tailed, 29, 49; Rufous-sided, 43
Trail: description, 18; guides (*see* Guide); points, in maps, 20
Trailhead, definition of, 6–7. *See also* Access points; individual trailheads by name

Trail Ridge Road, *xii,* 9, *30,* 41, 141, 157, 179, 181
Transition Life Zone, 177
Trash bag, 13, 15
Tree: broad-leaved, 184–186, *185* (figure); coniferous, 63; where to see, 73, 77
Tree line, 56, 59, 63, *104,* 105, 106, *126, 136, 160,* 161
Trees and shrubs, 182–186
Trout: Brook, 187; Brown, 187; Cutthroat, 118, 187; Rainbow, 187
Tundra, 60, 61, 63, *126,* 129, 130, 131, 162, 163, 164, 179, 181
Tundra & Glaciers Circuit, 71, 113, 126 (map), **127–131,** *132,* 133
Turtle, 188
Twinflower, 83, 89, 125, 181, 186
Twin Owls Trailhead, *24,* 25, 26, 28, 29
Twisted-stalk, 108
Two Rivers Lake, *120,* 124, 125
Tyndall, John, 130
Tyndall Creek, *110,* 112, 113, *126*
Tyndall Glacier, *126,* 127, 129, 130
Tyndall Gorge, 112

Ultraviolet (UV) radiation, 9, 12
Ungulates, 188, 189
United States Geological Survey (USGS), 20
University of Colorado, 144
Upper Beaver Meadows, *30,* 32, 33, 35, 37, *38,* 39, 41, 42 (photo), 179
Upper Beaver Meadows Picnic Ground, *38*
Upper Beaver Meadows Trailhead, 39, 41
Upper Mill Creek backcountry site, 122, 125
US Forest Service, 167
Ute Meadows, 41

Vaille, Agnes, 59
Valley: hanging, 177; U-shaped, 177
Valley Trail, *152,* 153, 154
Vertebrates, 187–193
Vest, fleece, 12
Vireo: Solitary, 92; Warbling, 43, 49, 77, 180
Visty, Judy, xi
Volcanic action, 176
Vole, 191; Southern Redback, 125

Walking stick, 12
Wallflower, 43, 55, 77, 83, 89, 125, 187
Warbler, 170; Wilson's, 29, 115, 179;
  Yellow-rumped, 29, 43, 63, 77, 92, 108,
  115, 125, 145
Water: bottle, 8, 13; drinking, 7–8, 18;
  purifying, 7
Watercourse, in maps, 20
Weasel, 191; Long-tailed, 191, 192; Short-
  tailed, 191
Weight, body, 4
Welton, Carrie, 59
West Portal, 169
West Portal Road, 161
West Side Circuits, 135–173, 172 (map);
  access points, xii, 3, 135; combining,
  173; introduction to, 135
Wheelchair-accessible, 1, 51, 91, 117
Whistle, 13
Wild Basin, 22 (photo), 56, 66
Wild Basin Loops, 64 (map), 65–66; East
  Loop, 64, 65, 66, 67; West Loop, 64, 65
Wild Basin Ranger Station, 65
Wild Basin Trailhead, 64, 65, 66, 67
Wildflower, 186–187; in hiking notes, 19;
  picking, 15; top ten, 186–187; where to
  see, 26, 46, 47, 73
Willow, 47, 49, 77, 79, 179
Windbreaker, 8
Wind River, 11, 15, 47, 49

Wind River Circuit, 23, 44 (map), 45–49,
  68, 69, 71, 132, 133, 169
Wind River Trail, 46, 69
Winter hiking, xi, 2, 25, 31, 39, 45, 65,
  85, 91, 95, 99, 117, 147, 153, 157, 167
Wisconsinian Glaciation, 74, 176
Wolf, 144, 193
Woodchuck, 124, 189
Woodpecker, 188; Downy, 67; Hairy, 29,
  43, 63, 67, 77, 108, 151, 170; Three-
  toed, 37, 43
Wood Pewee, Western, 77
Words, Native American: Haiyaha, 113;
  Haynach, 163; Kawuneeche
  (Cowoonache), 153; Nanita, 163;
  Onahu, 148; Tonahutu, 158; Wuh
  (Woo), 122
Worman, Odessa, 123
Worman, W. J., 123
Wrangler. See Equestrians
Wren: House, 43, 47, 83, 180; Rock, 37,
  49
Wyoming, 148, 162

Yarrow, 37, 55, 63, 108, 115, 145, 159,
  164, 170, 180, 186
Yellowstone National Park, 1
YMCA, 45, 53; livery, 46, 49
Yosemite National Park, 28, 100
Yucca, 55